MEDITATIONS

ON THE

MYSTERIES OF OUR HOLY FAITH.

HIC MAGNVS VOCABITVR QVI FECERIT, ET DOCVERIT
Venerabilis P. Ludovicus de Ponte
Soc. Iesu Vallisoletanus. obijt magna cũ
opinione Sanctitatis Vallisoleti in Collegio
S. Ambrosij decimo sexto Februarij Anno M.DC.
XXIV. Ætatis suæ Septuagesimo.

MEDITATIONS

ON THE

MYSTERIES OF OUR HOLY FAITH;

TOGETHER WITH

A TREATISE ON MENTAL PRAYER.

BY THE VEN. FATHER LOUIS DE PONTE, S.J.

BEING THE

TRANSLATION FROM THE ORIGINAL SPANISH BY JOHN HEIGHAM.

REVISED AND CORRECTED.

TO WHICH ARE ADDED

THE REV. F. C. BORGO'S

MEDITATIONS ON THE SACRED HEART.

TRANSLATED FROM THE ITALIAN.

IN SIX VOLS.—VOL. V.

Permissu Superiorum.

SAINT LOUIS

LIBRI SANCTI PRESS

MMXXIII

NIHIL OBSTAT
GEORGE PORTER, *SJ.*

IMPRIMATUR
✠ HENRY EDWARD,
Archbishop of Westminster

*Originally published by
Richardson & Son, 1852*

SECOND PRINTING

ISBN 979-8-8690-0996-8

TABLE OF CONTENTS OF VOL. V.

CONTENTS.

PAGE

III.—FOR THE PERFECT IN THE UNITIVE WAY.

(A.)—MEDITATIONS ON THE MYSTERIES OF CHRIST OUR LORD GLORIFIED.

HIS RESURRECTION, APPEARANCES, AND ASCENSION, UNTIL THE COMING OF THE HOLY GHOST, AND PUBLICATION OF THE GOSPEL.

THE INTRODUCTION—ON UNION WITH ALMIGHTY GOD, WHICH IS THE END OF THE UNITIVE WAY.

1. The meditations, which belong to those who have entered upon the way we call *unitive*, have for their end that union with God our Lord, of which the apostle St. Paul says, —" He who is joined to the Lord is one spirit."(1) And, although this union belongs peculiarly to the *perfect*, yet all ought to aspire to, and exercise themselves in it, even those that are but new beginners.—For the better understanding of this, I presuppose that this union comprehends three particular acts.

i. The first is, *the union of the understanding*, the office of which is to carry God within itself, and lodge Him in the memory, thinking of Him, and knowing Him with a true, proper, entire, and perfect knowledge, so as to become an image and lively portraiture of God Himself, into whom it is transformed according to that of the apostle: " We all, beholding," as in a glass, " the glory of the Lord, with open face," not veiled like that of Moses, " are trans-

(1) 1 Cor. vi. 17.

formed into the same image from glory unto glory, as by the Spirit of the Lord."(2) In these words the apostle St. Paul teaches us, that the meditation and contemplation of the glorious things of Almighty God has no other aim than to produce a knowledge and lively image of them in us, that whatever God has glorious in Himself we may have the same in ourselves by knowledge, endeavouring to have it daily more distinct and clear.

ii. From this knowledge proceeds a second act of union, the *union of the will*, which is carried out of itself with great violence, to embrace that good which it has discovered by the understanding, loving it, delighting in it, and desiring, with the greatest possible eagerness, to enjoy it. This union is set forth in that first and highest commandment of love,—" Thou shalt love the Lord thy God with thy whole heart, and with thy whole soul, and with thy whole strength."(3) In these words we are enjoined a love so perfect and excellent as to draw after it all our affections and desires, and transfer them to Almighty God with the greatest and most uninterrupted intensity possible. The affections which spring from this union and in which those ought to exercise themselves, who aim at it by means of these meditations, are the following,—admiration of the majesty of Almighty God, of His perfections, and of His wonderful works;—joy that He is what He is, and that He has in Him so many excellencies, and does so many glorious things ;—*praise* and *thanksgiving* for the gifts which proceed from Him ; an inward *desire* to see and possess Him, and to be always united to Him ;—very ardent desires also to honour and obey Him, and with a determination to please Him in all things, and that all men may know, love, and serve Him ;—a fervent zeal for His glory and for the *salvation of souls*, accompanied by a great sor-

(2) 2 Cor. iii. 18.   (3) Deut. vi. 5 ; Luc. x. 27.

row for the offences which are committed against Him ;—
confidence in His bounty and providence ; *fear* of His justice—not that servile and abject *fear*, " which perfect charity casteth out," (4)—but that filial and reverential fear
which dreads to be separated from Almighty God, or to do
anything that may offend Him, even in a matter of very
small importance ;—and to this affection must be united
that *sorrow for sins* which proceeds from *pure love*, for, as
we have already said, the higher degree of sanctity always
exercises the acts of the lower, although in a more perfect
manner.

iii. From this union results a *third*,—the *union of similitude*, consisting in imitation of life and manners, grounded
on a perfect conformity with the divine will, and readiness
to will, or not to will that which Almighty God wills or
does not will, in all circumstances, as well adverse as prosperous. Hence proceeds the continual exercise of all virtues belonging to the perfection of a Christian life, and
thus that highest degree is attained to which Christ our
Lord exhorted us, when He said,—" Be you, therefore, perfect, as also your heavenly Father is perfect ;"(5) that is,
in other words, be ye pure, charitable, merciful, prudent,
just, temperate, and holy as is your Father who is in
heaven. And in this sense is perfectly accomplished that
which the apostle said ;—" We, beholding the glory of
the Lord with open face, are transformed into the same
image,"(6) for, by receiving the glorious virtues of God
Himself into our souls, we are made like to His glorious
divinity, and pass from one brightness to another brightness ; from the brightness of *knowledge* to the brightness of
affection, and from this brightness to the brightness of

<hr>

(4) 1 Joan. iv. 18.   (5) Matt. v. 48.
(6) 2 Cor. iii. 18.

virtues, ascending from one virtue to another until we clearly see the God of gods in His mountain of Sion.(7)

2. From what has been said it follows that the contemplative life, when perfect, embraces these three sorts of union which are linked together in such a brotherly manner, that the one greatly helps and advances the other.(8) For the knowledge of Almighty God leads to the love of Him, and this to the imitation of His virtues; and this love and imitation bring the understanding to a wonderful perfection. For, as masters of the spiritual life commonly say, there are two means of knowing Almighty God.— i. One, the speculative, which proceeds from the natural light of our understanding, when it is enlightened by the holy light of faith, and ascends by reasoning and meditation to contemplate the glory and excellency of Almighty God, in the things which it beholds in creation, or which are revealed in Holy Scripture, which are, as it were, two mirrors or looking-glasses for discerning God in this life ;— the other, the *practical, experimental,* which proceeds from that most excellent gift of the Holy Ghost, called *wisdom,* or, as the word "sapientia" implies, a knowledge of God by taste. This, as was suggested in the introduction to the fourth part, is grounded on the wonderful sense of the charity and love of God which we experience in our souls by heavenly illuminations and sweet affections.(9) Of this knowledge, David said, " O taste and see that the Lord is sweet."(10) as if he had said, prove by experience the sweetness of Almighty God, and His wonderful operations, for by this means you will be able to see Him, so far as is possible in this life. And the apostle exhorts us to be

(7) Ps. lxxxiii. 8. (8) S. Th. ii. 2, q. clxxxvi. art. 1.
(9) S. Dionys. de Divin. Nom. c. 2. S. Bon. de 7. Itin. , Itin. 6. Gers. 3, p. Tract de Mist. Theol. S. Ber. ser. 23 et 24, in Cant. S. Th. . 2, 2, q. xlv. art. 3, etc.
(10) Ps. xxxiii. 9.

"rooted and founded in charity,"(11) and to devote ourselves to the sweet practice of it, that so we may "comprehend,"—that is, palpably touch and feel by experience, the greatness of God, the *breadth* of His charity, the *length* of His eternity, the *height* of His divine being, and the *depth* of His wisdom, and also know the excessive charity of Jesus Christ, which far "surpasses all knowledge" that the human understanding can attain to. And by virtue of this sublime and sovereign knowledge, we shall be "filled unto all the fulness" of Almighty God, and transformed unto Him by a perfect union; for as the Wise man speaking to God, says, "To know Thee, is perfect justice; and to know justice and Thy power, is the root of immortality,"(12)—for immortal and eternal life proceeds, as has been said, from the knowledge of the eternal God, the love of Him, and imitation of His holy virtues; so that, as St. John says, "he that loveth not, knoweth not God, for God is charity,"(13) and uncreated charity can only be known by experiencing within ourselves the acts and affections of created charity, just as the sweetness and strength of wine and honey are never well known, unless they have been tried and tasted.(14) And thus St. Thomas teaches, that it is lawful to desire to know God in this manner, and to prove His bounty, and His "good," "acceptable," and "perfect will,"(15) in order not to err a jot from it.

3. From what has been said, we may easily understand the principal end of these fifth and sixth parts, which are directed towards the first knowledge of Almighty God, that from that we may proceed to the second, and enjoy union with His infinite goodness and will, in the manner

<hr>

(11) Ephes. iii. 17.   (12) Sap. xv. 3.

(13) 1 Joan. iv. 8.

(14) Cass. col. 12 c. 13. S. Th. 2, 2, q. xcvii. art. 2, ad 3.

(15) Rom. xii. 2.

already described. And although it is true that this contemplation and union have for their principal end the
divinity and perfections of Almighty God, with whom we
are thus made one spirit, (16) yet they also have respect to
the humanity of the same God Incarnate, and His glorious
works and virtues, in which the divine perfections shine most
brightly; for, as the same Lord says, "life everlasting" consists in this, not only "that they may know Thee the only
true God," but also, "Jesus Christ whom Thou hast sent,"
(17) the Saviour of the world. And those who would exclude
from contemplation the mysteries of His sacred Humanity
will be themselves excluded from enjoying the blessings
and delights of the life eternal, for He Himself has said,
" I am the door, by me, if any man enter in, he shall be
saved; and he shall go in and go out, and shall find pas-
tures ;"(18) that is,—I in my human nature am the door,
by which to enter to Almighty God; if any man enter by
me, believing with a lively faith in me, and in my Father,
he shall obtain health and everlasting life—he shall go in
and shall go out, proceeding from the consideration of the
mysteries of my humanity, to the sublime secrets of my
Divinity, and from these he shall return again to those,
and shall find in all the spiritual pasture of devotion for
his soul.

4. Now, the life of Christ our Lord comprehends two
parts ;—one *mortal and passible*, of which we have been
treating in the preceding meditations ; the other *immortal
and impassible*, which commenced upon the glorious resurrection, and which He still leads, in which the glorious
perfections of His divinity shine most conspicuously, " for
although," as the apostle says, " He was crucified through
weakness, yet He lives by the power of God;" (19) and

<hr>

(16) S. Th. 2,'2, q. clxxx. art. 4.
(17) Joan. xvii. 3.   (18) Joan. x. 9.   (19) 2 Cor. xiii. 4.

hence it is, that the meditations on the glorious life of Christ our Lord, which are the subject of this fifth part, belong principally to the perfect, who have already passed through the previous ones. It is in their name that the same apostle speaks, when he says, " We have known Christ according to the flesh, but now we know Him so no longer," (20) that is, as St. Thomas explains it, (21) although we have hitherto known Christ clothed with mortal flesh, and subject to the miseries of our mortal body, and loved Him with a love mixed with some carnal affection, yet now we no longer know Him, or love Him in this manner, but contemplate Him clothed in flesh wholly immortal and glorious, and love Him with a pure love, free from all taint of flesh and blood, as we shall find in the use of the following meditations.

(20) 2 Cor. v. 16.   (21) Lect. 4.

I.—MEDITATIONS ON OUR LORD'S RESURRECTION, AND THE VARIOUS APPEARANCES MADE BY HIM UNTIL HIS ASCENSION.

MEDITATION I.

OF THE GLORIOUS DESCENT OF CHRIST OUR LORD TO LIMBO, TO FETCH THENCE THE SOULS OF THE JUST, AND OF THE GLORY HE GAVE THEM.

POINT I.

1. For the foundation of this meditation we must consider: i. *What Limbo is.*—ii. *What persons* are *detained* there.—iii. *How* they were until the death of Christ our Lord.

i. Limbo is a certain *place under the earth*, and is therefore called *Hell*, as when we say that Christ our Lord descended into Hell; and it is likewise described as "the pit wherein is no water," (1) and a prison of captives,—dark, and secured with "gates of brass," and "bars of iron," so strong, that no power, either of man or angels was sufficient to break them, or to bring out thence any one that had once been shut up there.

ii. In this Limbo, the souls of all the just, however perfect and holy, were shut up and imprisoned, because on account of Adam's sins, none could enter heaven until Christ had died for all. Here, therefore, were Adam himself, and Eve, Abel his son, Noah, and Abraham, with the other holy patriarchs. Moses and David with the other prophets, the souls of the great Baptist and St. Joseph, and all the just who died before the Passion of Christ.

(1) Zach. ix. 11. Isa. xlv. 2.

iii. Their continual *occupation* was, *to sigh for the coming of the Messiah*, to set them at liberty and impart to them the clear vision of Almighty God. Each one of them repeated, with longing desire, the prayer that David was wont to offer in his lifetime: " Show us, O Lord, Thy mercy, and grant us Thy salvation." " Stir up Thy might, and come to save us." " As the hart panteth after the fountains of waters, so my soul panteth after Thee, O God. My soul hath thirsted after the strong-living God, when shall I come and appear before the face of God ?" And that of Isaiah,—" O that Thou wouldst rend the heavens and wouldst come down; the mountains at Thy presence would melt away." " Drop down dew, ye heavens, from above, and let the clouds rain the just; be the earth opened, and bud forth a Saviour."(2) The other saints burnt with like desires, and sighing without ceasing, looked forward to the blessed day of their redemption, not without some sorrow, because, as the Wise man says, " Hope that is deferred, afflicteth the soul ;" (3) and when the fulfilment of the desire approaches, the soul rejoices. All those holy prisoners then greatly rejoiced when the soul of the great Baptist entered among them, to discharge there the office of precursor, which he had discharged in the world, and said, " Rejoice, and lift up your heads, because your redemption is at hand."(4)

2. From this consideration, I will endeavour to draw forth similar affections, I will imagine my soul a prisoner and captive in this body, as in a limbo and prison of darkness, where she sighs and longs for Christ our Lord to come and deliver her, and lead her with Him, saying with St. Paul,—" I desire to be dissolved and to be with Christ ;"

<hr>

(2) Ps. lxxxiv. 8.   Ps. lxxix. 3.   Ps. xli. 1.   Isa. lxiv. 1.   Isa. xlv. 8.
(3) Prov. xiii. 12.   (4) Luc. xxi. 28.

(5) and again, groaning out with Him,—"Unhappy man that I am, who shall deliver me from the body of this death!" (6) and with David, "Bring my soul out of prison, that I may praise Thy name." These and other such affections are very proper for perfect men, who have begun to taste the sweetness of union with God, and finding His absence heavy and grievous to be borne, say with David,—"My tears have been my bread day and night, whilst it is said to me daily, Where is thy God?" (7)

POINT II.

As soon as Christ our Lord had given up the ghost upon the cross, leaving there His body united to the divinity, His most holy soul united also to the same divinity, (8) descended into Limbo to deliver the souls of the just there detained. In this the Word Incarnate discharged the same virtues as He had manifested at His entrance into the world, to show us that even after His death, He was not unmindful of them. We have good reason to meditate on these virtues, in order to inflame ourselves with the love of our Lord, and especially on the two following:

1. The first virtue was His *boundless goodness and charity*, which moved Him to come *in person* to deliver these souls from prison. As He came in person to save the world, though He might have done it by other means, so although He might have delivered these souls from Limbo with a single word, as He raised Lazarus from the grave, by merely saying, "Lazarus, come forth;" or might have sent angels to bring them to His presence, yet would He do none of these, but willed that His own soul should descend really and truly to Limbo, to show the love which He bore them, and the great esteem in which He held

(5) Phil. i. 23. (6) Rom. vii. 24.   (6) Ps. cxli. 8.   (7) Ps. xli. 4.
(8) S. Th. 3, p. q. lii. in Symb. descendit ad inferos.

them, and what satisfaction He took in the services which they had done Him, and to apply to them by His presence the fruit of His death and Passion, according to those words of the prophet:—" Thou also, by the blood of Thy testament, hast sent forth thy prisoners out of. the pit wherein is no water." (9)

Colloquy.—O everlasting Lover of souls, how art Thou inebriated with love of them! Thou canst not be a moment without them! No sooner hadst Thou ceased to live with men than Thou didst ordain Thy soul to live with these souls, and remain among them, doing them the same good as before Thy death Thou hadst done to men. Come, Lord, and visit my soul, join Thyself to it, and so inebriate it with this Thy love, that it may never be separated from Thee, nor ever desire anything else than for ever to be united to Thee. Amen.

2. The second virtue was His most profound *humility,* which He vouchsafed to exercise by descending not only to this miserable earth, but even to the lowest parts of it, and to that which was a prison and place of punishment for sin, and by remaining there for some hours, not indeed as a captive, but as a deliverer of the captives; that by this humiliation to the lowest depths of the earth, He might merit exaltation to the highest heaven, according to what the apostle said,—" That He ascended, what is it, but because He also descended first into the lowest parts of the earth." (10)

Colloquy.—O humble Lord, who after gaining Thy victory, art pleased to mingle so many tokens of humility with Thy enjoyment of it : grant me grace to humble myself, and descend even to the lowest place, and continue to sit there, for well I know, that accord-

(9) Zach. ix. 11.   (10) Ephes. iv. 9.

ing to the measure in which I humble myself on earth,
I shall be exalted by Thee in heaven. (11)

POINT III.

1. Although the entrance of Christ our Lord into Limbo
took place in a moment, and without any resistance whatever, yet we may consider, *after what manner*, and with
what great majesty He entered it.

i. We may imagine how His holy soul descended *accompanied by many angels*, His servants and attendants, who
repeated those words of the Psalm, (which, however, as we
shall hereafter see, are to be understood primarily of Christ's
entrance into heaven,) " Lift up your gates, ye princes,
and be ye lifted up, O eternal gates, and the King of glory
shall enter in ;" and on the princes of darkness demanding
" Who is this King of glory?" they answered,—" The
Lord, who is strong and mighty ; the Lord, mighty in battle." (12)

Colloquy.—O glorious King, I rejoice that Thy
glory and might are proclaimed by angels, and published amongst devils, that they may know Thee, and
come and prostrate themselves at Thy feet.   O most
strong and mighty King, what new kind of valour is
this, and how great is Thy power, dying in the battle,
to depart with victory, killing death itself, and van-
quishing its author.

ii. The princes of darkness feigned themselves deaf to this
first demand of the angels, and when it was repeated a
second time, they asked the same question as before, to
which the angels answered: " *The Lord of virtues is the
King of glory.*"   O King of glory, how justly does the
name of Lord of " virtues " belong to Thee, Thou art
indeed the Lord of charity, of humility, of obedience, of

(11) Luc. xiv. 11.   (12) Ps. xxiii. 7.

patience, and of the other heavenly virtues, all which Thou gainedst for us in the battle of Thy Passion, and dost divide as spoils among Thine elect. Thou art also the Lord of "virtues," because from Thee proceed all holy, strong, and glorious works, by which Thou displayest the glory of Thy kingdom, and also makest Thy subjects glorious. Thou art the Lord of heavenly virtues, since to Thy dominion, the powers, dominations, and the whole army of the court of heaven are all subject, and in Thy presence they all tremble, and prostrate themselves, adoring Thee as their God, their King, and sovereign Lord.

Colloquy.—O Lord of "virtues," make me likewise to partake of them, since Thou hast gained them for me also. O Lord of charity, infuse charity into my heart, that it may be wholly melted in Thy burning love. O God of humility, root humility very deeply into my soul, that I may find grace and favour in Thine eyes. Amen.

2. I will consider further the omnipotence of this glorious King, who by virtue of His blood, destroyed and broke in pieces the bolts and gates of hell, penetrated without resistance to the lowest depths of the earth, even as deep as hell, to draw from thence those who were held captives, and to unloose their chains. This consideration should make me rejoice, and say with David,—" *Let the mercies of the Lord give glory to Him and His wonderful works to the children of men...Becaase He has broken the gates of brass, and burst the iron bars.*" (13) The *gates of brass* are my sins, which hinder the entrance of Almighty God into my soul. The *barriers of iron* are the impediments set by the devil and the flesh, to hinder those gates from being opened by God. The *strong chains* are the

<hr>

(13) Ps. cvi. 3, 16.

strong passions by which I am held fast, so that I cannot do the good that I desire.

Colloquy.—Let all Thy mercies, O my Saviour, give glory to Thee, and let all the world bless Thee for the " wonderful works" which Thou dost " to the children of men," who by Thine omnipotence breakest all the gates, bars, and chains of iron, that Thou mayest enter into our souls, and set them at perfect liberty. Break all these in pieces within me, O Lord, and vouchsafe to enter into my soul, that I may glorify Thee, and sing of Thy mercy, world without end. Amen.

POINT IV.

The most holy soul of Christ our Lord, entering into Limbo, illuminated with a heavenly light all those dark regions, and thus the divine wisdom Incarnate, accomplished that which He had promised :—" *I will penetrate to all the lower parts of the earth, and will behold all that sleep and will enlighten all that hope in the Lord.*" (14)   And in an instant He poured into all these souls which were there awaiting Him, a certain ray of glory, by which they beheld the divine essence, and the majesty of their deliverer, so that all of them were glorified ; Limbo was being converted into a heaven, and that prison of captives into a paradise of the blessed.

1. And here we must consider, first, the *unspeakable joy of those holy souls,* on account of that sudden and wonderful change in their state, by which they passed at once to the clear vision of Almighty God which constitutes that supreme blessedness which they now enjoy. Oh how fully and abundantly satisfied did they remain, and how well rewarded did they reckon themselves for all their past labours ! Oh how grateful did they show themselves

(14) Ecclus. xxiv. 45.

to Him, who had purchased them so great a good, at so great a cost to Himself! All adored Him, all praised Him, all congratulated Him on this His victory. We may likewise imagine that they came by choirs to acknowledge Him, as is usually done when a new king enters upon his reign.—i. The first was the choir of Patriarchs, with all their sons, the true heirs of their faith and sanctity; all of whom adored Him, and acknowledged Him as their supreme Patriarch, and "the Father of the world to come," professing themselves His sons, and praising Him for the heavenly inheritance which He had given them.—ii. Next followed the second choir of Prophets, who acknowledged Him as the head Prophet, and thanked Him for having entirely accomplished all the prophecies and promises, which He had made and delivered by them.—iii. After these came the third choir of Priests and Levites, adoring Him as High Priest over all land, thanking Him for the sacrifice which He had offered on the cross, to deliver all from their sins.—iv. After these followed the fourth choir of holy captains, judges, and kings, with the rest of the elect people of Almighty God, adoring Him as supreme King of heaven and earth, and congratulating Him upon the victory He had gained over the princes of darkness, and upon having vanquished the pride of him that called himself, "king over all the children of pride."—v. The fifth choir was that of illustrious Martyrs, from Abel to the innocent infants who were put to death by command of Herod, all of whom adored Him, acknowledged Him as the glorious King of Martyrs, and thanked Him for that noble martyrdom which He had suffered upon the cross.

All these five choirs took for their captain and standard-bearer, the glorious, prophet, martyr, and precursor of Christ, St. John the Baptist, and all with one voice and heavenly harmony, sung that divine Canticle of the Apocalypse:—"*The lamb that was slain is worthy to receive power, and divinity, and wisdom, and strength, and honour, and glory, and benediction.*" "*Thou art worthy, O Lord, to open*" these internal gates, "*because Thou wast slain, and hast redeemed us to God in Thy blood, out of every tribe, and tongue, and people, and nation, and hast made us to our God, a kingdom and priests, and we shall reign on the earth.*" (15) And then taking off the crowns of glory which they had on their heads, and confessing that they did not belong to them, but to this Divine Lamb, they cast them before His holy feet, saying:—"*Thou art worthy, O Lord, our God, to receive glory, and honour, and power, because Thou hast created all things, and for Thy will they were, and have been created.*" (16) Thou hast redeemed us, and hast gained these crowns for us; therefore as they are Thine, to Thee be all the glory, world without end. Amen.

With each of these five choirs ought I to join in praising Christ our Lord, as *Patriarch,—Prophet,—Priest,—King,—*and *Martyr*, incomparably excelling all others.

2. Hence will I ascend to consider the *boundless love which Jesus Christ our Lord felt* at the sight of such a multitude of souls, redeemed with His precious blood. Oh. how greatly did He rejoice that He had come into the world to redeem them! Oh how well-spent did He account the labours of His Passion, when He beheld the glorious fruits which He gathered from them! There He saw fulfilled that promise of the eternal Father:—"*Because His soul hath laboured He shall see, and be filled...Therefore will I distribute to Him very many, and He shall divide the spoils of the strong, because He hath delivered His soul unto death, and was reputed with the wicked.*" (17.)

(15) Apoc. v. 9.—12.   (16) Ibid. iv. 11.
(17) Isa. liii. 11.

Colloquy.—O most sweet Redeemer, I rejoice with Thee for the joy and satisfaction which Thou receivest in recompense for the sorrow and anguish which Thou hast endured. Well do these five choirs of saints answer to the five wounds, by which Thou hast redeemed them from the bondage of the Devil; it is just and right that Thou shouldest rejoice in so great a multitude of sons, as Thy Eternal Father hath bestowed upon Thee. I give Thee thanks, for the division of the spoils, which Thou hast made amongst them, imparting to every one a recompense proportionable to his labours. Bestow, dear Lord, some part of these spoils on me also, that I may serve Thee as the blessed saints served Thee, and may come to enjoy that happy recompense which they have obtained. Amen.

3. Lastly, from all this I will draw a very great confidence in Almighty God, so as never to be weary of hoping in Him, nor anxious if He tarry and delay; for there is no period of time which will not at length come, and in a moment, when unlooked for, He can infuse such a joy, as abundantly to recompense the labours of many years.

POINT V.

Christ our Lord remained in Limbo all the time that His body remained in the sepulchre, that is to say, some thirty-six or forty hours, exercising in that prison His humility and charity, and giving rewards to the just, in that very abode which had been the scene of their affliction. (18) Meanwhile He ceased not to perform there very wonderful works, with which to increase the joy and satisfaction of those holy souls.

1. In the first place, a few hours after He Himself had descended to Limbo, *the soul of the good thief came thither*

(18) S. Th. 3, p. q. lii. art. 4.

also, and then it was that our Redeemer fulfilled the promise that He had made upon the cross,—"*This day thou shalt be with me in Paradise;*" for as soon as he came thither, He placed him in a celestial paradise, that is, He imparted to him the clear vision of Almighty God, from which flow all the delights of Paradise. And as Christ our Lord is wont highly to honour those who honour Him, He there, in the sight of all the just, vouchsafed to honour that blessed soul, and recounted to all that holy company how he had acknowledged Him as their King and God, in the midst of so many who were insulting and blaspheming Him. And then all the just congratulated the good thief upon the confession which he had made to the honour of his God, and exceedingly rejoiced with him ; and he on his part greatly praised his Lord, who had bestowed upon him so great a reward, for so little and small a service.

Colloquy.—Be glad, O my soul, and rejoice in God thy Saviour, embrace right willingly His holy cross, since from a cross a thief descended to Paradise, and was glorified with Christ, because upon it he had confessed Christ.

2. Secondly, it is to be believed that during this time, whilst Christ our Lord was in Limbo, *He despoiled purgatory* also, and drew out the souls contained in it, either accelerating the payment of the debts they owed, or applied to them some indulgence in virtue of His precious blood, so newly and freshly shed in His holy Passion. Perchance, therefore, He despatched some angels to purgatory, who brought Him first one and then another of those souls. Oh how exceedingly did these souls rejoice as they were brought before Him, not only to see themselves freed from such great pains, but also to behold the glory of their deliverer, and the delightful companionship into which

they were admitted! and how did those also who were there rejoice anew, with those who had newly come to them, accounting their joy their own, according to the law of charity.

Colloquy.—O most liberal Redeemer, remember us also in this our day, who are living in this mortal life, purge us from our sins, and from the miseries which we suffer from them: turn our mourning into joy, purify us from our offences, and remit the penalty which our sins have deserved. Amen.

3. Lastly, I may consider the rage and fury of the damned, when they became aware of the entrance of our Lord into Limbo, and found that He left them to themselves, and took no notice of them, as not being worthy to be visited by Him, or comforted with His presence, but rather deserving confusion, because they would not avail themselves of the means which He had given them for obtaining pardon of their sins. In particular I may imagine the grief and rage of the accursed Judas, and of the impenitent thief, and how they were filled with a most devilish fury against themselves, because they had not profited by the opportunities which they had had, the one in the school· of Christ, and the other on the cross. From them I will take warning to be very careful as to my own manner of living, since the blood of Jesus Christ does not bring out of hell those who have fallen into it through their own obstinacy, and who, with a perverted free will, have despised and made light of that same blood.

4. I will likewise ponder the *shame and confusion of proud Lucifer*, and the other princes of that darkness, when they saw themselves vanquished by Christ, and put in chains by His Almighty power; and the captives, whom for the space of about five thousand years they

had kept prisoners, loosed and set free. Oh how great was their rage, to see themselves prostrate at the feet of Christ! And how great glory was it to Christ, to see them placed under His feet; for then, as the apostle says, (19) " He despoiled the principalities and the powers," stripping them of their power with great authority, and tearing away their prey like a mighty conqueror, " triumphing over them in Himself," and openly displaying His justice before a multitude of angels at this judgment.

Colloquy.—I rejoice, O my Saviour, in this Thy triumph over the princes and potentates of hell, and that Thou hast with so great valour taken from them all their spoils, and deprived them of their whole armour in which they trusted. (20) Triumph, likewise, dear Lord, over the same enemies in me, giving me Thy grace to overcome them, and so my victory will be Thine; for all who overcome them, overcome them only by Thee, to whom be honour and glory world without end. Amen.

MEDITATION II.

ON THE RESURRECTION OF CHRIST.

POINT I.

In the morning of the third day after the Passion, which was Sunday, the soul of Christ our Lord *departed from Limbo,* together with those choirs of just souls which He had in company with Him, and went directly to the sepulchre in which His body lay entombed.(1)

i. Here is to be pondered, first, the *cause for which Christ our Lord hastened His Resurrection:* for, although

(19) Col. ii. 25.   (20) Luc. xi. 22.
(1) S. Th. 3, p. q. liii. et liv.

He had said, that, as Jonas was in the whale's belly three days and three nights, so should "the Son of man be in the heart of the earth three days and three nights," (2) yet He abridged that time as far as was possible, without prejudice to the truth of His word, and contented Himself with part only, and that a very small part, of the first and third days, namely, the close of the Friday, and the first dawn of the Sunday. The cause was, His immense charity, which moved Him to succour speedily His disciples, who were in the darkness of unbelief, and to make haste to comfort His afflicted Mother, and all His dear and beloved friends, as also to illuminate and rejoice the world with the glory of His body, as He had illuminated and rejoiced Limbo with the glory of His soul.

Colloquy.—I give Thee thanks, O most sweet Saviour, for the care that Thou hast of those that are Thine, and for the speed with which Thou hastenest to comfort and relieve them. Thou hast accomplished Thy course like the sun, rejoicing "as a giant to run the way;"(3) and Thou hast made Thy day much longer than the night, for the day of Thy life lasted thirty-and-three years, illuminating the world which was in darkness, but the night of Thy death lasted but six-and-thirty hours, after which Thou didst immediately return and rise again with a new light, to comfort those whom Thou hadst left oppressed with sorrow for Thine absence. Hasten, Lord, I beseech Thee, enlighten me with the vision of Thyself, that my soul may rejoice in the presence of Thy grace. Amen.

2. Christ our Lord ordained also, that His *death* should be in the *evening*, at the setting of the sun, but His *Resurrection* in the *morning* at the *rising* of the sun. By

____

(2) Mat. xii. 40.   (3) Ps. xviii. 6.

which is signified that He died *for our sins*, by which we had deprived ourselves of the light of heaven, and of the splendour of His divine grace, and "*rose again*," as the apostle says, "*for our justification*," (4) to restore to us the life of the same grace, together with the joy of it, and to wipe away the tears of our former sadness, according to the words of David,—" In the evening weeping shall have place, and in the morning gladness." (5)

3. Then ponder the *exceeding joy with which the most holy soul of Christ our Lord went forth out of Limbo*, surrounded by that glorious and shining company, and triumphed over hell, which He had despoiled of so great a prey. We might imagine Him repeating those words of Jacob, " with my staff I passed over this Jordan, and now I return with two companies." (6) I passed through the world with only the staff of my cross, not having any with me to help me, and now I return with two companies of just souls of the two laws, the *natural*, and the *written*. Oh how joyfully did those two noble troops ascend, and how did they sing by turns the triumph of their captain, saying, (7) " Let us sing to the Lord, for He is gloriously magnified, the horse and the rider He hath thrown into the sea. The Lord is my strength and my praise, and He is become salvation to me. He is my God, and I will glorify Him, the God of my Father, and I will exalt Him. The Lord is as a man of war, Almighty is His name. Pharaoh's chariots and his army He hath cast into the sea, his chosen captains are drowned in the Red Sea." Join thyself, also, my soul, to these companies of glorious souls, and extol with them this thy sovereign captain, hoping thyself also to participate in their glory.

. (4) Rom. iv. 25.   (5) Ps. xxix. 6.   (6) Gen. xxxii. 10.

(7) Exo. xv. 1.

POINT II.

1. When Christ our Lord arrived at the Sepulchre, He first of all *showed that company the sad and lamentable spectacle of His body*, that so they might see at how dear a rate He had purchased their deliverance. And when those blessed souls saw the body, lying in such a state in the sepulchre, with the flesh torn and the bones out of joint, dyed all over with its own blood, and pierced in so many places, with the wounds of the feet, hands, and side, they began anew to praise their deliverer, and gave Him boundless thanks for the liberty which He had procured them at so great a cost to Himself.

2. Then Christ our Lord, by His omnipotency, and probably also by the ministry of angels, *gathered up and replaced all the blood which He had shed in His Passion.* Some angels, therefore, went to the garden of Gethsemane, others to the hall of Pilate, and others to Mount Calvary, to gather up the blood of their Lord which was scattered in those places, and this they did with great reverence, because it was united to the divinity, and then they returned to fill the veins of that blessed body. They brought likewise the hairs which had been plucked off from His head and beard, so that what Christ had promised to His servants was fulfilled in Himself: " A hair of your head shall not perish." (8)

Colloquy.—O most precious blood, I rejoice that thou art restored to thy former place, for such blood was not to be anywhere, but in such a body, and the blood of God was not to fill other veins than the veins of God, in which thou shalt now remain for ever, to be the price of our redemption, the fountain to wash away our transgression, and sustenance and drink in the Blessed Sacrament, and Sacrifice of the Altar.

(8) Luc. xxi. 18.

3. Then *His blessed soul entered into His body,* and by her entrance changed and transfigured it, much more gloriously than before in Mount Thabor. She stripped it of the winding sheet in which it was wrapped, wiped away the myrrh with which it was embalmed, cleansed it from all the filth and spots with which it was defiled, and communicated to it for ever the four properties of a glorious body—*brightness—immortality—impassibility,* and *subtilty.* And thus that body became a thousand times more beautiful and radiant than the sun, or rather, each particular part of it, resembled a sun of immense brightness and beauty : and more especially those five wounds, which were still left remaining in it, for reasons which will be noticed hereafter, cast forth beams of great splendour, which adorned His feet, hands, and side, in a wonderful manner : the wounds, also, which the crown of thorns had caused, formed, as it were, a glorious diadem of marvellous beauty, to adorn His sacred head. At the same moment availing Himself of the property of subtilty, He went forth out of the sepulchre, passing through that great stone, which had closed Him in, but which, hard as it was, could not hinder Him. Oh what joy did that blessed soul receive, when she saw her body so exceedingly glorious, and how gladly did she embrace it, choosing it for her perpetual habitation ! how cheerful, likewise, was that blessed body, when it saw itself adorned with those properties of glory, in recompense for the pains and ignominies which it had endured ! O King of glory, who, like a new man, comest again the second time into the world, with Thy garments renewed, to live a new life full of majesty, I congratulate Thee upon this Thy *new nativity,* no less admirable than the first. *In that* Thou wentest forth from the womb of Thy mother, leaving the gate shut to preserve her virginity :—*in this,* Thou issuest forth from

the earth, leaving the sepulchre shut, to manifest Thy majesty, and the subtilty of Thy body. *In that* Thou camest forth as a new man, free and exempt from all sin, but subject notwithstanding to pain : *in this*, Thou comest forth all renewed, quite exempt from all pain, and crowned with a crown of unspeakable glory, and therefore we may now say with great exultation :—" We saw His glory, the glory as it were of the Only-begotten of the Father."(9)

4. Lastly, it is to be believed, that Christ our Lord, according to His custom, lifting up His eyes and hands towards heaven, *gave thanks to His Eternal Father, for His Resurrection,* and the glorification of His body, in those words of the psalm :—" Thou hast turned for me my mourning into joy: Thou hast cut my sackcloth, and hast compassed me with gladness, to the end that my glory may sing to Thee, and I may not regret" (10) or be subject to any further sadness. In imitation of this glorious Lord, I will likewise say to the Eternal Father :—

Colloquy.—I give Thee infinite thanks, O heavenly Father, that Thou hast turned the mourning of Thy Son into so great joy, cutting the sackcloth of His mortality and sorrow, and clothing Him now once more with immortality and joy. Let the selfsame glory which Thou gavest Him praise Thee ; let His blessed soul, which is His glory, and Thy glory, praise Thee ; and let my soul also praise Thee, and never cease to praise Thee for all eternity. Amen.

POINT III.

As soon as Christ our Lord was risen, *the hierarchies and choirs of Angels descended by the decree of His Eternal Father, to congratulate Him,* and to celebrate the feast of His glorious triumph: for if a whole host came from

(9) Joan. i. 14.　　　　　　　　(10) Ps. xxix. 12.

heaven to celebrate the festival day of His nativity, when He entered into the world to lead a mortal life; how much more is it to be believed that they came at His holy Resurrection, when He began to lead an immortal life, not coming to combat but to triumph for the victory? And so the blessed apostle intimates, saying :—" When He bringeth in the first-begotten" again into the world, He saith: " and let all the angels of God adore Him." (11) This is the day, when the Father brought Him into the world the second time, and all the angels adored Him as their God, and their supreme Lord, renewing that canticle first sung at His nativity, " Glory to God in the highest, and on earth peace to men of good will." (12) And great reason they had for doing so, since the resurrection was a work of great glory to Almighty God, and of great peace to mortal men, for by it men are reconciled to Almighty God, and their enemies overthrown: so that we may say in the words of the Psalm :—" This is the day which the Lord made, let us be glad and rejoice therein."(13)

Colloquy.—I give Thee thanks, O Eternal Father, for the care with which Thou glorifiest Thy Son, fulfilling the promise which Thou madest Him when a voice came from heaven saying, " I have both glorified" Him, " and I will glorify" Him " again." (14) I rejoice, O my Saviour, that Thy angels adore Thee, and I together with them adore and glorify Thee in this day, which is wholly Thine, and not mine, because whatsoever Thou didst in it, belongs to the greatness of Thy divinity, and not to the baseness of my humanity. Oh that all the world would acknowledge Thee, and rejoice in this Thy victory, that so they might enjoy the spoils thereof! Amen.

(11) Heb. i. 6.   (12) Luc. ii. 14.

(13) Ps. cxvii. 24.   (14) Joan. xii. 28.

POINT IV.

Christ our Lord being thus raised up, would not retain this glory for Himself alone, *but was pleased to give a share of it to others*, together with Himself, and so He appointed that some of these holy souls, whose bodies lay in the sepulchres of Jerusalem, which had opened on the day of His Passion, should be joined to their bodies, made glorious and brilliant like His own. Oh how happy were those just souls, when they saw themselves with their bodies now glorified and brilliant like the sun.(15) They approached no doubt immediately to the body of Christ, which shone incomparably more than their own did, and kissed His feet and hands, adoring Him, and praising Him for the singular favour which He had done them.

1. The *causes also* are to be pondered, for which Christ our Lord did this :—

i. The first cause was, to *display His omnipotence, charity,* and *liberality,* for His goodness could not endure, not to communicate that good to others which it enjoyed in itself.—ii. The second cause was, in order that some *few bodies might be witnesses of His Resurrection,* and that from them we might conceive a hope of all rising again with Him in our turn, with glorious bodies like to His.—iii. The third cause was, to give us to understand that His will was, that *we should all forthwith rise again in spirit,* and begin a new and glorious life like His; that according to the words of the apostle, " as Christ is risen from the dead by the glory of the Father, so we also, " in novitate vitæ ambulemus," should " walk in newness of life." (16) Therefore, as Jesus Christ stripped Himself of His funeral

(15) Mat. xxvii. 53. S. Amb. et alii. quos citat Suar. 3, p. q. xliii. art. 3, et Cajet. ibid.

(16) Rom. vi. 4.

garments, and issued forth from the sepulchre alive, and with His body glorious, entire, immortal, impassible, brilliant, agile, subtil, and most beautiful: even so I must strip myself of the garments of the old Adam, and of the funeral garments of my passions and bad habits, in which I used to be wrapped, and begin to lead the perfect life of grace, the conditions of which are:—that it be *entire* in all virtue; *immortal* by a fixed purpose to return no more to deadly sin, as Christ arose to return no more to die;—*impassible*, not giving entrance to any passions which may cause sickness in the soul: brilliant by the light of an inward knowledge of heavenly things;—*agile*, or nimble to accomplish without repugnance whatever is the will of God;—and *sublil*, or spiritual, renouncing all earthly things, and taking no more of them than is necessary, that my conversation may be in heaven with the holy angels, although my body is on earth amongst men. These are signs of my having risen again with Christ our Lord, after which I ought to aim, because, as St. Gregory says, (17) the just man ought daily to imitate His Resurrection, endeavouring to obtain virtues for the renewal of his soul, corresponding to those endowments of glory which his body shall hereafter possess.

2. Concerning this point, *two things* are to be noted of great importance :—i. The first is, that as all the dead who were in Jerusalem did not arise with Christ, but *only those whose sepulchres had opened during His Passion:* so neither do all sinners rise again with Christ to the life of grace, but only those who through the virtue of His Passion open their sepulchres, by manifesting their consciences to their confessors, and rending their hearts with contrition. In the same manner, it is not all the just that attain to a participation in the joy of the Resurrection, but only those who have rent their hearts with the affection

(17) In Prolog. in Cant.

of compassion for the sorrows and pains of Christ, according to the saying of the apostle :—"if we suffer with Him" we shall " be also glorified with Him."(18)—ii. The second is, *the difference between the perfect and imperfect spiritual resurrection:* for the imperfect arise again, wrapped in their funeral garments, as Lazarus did, who came forth out of his grave, " bound feet and hands, with winding bands, and his face was bound about with a napkin :"(19) that is, they come forth with the remains of their former life, their sinful habits and customs, and unbridled passions, and consequently with peril of relapse, and in danger of dying another death, unless they unbind and strip themselves by mortification, put off these garments of their mortality and spiritual decrepitude. But the truly perfect, in imitation of their captain, Jesus, who left both His winding sheet and His napkin in the sepulchre, rise again with a new fervour, casting away all these garments of the dead, and putting on other new garments of life eternal, " stripping" themselves, as the apostle says, " of the old man with his deeds, and putting on the new,"(20) so as to be wholly renewed in perfect sanctity.

Colloquy.—O glorious conqueror, make me partaker of Thy Passion, that I may also be partaker of Thy Resurrection ! I will not arise with Thee as Lazarus and others, who rose to return to death again, but as Thou, being risen from the dead, now diest no more, so will I rise to a new life, never more to die the death of sin.(21) Let me suffer much in my body, that so my soul may be made *impassible ;* cover me with outward ignominy, that my spirit may shine with inward light ; and let it be *agile,* and ready to obey, that after this life, it may come to enjoy Thee in life everlasting. Amen.

(18) Rom. viii. 17.   (19) Joan. xi. 44.   (20) Col. iii. 9.
(21) Rom. vi. 9.

MEDITATION III.

OF THE APPEARANCE OF CHRIST OUR LORD TO HIS BLESSED MOTHER,
AND THE ANGEL'S MANIFESTATION OF THE RESURRECTION TO THE
WOMEN.

POINT I.

After Christ our Lord was risen again, He was pleased to manifest His Resurrection to the world, in order that many might enjoy the fruit of it.(1)

1. *In three different ways was this manifestation made.* i. The first was *by means of the Saints*, who rose with Him, and who, as St. Matthew says, " coming out of the tomb...came into the holy city, and appeared to many,''(2) no doubt declaring to them that He who was crucified was the true Messiah, King of Israel, Saviour of the world, and was now risen again. And it is to be believed that they appeared amongst others to Joseph of Arimathea, and Nicodemus, to comfort them, and confirm them in the faith of their Master.—ii. The second was *by sending angels* to make known His resurrection to the devout women, who went to the sepulchre to anoint Him; telling them that He was risen, and showing them the sepulchre empty.—iii. But Christ our Lord did not content Himself with these two means, but added a third, and *showed Himself to His friends,* to display more clearly the greatness of His charity. Which charity was the cause that, although He might have been expected to ascend immediately after His holy Resurrection, to the empyreal heaven, as to the place assigned to glorified bodies, yet He chose to remain in the world for some days, and, like a good pastor, gather together His dispersed flock, not trusting this to any one else, but comforting His disciples in person, " appearing

(1) S. Th. 3, p. q. lv.   (2) Mat. xxvii. 53.

to them, and speaking of the Kingdom of God,"...showing
" Himself alive after His Passion by many proofs,"(3) that
they might publish His Resurrection abroad as eye-witnesses.

Colloquy.—O King of glory, let all angels and men
praise Thee for this excellent love that Thou hast
showed us. The world was not worthy that Thou
shouldst remain in it a single moment after Thy Resurrection, but Thy charity which held Thee in Limbo
almost forty hours, held Thee on the earth forty days,
to purify and honour it with Thy presence, and to
show us that although Thou hast changed Thy condition of life, yet Thou hast not changed the manners of
Thy former life, and hast not forgotten in Thy prosperity those who kept Thee company in adversity.

2. Hence we are to gather, spiritualizing what has been
said, that Christ our Lord employs *three means* of making His
mysteries known to us, comforting and instructing us.—i.
The first means is, that of *holy men*, who, having risen again
with Him, and knowing by experience the sweetness and
excellency of this their God, with a holy zeal teach others
what they have learned themselves, in order that God may
be known and glorified.—ii. The second means is that of
the holy angels, who, by inward and secret suggestions,
enlighten, teach, and comfort us, and help to remove the
difficulties which hinder us from enjoying Christ glorified.
—iii. The third means is to *speak to our hearts* Himself,
and give us inward testimonies of His divine presence;
which is the means that He employs with His best beloved
disciples, to whom He fulfils even in this life that promise
which He made in His discourse at the last supper: " He
that loveth me, shall be loved of my Father, and I will
love him, and will manifest myself to him."(4)

(3) Act. i, 3.   (4) Joan. xiv. 21.

Colloquy.—O my beloved, I will love Thee with my whole heart, since it is so great a good to love Thee, who lovest him that loves Thee, and dost manifest Thyself to him, the more to inflame him with Thy love.

POINT II.

The first visit and appearance of Christ our Lord was to *His holy mother*, who was very greatly afflicted, on account of His passion, although not without a lively faith and hope of His Resurrection.

1. As the third day began to dawn, being settled in most lofty contemplation, and with fervent desires, and profound sighs, she besought *her Son to hasten His coming* to her, seeking like the lioness with her roaring, to awake the lion of Judah, who rested in His couch.(5)	Perhaps also she repeated those words of the psalm:—" Arise, O my glory, arise psalter and harp ;" (6) come forth gloriously out of the sepulchre, and make us all glorious ; arise, my psaltery and harp, and come forth out of this case in which Thou art enclosed, and with Thy music rejoice those who, on Thy account sit in sorrow; for Thou hast said : " I will arise up early."	Come, then, O sun of justice, before the rising of the early sun, to disperse the darkness by Thy light.

2. While the Blessed Virgin was wholly inflamed with these desires, *Christ our Lord entered*, together with those three shining companies of angels, of souls, and of glorified bodies, by which He was attended, and manifested Himself to her in all His glory and splendour, strengthened the sight, as well of her body as of her soul, that she might both see and enjoy Him.	Oh what comfort, satisfaction and glory did the Holy Virgin receive from so glorious a sight, in which was accomplished in part that which was

(5) Gen. xlix. 9.	(6) Ps. lvi. 9.

Vol. V.—3.

spoken by the prophet:—" I shall be satisfied when Thy glory shall appear."(7) Oh what sweet embraces mutually passed between the mother and the Son, and what loving discourses did they hold together! The Blessed Virgin kissed those precious and radiant wounds of her Son, drawing out of those fountains abundant streams of consolation, as before of desolation, for according to the measure of afflictions, God is wont to refresh the soul with consolations.(8) Then that illustrious train began to congratulate the holy Virgin, and to acknowledge her for the Mother of God, their Redeemer, thanking her for the toils and pains which she had undertaken in the work of their redemption. Oh what new joy did the Virgin conceive when she beheld this fruit of her Son's Passion, and so many souls redeemed by it. She congratulated her Son upon this great gain; and the angels celebrated the festival with heavenly music, to the glory of the Son and of the mother, and in honour of their mutual joy.

3. Finally, after Christ our Lord had remained thus a considerable time with His Blessed Mother, discovering to her many great and heavenly mysteries, and telling her that He would remain some days longer in the world, and often come to visit her; at last He took His leave of the holy Virgin, who remained full of wonderful consolation from this visit; which, however, she kept to herself in great silence, as before she had done the mystery of the Incarnation. For, as she would not reveal that mystery to her spouse St. Joseph, until an angel had declared it to him; so she would now conceal the visitation of Christ risen, without telling it to the apostles, or to the devout women who were in her company, until the angel, or Christ Himself declared it to them.

Colloquy.—O sovereign Virgin, I congratulate

(7) Ps. xvi. 15.   (8) Ps. xciii. 19.

thee on the Resurrection of thy Son. "Rejoice thou queen of heaven, Alleluia—Because He whom thou didst deserve to bear, Alleluia—Is risen as He said, Alleluia. Pray for us to God, Alleluia." (9) And make us partakers of that eternal Alleluia, which is sung in the streets of the celestial Jerusalem. Amen.

POINT III.

At the same time, Christ our Lord, by His holy angels, would manifest His Resurrection to the devout women who had followed Him, whose piety and devotion the Evangelists declare, saying,—" Mary Magdalen, and Mary, the mother of James, and Salome, and other devout women, who, on the Sabbath, rested according to the commandment ;" for reverence of the solemn feast, on the first day of the week, that is the *Sunday, came very early to the Sepulchre,* whilst it was yet dark, carrying the spices, which they had prepared: and they said one to another, " *Who shall roll away the stone ?*" (10)

In these women, is set before us the devotion with which we are to seek Christ our Lord, accompanied by the virtues which they exercised.

i. The first was, of *obedience to the law;* for although they burned with a great desire to anoint the body of Christ our Lord, yet they refrained from doing so upon the festival day, lest they should fail in their obedience to the commandment of God.

ii. The second was, great *diligence* in going thither before it was day, setting forward on their journey although the morning was yet dark; and although women are naturally fearful, yet they feared not to set out, and to go that journey by night, to accomplish the desire they had to offer this service to their Master. With this dili-

(9) Hym. Eccles.
(10) Luc. xxiii. 55.   Mat. xxviii. 1.   Marc. xvi. 1.   Joan. xx. 1.

gence will the divine wisdom Incarnate be sought, which said;—" They that in the morning, early, watch for me, shall find me." (11)   And if I desire to find the manna of celestial consolations, I ought to prevent the rising of the sun, to gather it with God's blessing, because the slothful do not find it, and the diligent only are those that enjoy it. (12)

iii. The third was, *confidence in God*, and *perseverance* in well doing, without desisting for fear of difficulties: because, although these devout women were not ignorant that they wanted strength to remove that great stone from the door of the sepulchre, yet did they prosecute their journey, trusting in Almighty God, that He would send them some assistance : and, so, accordingly, when they came hither, they found it removed in recompense of their confidence.   For the divine providence is never wanting to those, who, after this manner rely upon God, in things belonging to His service.

POINT IV.

The manner that this came to pass, the Evangelists declare, saying,—" Behold there was *a great earthquake*. For an angel of the Lord descended from heaven, and coming rolled back the stone, and sat upon it; And his countenance was as lightning, and his raiment as snow; And, for fear of him, the guards were struck with terror, and became as dead men.   And the angel answering, said to the women: Fear not you, for I know that *you seek Jesus who was crucified*.   He is not here,—for He is risen, as He said.   Come, and see the place where the Lord was laid." (13)

1. Here is to be considered first, the *majesty, beauty,*

(11) Prov. viii. 17.   (12) Sap. xvi. 18.
(13) Mat. xxviii. 2, and Marc. xvi.

and power of this angel, as well in the fearful earthquake which he caused, as in the facility with which he rolled away that huge and great stone from the sepulchre, which wrought great fear, both in the wicked, and the good, although in a different manner.   For the soldiers, as wicked, he struck and prostrated upon the earth, leaving them, as it were, dead, that they should not enjoy that good and felicity ; but he comforted the devout women, saying, Nolite timere vos, "Fear not you ;" as if he had said, These watchmen fear, because they are wicked ; but you, do not you fear nor terrify yourselves, because I bring you grateful news of the Resurrection of that Lord and Saviour, whom you seek for.

2. Next, I will meditate on that *new surname*, which the angel gave to Christ our Lord, calling Him " Jesus of Nazareth crucified ;" as he that well knew the manner of our good Jesus, which was to glory when He was despised, and to hold it for an honour, to be crucified for us.

Colloquy.—O sweet Jesus of Nazareth crucified, and never so true a Nazarite as when Thou wert crucified, since on the cross Thou didst send forth the flowers of Thy virtues, and the fruits of our sanctification, of which Thou dost glory in Thy glorious resurrection.   Oh that I may seek Thee with so great fervour, that I may not glory in knowing any other thing than Jesus Christ, and Him crucified.   O most blessed angel, come, I beseech thee, to my help, stay me up with these flowers, and strengthen me with these fruits, (14) because I languish with love, desiring to see Jesus of Nazareth, who was crucified for me.   Amen.

3. These women, *because of their little faith, were not worthy that Christ our Lord should appear to them,* and

(14) Cant. ii. 5.

therefore, *the angels disposed them* for it by exciting and assisting their faith, saying, " Come and see the place where the Lord was laid," in order that you may believe that He is risen again. He likewise aided their charity, saying, Going quickly, " tell His disciples, and Peter," that He is risen. He named Peter, in particular, that he hearing this news, might not think himself forsaken because of his denial : for since he had now deplored his sin, he was also worthy of this comfort. From whence I will gather that the hindrance of seeing Christ our Lord, and of enjoying His sweet presence, proceeds oftentimes from the imperfection of our own faith, and from our little disposition for such blessing; for which cause I ought to endeavour that those virtues be increased in me, which may dispose me to see our Lord, not despairing because I have been a sinner, seeing, that to Peter, hope was given of seeing Him.

4. These devout women, entering into the most inward part of the sepulchre, " *Two men stood beside them in shining apparel.* And as they were afraid, and bowed down their countenance towards the ground, they said unto them: Why seek you the living with the dead ? He is not here, but is risen. Remember how He spoke unto you, when He was yet in Galilee, saying: The Son of Man must be delivered into the hands of sinful men, and be crucified, and the third day rise again. And they remembered His words, And going back from the sepulchre with fear and great joy, they ran to tell all these things to the eleven, and to all the rest."(15) In which it appears, that *perseverance in devotion* towards Jesus Christ, is always worthy of new consolation. For first, these devout women saw one angel, but persevering in their pious search, they saw two others, who said to them the

(15) Luc. xxiv. 4. Mat. xxviii. 8.

same that the former had, confirming them in faith, yet
with a kind of gentle reproof, as if they had said:—" Why
are you so senseless, in seeking amongst the dead Him
who is now above, and is risen?"   I may likewise consider
how it belongs to angels, to bring back to our minds the
words of Christ, and with them to instruct us, comfort
us, confirm our faith, excite our hope, and kindle
our charity, that so we may become worthy to see Him
glorified.

Colloquy.—O blessed angels, to whom Almighty
God has committed the care of souls, if you see that
mine seeks "the living with the dead," seeking Christ
amongst the dead things of this world, correct, instruct,
and direct her, that she may seek Him where He is,
that is, in the land of the living, where He reigns with
those that are His, world without end.   Amen.

<hr>

MEDITATION IV.

OF THE APPEARANCE TO MARY MAGDALEN.

POINT I.

These devout women, returning from the sepulchre,
recounted to the apostles the discourse of the angels, upon
which they all returned the second time, and then, as St.
Mark says, Christ our Lord "*appeared first to Mary
Magdalen,* out of whom He had cast seven devils."(1)

1. First here is to be considered, the *infinite charity of
our Redeemer,* in so greatly honouring converted sinners,
choosing for the first eye-witness of His resurrection, a
woman who had been the habitation of seven devils, and
of the seven mortal sins which proceed from them: to

(1) Marc. xvi. 9.

give us to understand, that the multitude and enormity of sins past, do not hurt us, when they are compensated by a greater present fervour.

2. He who was the first in *the service* of Almighty God, will also be the *first in receiving favours* of Christ: and if I am singular in *serving Him*, He, also, will be singular in *rewarding me*, as was the case with Mary Magdalen, who made herself singularly remarkable in the love and service of Christ our Lord, doing for His love many things which others did not: such as were to wash His feet with her own tears, to wipe them with the hair of her head, to kiss them with her lips, to anoint them with a precious ointment, to sit at His feet, to hear His doctrine, with great delight, to remain with Him on the mount of Calvary, and lastly, to arise early in the morning, before it was day, to anoint His dead body, and that with greater fervour than all her companions, and, therefore, she merited to see Christ before the rest, as it is said in her hymn : "Prima meretur gaudia, quæ plus ardebat cæteris :"

> " The early joy was hers to claim,
> When love burnt with a brighter flame."

This will be shown in the points ensuing.

POINT II.

" Mary stood in the sepulchre without, weeping. Now as she was weeping, she stooped down and looked into the sepulchre, and she saw two angels in white, sitting, one at the head, and one at the feet, where the body of Jesus had been laid. They say to her,—'Woman, why weepest thou?' She saith to them, 'Because they have taken away my Lord, and I know not where they have laid Him.' " (2)

1. In these words are to be considered :—

i. The *fervour of Mary Magdalen*, which shone, first, in the great longing which she had to behold the body of her Master, which, although it was founded in some defect of faith in the Resurrection, yet because it proceeded from a fervent love and a pious intention, was grateful to her Beloved.

ii. From this longing arose *inquietude* or *solicitude in seeking* Him: and for this cause she sat not down by the grave, but was always on foot, as in a readiness, to seek Him out here and there, stooping down once and again to look into the sepulchre, to see if perchance she could find Him the second time, whom she could not find the first; for he that fervently loves Almighty God, does not cease often to repeat the self-same prayers, and to multiply the same endeavours to find Him.

iii. Hence it was, that although her companions returned from the sepulchre, contenting themselves with that which the angels had told them, and St. Peter and St. John returned to their dwelling, contenting themselves with having seen the funeral clothes, yet she contented herself with none of this, but *stood by the sepulchre with great perseverance*, as if she had said :—" Here I lost Him, whom I so greatly loved; here, therefore, I will find Him, or here I will die unless I find Him."

iv. Finally, she manifested her fervour *in the tears which* she there shed on this account, which tears the sight of the *angels, although so bright and shining*, could not check, because she could find no comfort in the sight of creatures, *who had placed all her desire in the sight of her master, who was her Creator.*

2. In these four things I am to imitate this fervent woman, seeking our Lord with a desire, *vehement, solicitous, constant, and devout,* resolving not to take any superfluous comfort in any creature, till I find out my Creator, saying

that which David said to another purpose :—" If I shall enter into the tabernacle of my house, if I shall go up into the bed wherein I lie, if I shall give sleep to my eyes, or slumber to my eyelids, or rest to my temples : until I find out a place for the Lord, a tabernacle for the God of Jacob," (3) to 'enter therein, and to abide for ever in His company.　In which I will also imitate the fervour of the spouse with which she sought out her beloved, through all "the streets and the broad ways" (4) of the city, not staying with the watchmen, nor resting one minute, till she had found Him ; for of those that seek Him in this manner, is understood that which Christ our Lord said :—" He that secketh findeth."(5)

3. Next is to be considered, the *cause* and *motive* of these fervent tears, which the same Magdalen told the angel, saying :—" Because they have taken away my Lord, and I know not where they have laid Him :" as if she had said :—" Does it not seem to you a sufficient cause for me to weep, that they have taken away from me my God, and all my good, without my knowing who has taken Him away, or where they have laid Him?　Before, indeed, I bewailed His death, but yet I comforted myself that I had His body : but now they have taken from me that comfort which He had left me, and this is that which I bewail, without finding any remedy for my tears."

4. Here I will consider that tears are *well employed, principally for two causes.*—i. *When our own sins have banished God* from our souls, depriving us of His grace and friendship ; and these tears are like those which the glorious Magdalen shed at the feet of Jesus Christ, when He cast seven devils out of her, and forgave her all her sins.—ii. The second is, *when unknown to us, God withdraws Himself from us,* and leaves us in darkness and dry-

(3) Ps. cxxxi. 8.　　(4) Cant. iii. 2.　　(5) Mat. vii. 8.

ness of spirit, with such great obscurity, that we hardly know where, or how to seek Him; and these tears resemble those which Mary Magdalen shed on this occasion, seeking out her master and Redeemer; and both sorts of tears give us great hope that we shall find God our Lord, if with them we desire Him, and seek Him, saying with the kingly prophet:—" My tears have been my bread, day and night, while it is said to me daily, where is thy God?" (6)

Colloquy.—O my God, who wast wont to lodge in my soul as in Thy sepulchre, rejoicing and refreshing me with Thy blessed presence, where art Thou now? Who has taken Thee from me, and has plucked Thee from my heart? Why leavest Thou me alone, dry, heavy, and comfortless? If my sins and my great offences have taken Thee forth from the place where Thou wast, take them from me of Thine own infinite mercy, that Thou mayest return to Thy place, and that I, by the help of Thy grace, may preserve it always clean, in order that Thou mayest never more withdraw Thy presence from me.   Amen.

POINT III.

Christ our Lord, taking compassion on the abundant tears of Mary Magdalen, resolved to comfort her, to fulfil the word which He had spoken when He said—" Blessed are they that mourn, for they shall be comforted :" (7) but Christ proceeded in this *by little and little*, and all for the greater good of Mary Magdalen.

1. For, first, He appeared to her, *not setting Himself before her eyes*, but behind her back, making some little noise, in order that she might turn to behold Him, upon which, " she turned herself back, and saw Jesus standing." (8)   Where is represented to us the manner in which

<hr>

(6) Ps. xli. 4.   (7) Mat v. 5.   (8) Joan. xx. 14.

God our Lord seeks souls, who turning their backs towards Him, forsake Him, and do not know Him, nor respect Him, as it is fitting they should: to whom He said by the prophet Isaiah:—"Thy ears shall hear the words of one admonishing thee behind thy back: this is the way, walk ye in it; and go not aside neither to the right hand, nor to the left."(9) These voices are certain inspirations, and interior touches, by which God our Lord invites these souls to turn their face to Him whom they have behind their back, in order that He may also behold them, and be touched with compassion towards them, saying that of the Canticles:—"Return, return, O Sulamitess: return, return, that we may behold Thee."(10) Four times does He bid her turn her face towards her God: to signify that He desires such a conversion as is very *fervent*, and very *perfect*, converting them to God with their *heart, soul, spirit,* and *strength,* fulfilling the commandment of love with these four conditions before specified.

Colloquy.—O my soul, Sulamitess, and captive of thy disorderly affections, behold how the three divine Persons exhort thee to turn thy face, because They desire to behold thee with Theirs. And since all thy good consists in being beheld by God, delay not to turn to Him, who invites thee to behold Him, in order that He may behold thee, and have compassion on thee.

2. Although Mary Magdalen beheld Christ our Redeemer, yet *she did not know Him*, because He appeared to her in a disguised habit like a gardener, since she deserved not to see Him plainly, on account of her little faith and her imperfect disposition. By which we are admonished, that the deadness and lukewarmness of our faith, is the

<hr>

cause that we know not God, who is present in every place, and Christ our Lord who is present in the Blessed Sacrament, and do not respect them, nor treat with them as present with us; and therefore He appears to us in the form of a gardener; to show us the need which the imperfect have, that Christ should weed and cultivate the garden of their souls, rooting up the evil weeds of sins and imperfections, and planting perfect virtues in them.

Colloquy.—O sweet Jesus, since Thou knowest that " neither he that planteth is anything, nor he that watereth," but He " which giveth the increase," (11) who is Almighty God, increase my faith and virtues, weeding out and separating from me their imperfections, that I may be accounted worthy so to know Thee, that I may perfectly love and serve Thee. Amen.

3. Mary Magdalen, turning her face towards Jesus Christ, He with a voice different from that which He was wont before to use, said to her, " *Woman, why weepest thou?   Whom seekest thou?*"   Where is to be considered, that when Almighty God, in the like case, makes such demands as these, seeming as if He knew not the matter concerning which He questions us, He would give us to understand that there is something in it which He does not like, or knows not with that knowledge, which is called the knowledge of approbation.   And, therefore, when the same Magdalen stood behind at His feet, weeping, and watered them with her tears,(12) He did not say to her,— " Why weepest thou?   Whom seekest thou?"   Because those tears were grounded in the true knowledge of her sins, and in a lively faith and love of that Lord, whom she had there before her, who well knew them and ap-

<hr>

(11) 1 Cor iii. 7.   (12) Luc. vii. 38.

proved them. But in this case, because her tears proceeded from ignorance and lack of faith, lamenting Him as dead who was alive, and seeking the living amongst the dead, He said to her:—"Why weepest thou? Whom seekest thou? As if He had said: "Knowest thou wherefore thou weepest, and whom thou seekest? Doubtless thou dost not well know, for if thou knewest, thou wouldst not lament Him after this manner as dead, nor seek Him as absent, whom thou hast so present." By which Christ our Lord instructs us, that it is His will, that we should examine well the cause of our tears, and of our sighs: as also what it is we seek and make our aim in His holy service, in order that nothing intermix itself with it contrary to God, or unworthy of His greatness, and of our perfection. For many times I think that I weep for my sins, and yet do not, but rather for some temporal loss or damage which results from them; I think that I weep to go and see God, when in fact I weep to fly from the toil and misery which oppress me. It likewise happens, that I suppose that I seek God and His glory, when in very deed I seek myself, and my own honour, or convenience. And if I seek God, yet I do it, mixing with it many imperfections: and therefore with great reason God our Lord says to me:—"Why weepest thou? Whom seekest thou?"

Colloquy.—O God of my soul, grant to me that I may weep for my own sins, and for Thy absence, in such a manner that Thou approve my tears, and that I may so seek what I desire, that Thou allow of my endeavours. Amen.

POINT IV.

Mary Magdalen, "thinking that it was the gardener,

saith to him, *Sir, if thou hast taken Him hence, tell me where thou hast laid Him*, and I will take Him away."(13)

1. In these words Mary Magdalen discovered the *excess of her fervent love,* which with great violence held her as one taken out of herself, and drew strength out of her weakness, to offer herself to more than she was able. So that there are here expressed, after a very lively manner, the properties of inflamed charity, which is called *unitive* and violent.

i. The first property is, that it so transports out of himself the heart and tongue of him that loves, that he is *always thinking of his beloved,* and supposes that all think of Him, and is always speaking of Him, imagining that all understand Him ; and, therefore, Mary Magdalen did not say, " If thou hast taken away the body of my master," but only, " if thou hast *taken Him hence ;*" because she imagined that the gardener understood, and knew of whom she spoke, so absorbed was she in thinking only of her Beloved. By this sign I shall come to know, if I bear a great love towards God; for, as He Himself said—"Where thy treasure is, there is thy heart also ;" (14) and consequently, there is thy tongue, thine eyes, thy feet, and thy whole spirit, employed in the sight and love of thy treasure, and in keeping it, and carefully adding to it.

Colloquy.—O infinite God, be Thou my treasure, and transport my heart, and whatsoever is within me, that where Thou art, I also may be, seeing Thee and enjoying Thee, world without end.   Amen.

ii. The second property of this inflamed charity is, to cause in him that loves, an *entire forgetfulness of himself,* and of all that he has, and to move him to humble and subject himself to every human creature, that so he may

<hr>

(13) Joan. xx. 15.   (14) Mat. vi. 21.

obtain his object. And sometimes he both says and does things, which to human judgment seem to be mere folly, but are indeed the excesses of love, after the manner that holy David, forgetful of his regal dignity, leaped and danced before the ark; who, when Michol his wife mocked him, made no account of it, but humbled himself so much the more in his own eyes, and leaped more before God, saying:—" I shall appear more glorious."(15) And the same Magdalen, wounded with the like love, came to the banquet, where Christ was invited, and cast herself at His feet, without regarding what the guests would judge of it, as entirely forgetful of all, as if she had been there alone. And on this present occasion, with the like abandonment of herself, with great humility and reverence, she called Him Lord, whom she deemed to be the gardener, so to win His favour, and to persuade Him to show her the place where the body of her master lay, saying to Him, " If Thou hast taken Him hence ;" not weighing that there was no reason why the gardener should take out of the ground, or pull out of the grave, the body of the dead, which his lord and master had placed in it. And by this second sign I shall know the greatness or littleness of my charity, for if the love of riches in the covetous, and the love of honour in the ambitious, and the love of delights in the voluptuous, have such great force as to transport them out of themselves, and make them so forgetful of themselves, and of their own affairs, that they humble and subject themselves to others, and do such things as appear mere madness, to Him that loves them not as they do themselves; how much more, and with what greater force does the love of Almighty God effect this in those, whom He has brought and made to enter into the cellars of His delicious wines?(16) For unless

<hr>

(15) 2 Reg. vi. 22.   (16) Cant. ii. 4.

the same God established this His charity in them, such excesses would plainly cause them to be accounted fools and madmen, but He does establish this charity in them; and if they do anything which to Him that does not love appears folly, yet it is wisdom in the eyes of Him, who knows what it is to love.

Colloquy.—O Eternal King, bring me into the cellars of Thy wines, inebriate me with the strong wine of Thy inflaming love, transport me out of myself, and transfer me into Thee, cause in my soul a total forgetfulness of my own affairs, that I may wholly attend to those that are Thine, and may humble myself before the world, so as even to be accounted a fool, that I may be truly wise before Thee.   Amen.

iii. The third property of fervent love is, *to draw force out of feebleness,* and to cause him that loves to offer himself to much more than he is able, in the service of his beloved, trusting not so much to his own strength, as to that which God will give him.   For even so Mary Magdalen, inflamed with this vehement love, offered herself manfully and valorously to go and fetch the body of her master, wherever it was, without exception of any place, or making any account of the sacredness of the season, and that the sun was now risen, and that she herself was a weak and feeble woman, the burden a dead body, and the body of one crucified, abhorred by the Jews, and condemned to death by the governor himself, without whose leave, Joseph of Arimathea was not so bold as to give it burial, yet, she, breaking through all these difficulties, said, " Ego eum tollam," " I will take Him away."

Colloquy.—O woman, great is thy confidence, great is thy courage, and great is thy fortitude, because thy love is great.   O love invincible, which vanquishest whatever is hard and difficult in this life, and art over-

come by none !   Thou bearest Him who bearest thee !
Thou makest the burden light which thou takest upon
thee !   Thou layest Christ upon our shoulders, and
yet makest Christ to carry us, helping us thyself to
bear the whole burden !   O most strong love, thou
art in very deed strong, and no less strong than death
(17) itself, since thou darest wrestle with the dead, and
break through the difficulties of death itself, in order
to serve and please thy beloved !   O eternal God and
infinite Lover, inebriate me with the sweetness of Thy
love, in order that my strength being thus renewed,
I may run in Thy service, going always forward, and
never fainting, undergoing whatever burden Thou
shalt impose upon me, ever hoping that Thou wilt give
me strength to support it.

2. In this spirit I will offer myself to carry Christ dead
upon me, that is to say, His mortification in my body, after
the manner that He mortified His, according to that of the
Apostle, "Always bearing about in our body the mortification of Jesus, that the life also of Jesus may be made
manifest in our bodies," &c.   "For you are bought," says
the same Apostle, "with a great price.   Glorify and bear
God in your body." (18)

POINT V.

1. Christ our Lord, beholding the fervour, the tears, and
the promptitude of Mary Magdalen, offering herself to
take away His body, at last discovered Himself to her,
calling her by her proper name, and with His accustomed
sound of voice, saying, "Maria,(19) Mary ;" and she instantly knowing Him, answered : " Rabboni !" that is, Master !
—i. Here we should consider the *omnipotence of Christ, full*

---

(17) Cant. viii. 6.　　　　(18) 2 Cor. iv. 10.   1 Cor. vi. 20.
(19) Joan xx. 16.

of sweetness and gentleness; since, with one single word, Mary, He so changed the heart of this His devout handmaiden, drove all sadness away from her, and filled her with incomparable gladness, enlightened her understanding with a new brightness, dissolving all the darkness of infidelity, and inflamed her will with the new fire of His love, that she might love Him, as the living God, whom before she loved as a dead man.

Colloquy.—O infinite God, how infinite is Thy love towards those whom Thou knowest by their proper name. (20)   To these Thou manifestest Thy divine face, and makest them joyful with Thy presence, because they have found grace before Thee.   O happy Magdalen, whom Christ knew by thy own name, and called thee by it; and calling thee, discovered Himself to thee, that thou mightest know Him that knew thee, and see Him whom thou desiredst to see, and find Him whom thou hast sought with so great fervour.   Let me, dear Lord, find grace in Thy sight, and do Thou know me in such a manner, that I may come to know Thee, as I am known by Thee, and love Thee, as I am beloved by Thee.   Amen.

2. Consider the answer of Mary Magdalen, which was, "Rabboni, Master!" for, taken by surprise by love, she called her Beloved by that name, which she was formerly wont to give Him.   When she spoke to the angels, she used a name of reverence, and named Him Lord; but now speaking to Himself, she gave Him a name of reverence and love, calling Him " Master;" for hearing that word, " Mary," she felt in her soul the effects of her divine master, by means of the fulness of light which He infused into her, and thereupon cast herself at His feet, at which she was wont to sit to hear His teaching.

(20) Exo. xxxiii. 12.

Colloquy.—O Sovereign Master, who with a single word didst teach this Thy fervent disciple such heroic virtues; vouchsafe to enlighten my understanding, that I likewise may know them, and knowing them, may love Thee as she loved Thee. Amen.

3. Christ our Lord, seeing Mary Magdalen prostrate at His feet, with a desire to kiss them, said to her,—" Do not touch me, for I am not yet ascended to my Father; but go to my brethren and say to them ; I ascend to my Father, and your Father, to my God, and your God."(21) Where the causes are to be considered, why Jesus permitted not that Mary Magdalen should touch Him, as she was wont to do at other times.—i. The first cause was, because with the fervour that she cast herself down, she sought to have touched Him *too familiarly*, and our Lord would teach her, that she was for the time to come, to behave to Him *with great reverence*, as to Him that now led a glorified life, and was upon the point of ascending to His Father; and generally His Majesty desires that we join *reverence* with *love*, in all our behaviour towards Him. ii. The second cause was, because her *faith* was yet *imperfect ;* for, as for this reason He discovered not Himself to her all at once, but *by little and little*, first in the guise and figure of a gardener,—and afterwards in His own figure and voice; so now He would not bestow all His favours on her at once, but first discovered Himself to her, so that she might know Him, and rejoice to see Him ; and afterwards, when her faith was more perfect, suffered Himself to be touched by her, and, therefore, He said,—" Do not touch me ;" as if He had said, " Do not touch me," because within thy heart I am not yet ascended to my Father, since thou dost not yet rightly believe me to be ascended in a glorified life to my Father.

(21) Joan. xx. 17.

Colloquy.—O most high master, ascend in my heart to the greatest possible height, giving me the highest faith and esteem of which I am capable of Thy majesty, in order that I may be worthy to see Thee, and with inward charity to embrace Thee. Amen.

4. Consider *the tenderness of that kind and loving* salutation, which Christ our Lord sent by Mary Magdalen to His disciples, by which He gave them to understand, that the glory of His Resurrection had not diminished His gentleness, and showed them greater signs of love than before, for " He is not ashamed to call them *brethren.*"(22)   And that which He commanded her to say to them was, " I ascend to my Father, and your Father, to my God and your God."   My Father by eternal generation, your Father by grace and redemption ; my God by unity of nature, your God by unity of charity.

Colloquy.— O most loving Jesus, I give Thee all the thanks that I possibly can, for this so singular grace with which Thou enrichest us, in giving us Thy Father for our Father, and Thy God for our God. O my soul, if thou hast such a Father, what dost thou desire more ?   If thou hast such a God, what canst thou require more ?   O my Father, show Thyself to be my Father, making me to be Thy son.   O my God, show Thyself to be my God, making me one spirit with Thee, by the union of perfect charity. Amen.

(22) Heb. ii. 11.

MEDITATION V.

OF THE APPEARANCE MADE TO THE OTHER DEVOUT WOMEN, AND TO MARY MAGDALEN.

POINT I.

Mary Magdalen, departing with great joy of mind from the sepulchre, met with her other companions in the way, and relating to them what had happened to her, they were all inflamed with a burning desire to see their master, who, beholding their great eagerness, and the fervour with which they went so early to seek Him, came to meet them, and, saluting them, said, " Avete, all hail."(1)

How careful Christ our Lord is *to reward the labours and watchings of His servants*, although He sometimes defers this visitation till they make themselves more worthy of it, that so it may turn to their greater profit ; whence I will learn never to desist from my pious exercises, though this visitation be long delayed.   And it is a source of great consolation to know the goodness of Christ our Lord, who bears with our imperfections when we seek to serve Him with a *true and fervent intention,* as was the case with these devout women ; who went to anoint Him with some defect of faith, and yet because they sincerely desired to serve Him, He, beholding this their pious intention, was pleased to comfort them.   Oh, how joyful and contented were they with the sight of Him, and how well employed did they reckon all their past labours, for with that single word, " Avete," that is to say, "God save you," or "rejoice you," they were replenished with spiritual health and excessive joy, because the words of Christ are *efficacious,* and effect all they signify.   Nor did our Lord use this word

(1) Mat. xxviii 9.

without the same mystery which the angel Gabriel had used when he announced the Incarnation to the Blessed Virgin, that so confirming what the angel had said, He might announce to these devout women, that, by His holy Resurrection, He freed them from the maledictions of that guilt which we all incurred by another woman.

Colloquy.—O my Saviour, come into my soul, and into all its powers, and say to them, '*Avete,*' 'All hail,' or 'God save you;' because at Thy word they will all be filled with that joy and benediction which Thou hast gained for us by Thy glorious Resurrection. Amen.

POINT II.

As soon as these devout women saw Christ our Lord, immediately "they came up and took hold of His feet, and adored Him." (2)

1. They did not cast themselves down precipitately, as Mary Magdalen did the first time, but *with great reverence came near to Him and adored Him,* and He Himself giving them leave, they took hold of His sacred feet, and kissed them with unspeakable love. And here Mary Magdalen obtained the full accomplishment of her desire, which was to touch and kiss the feet of her master, Christ. Oh, what sweetness did they feel in this touch, kissing those precious wounds which they went to embalm and anoint with so great desire! They went to the sepulchre to anoint Christ, but Christ anointed them with the same ointment with which He Himself was anointed, which was, " with the oil of gladness," (3) and with that spirit of holy devotion which He shed and poured upon them.

2. In imitation of these holy women, whom St. Mark reports to have been principally three, I am to take care

(2) Mat. xxviii. 9.   (3) Ps. xliv. 8.

that the *three faculties of my soul exercise themselves* in anointing Christ;—the *memory* with holy recollections;—the *understanding* with pious meditations;—the *will* with fervent affections, buying these perfumes of Him that said: " Come, buy without money and without any price;" (4) because He gives us for nothing the price with which we are to buy this holy ointment. With His help and assistance, therefore, I will offer to Him many exercises of mortification, as a grateful payment to Him, and I will beseech Him to impart to me these aromatical spices with which to anoint Him, since from His hand only all kinds of good comes to us.

Colloquy.—O Jesus Christ, anointed by Thy eternal Father "with the oil of gladness above Thy fellows," Thou hast no need to be anointed with such base and worthless ointments as mine are, but yet Thy charity is so great, that Thou acceptest it for the oil and anointing of gladness to Thyself, to see me inflamed with Thy love. Behold, I here offer to Thee the aromatic spices which I have bought, that is, affections of *praise* and of *gratitude*, of *love* and of *confidence*, with lively desires of obtaining all virtues, to anoint Thee with. But Thou, Lord, who preventest those that seek Thee, " let Thy mercies speedily prevent" (5) me ; give me leave to touch in spirit Thy sacred wounds, and to anoint my heart with that most precious liquor which flows from them, that, assisted by the grace of Thy divine Spirit, it may always employ itself in Thy love and service. Amen.

POINT III.

" Then Jesus said to them, Fear not. Go tell my brethren, that they go into Galilee, there they shall see me." (6)

<hr>

(4) Isa. lv. 1.　　　(5) Ps. lxxviii. 8.　　　(6) Mat. xxviii. 10.

1. In this joyful salutation is to be seen, how it is the property of the spirit of God, *to conform itself to the spirit of the angels*, and of His ministers, saying the same that they have said, and confirming that which they have spoken, but yet with greater signs of love.   The angels said,—" Tell ye, His disciples, that He is risen, and behold He will go before you into Galilee, there you shall see Him."   Christ our Lord said, *"Tell my brethren;"* and He who called not the angels brethren, called men His brethren, in sign of more tender and sweeter love, because of the relationship and resemblance which He bore to them by sharing their human nature.

Colloquy.—O most loving Jesus, how sweet to my ears is this word, which issues forth from Thy blessed mouth, *" tell my brethren!"*   Never shall I be weary of hearing it, although Thou repeat it an infinite number of times.   Speak it, dear Lord, to my heart, and grant me to feel the spirit, which Thou hast enclosed in these words, in order that I may obtain that resemblance of life, which ought to proceed from such a brotherhood.

2. I may likewise meditate on the cause *why Christ our Lord commanded His apostles*, as the angels had also told them before *to go into Galilee*, and promised that they should see Him there, when He intended and appointed to see them the same day in Judea and in Jerusalem, where they were at that very time.   The cause was, that the *country of Judea was very unquiet and much molested*, and they themselves also were there very full of trouble and fear: in order, therefore, that they might enjoy His presence with greater quiet and content, He commanded them to go to Galilee, a place of less noise and more quiet; giving us to understand, that although Almighty God sometimes visits us amongst the troubles and tumults of

the world, yet He desires that we should seek out a quieter place, where we may see Him for a longer time, and converse with Him in prayer and contemplation.(7) And the name of *Galilee* also, which signifies *transmigration*, implies something of the same sort; for they who desire to see and enjoy Christ risen, ought to *transfer* and change themselves from vice to virtue, from a loose to a stricter kind of life, from trouble to quiet, from lukewarmness to fervour, and from imperfection to perfection.

Colloquy.—O most sweet Jesus, since Thou art so great a friend of Galilee, transfer me with this transmigration so pleasing to Thyself; that I may be worthy to see Thee by contemplation in this life, and afterwards, being removed from this to the other, may see Thee face to face for all eternity.   Amen.

MEDITATION VI.

OF THE APPEARANCE TO ST. PETER, AND OF THE THINGS WHICH HAPPENED PREVIOUSLY TO IT.

POINT I.

The devout women going back from the sepulchre, told all these things which they had heard of the angels, "to the eleven, and to all the rest, who were mourning and weeping." And they hearing that He was alive, *did not believe them; " and these words seemed to them as idle tales ;"* nay, when Mary Magdalen affirmed that she had seen Jesus, as little did they believe her.(1)

1. In this fact is described to us, how difficult and how

(7) S. Greg. Hom. xxi. in Evang.
(1) Luc. xxiv. 9.   Marc. xvi. 10.

heroic the act of faith is, which lifts us up to believe some things, against that which we have perceived by our senses, and how ill and grudgingly men answer to Almighty God, for the manifold things He does for them, disbelieving what they heard to have been done by God, and looking upon the testimony as dotage, whereas it is more gross dotage in them not to believe what God has revealed. For Christ having said to His disciples that He was to be crucified, and that He should rise again the third day: and these devout women now telling them the message of the angels, and giving them a sign so certain as that they were to go into Galilee and there see Him, as He Himself had foretold them on the night of His supper: they did not believe for all this, but considered it dotage, to think that a man dead on the cross, left without blood, and wounded in so many parts of His body, should be risen again : quite forgetful, not only of the revelation of Christ Himself, but of the raising up of Lazarus, and of other miracles, which their master had done before their eyes.

Colloquy.—O supreme master, I am well contented to subdue my understanding to the obedience of faith, and to deny and wholly renounce all my senses, that I may believe what Thou hast revealed ; for I know that " I shall rise out of the earth, and I shall be clothed again with my skin, and in my flesh," after it has been converted into dust and ashes, "I shall see"(2) Thee, my God and my Saviour ; this my hope is laid up in my bosom, because I do not doubt Thine omnipotence, and much less Thy will, since Thou hast revealed and promised that it shall so come to pass.

2. Hence I am to learn carefully *to fly two extremes :*— One, that of those *who over-lightly believe* every revelation and vision of every woman, not without danger of believ-

<hr>

(2) Job. xix. 25.

ing many things, which are plain dotage and dreams, or mere inventions of their own imaginations:—the other, that of those who are *overhard and difficult to be convinced*, and take all that they hear for dotage, which is an egregious error; for sometimes even women, and ignorant men, for their devotion and their fervour, are worthy to have true visions of angels, and even of the Lord of angels, as is to be seen in this present case; and therefore such ought to be believed, especially when those visions tend to confirm the truths of our holy faith; nor is it a greater error to call the dotage of the imagination, God's revelation, than, on the other hand, to call God's revelation the dotage of the imagination.

POINT II.

Amongst the disciples, the two most fervent, who excelled most in the love of Christ our Lord, were Peter and John. *"Peter therefore went out and that other disciple, and they came to the sepulchre*, and they both ran together, and that other disciple did outrun Peter, and came first to the sepulchre,......but yet he went not in. Then cometh Simon Peter following him, and went into the sepulchre, and saw the linen clothes lying, and the napkin that had been about His head, not lying with the linen clothes, but apart, wrapped up in one place;" which was a certain sign that the body had not been taken away by stealth, but had risen; "and he saw and believed" (3) that which the women had related to them.

1. Here we may consider, that these two disciples were not in the same extreme as the rest, who took the revelation related by the women for mere dotage; but yet they *would try whether the ground and signs of that revelation were good or not.* For it is the property of such as are

(3) Joan. xx. 3.

wisely fervent, to use diligence, that they may attain to sufficient certainty in things relating to Almighty God, and because love overcomes all kinds of difficulties, therefore, although these disciples know what great persecutions the Jews would raise up against the disciples of Jesus Christ, and that they had set a guard to keep the sepulchre, yet they resolved within themselves to go to it, to see that which was related by the women.

2. But it was not without mystery that the angels did not appear to them as to the women ; the reason of which probably was, *that such* an appearance *was not needful,* since from the women's revelation, and from the sign which they themselves saw of the linen clothes, which remained there gathered together, they believed Christ to be truly risen, and reminded themselves on this occasion of the words which their master had spoken at His last supper. And hence it may be seen, that the visions and appearances of holy angels are not signs of greater sanctity, since they are sometimes granted to those who are more tender and weaker in virtue.

3. By these two apostles, Peter and John, are represented the principal virtues with which we are to seek Christ, namely, *faith and charity.* For faith discovers the truths, and enters, first with St. Peter into the sepulchre, and presently afterwards love enters, as St. John entered. and with this entrance, faith is increased and strengthened, and its knowledge rendered more perfect. In the same two apostles, are likewise represented the two lives, *active* and *contemplative,* which bring us to Christ; the active goes before, disposing and preparing, and then follows the contemplative, possessing and enjoying.

Colloquy.—O most loving Jesus, enlighten my faith and inflame my charity, that, laying aside all human fear, I may seek Thee and enter in where Thou desirest I should find Thee : perfect me with the exercises of the active life, in all kind of virtue, in order that I may ascend to the exercises of the contemplative life, and, by means of them, may enter into "the secret of Thy face,"(4) to see, and to enjoy, the beauty and splendour which Thou hast in Thy glory. Amen.

The mystery contained in the circumstance of Christ our Lord leaving the linen clothes in the sepulchre, is pointed out at the end of the second meditation.

POINT III.

St. Peter and St. John returning into the city, St. Peter went apart by himself, " secum mirans, quod factum fuerat." Wondering in himself at that which was come to pass,(5) that is, pondering with himself and ruminating upon what he had heard and seen in the sepulchre ; and as he was thus meditating, Christ our Lord appeared to him, as may be collected from those words which St. Luke reports to have been spoken by the other apostles : " Surrexit Dominus vere, et apparuit Simoni." " The Lord is risen indeed, and hath appeared to Simon."(6)

1. *St. Peter rendered himself worthy of this appearance* of Christ our Lord, disposing himself for it by the diligence which he used in going to the sepulchre, and by the meditation which he retired to make by himself on the things which he had seen. And, notwithstanding that St. John went also with him to the sepulchre, yet *we do not read that Christ our Lord appeared to him;* where we may observe, that Almighty God often imparts greater favours to such sinners as have truly repented, than to the just who have not sinned, in order to comfort and encourage such penitents; as is declared in the parable of the prodigal son,

(4) Ps. xxx. 21.   (5) Luc. xxiv. 12.   (6) Ibid. xxiv. 34.

It was not without cause, therefore, that the first man and the first woman, to whom, as the Evangelists relate, Christ our Lord appeared after His Resurrection, were such as had been first sinners; that so, "where sin abounded," "*grace*" also might "*more abound*."(7)   Hence I will encourage myself to put my confidence in Almighty God, although I have been a grievous sinner, and will dispose myself by prayer and fervour of life to receive His gifts, who on His part is ready to give, and liberal in giving.

2. I will consider the great *confusion and shame* which St. Peter felt when he saw himself before his master, remembering that he had denied Him; and it is to be believed that he cast himself at His holy feet, bitterly lamenting his former sins, and craving pardon of Christ our Lord, who, without doubt, comforted him, and assured him of pardon, and replenished his soul with unspeakable joy. Oh what tender words did Christ our Lord use to him, and what wholesome admonitions did He give him !   We may imagine that He said to him, " 'Pax tecum,'—peace be unto thee,—fear not, it is I,—thy sins are forgiven thee,— confirm thy brethren." (8)   Oh how was the heart of the holy apostle lightened by the sight and words of his blessed master !   How was he confirmed in faith, and how inflamed in his love !

Colloquy.—O sweet Jesus, how great is the multitude and sweetness of Thy mercies towards all sinners, who, from the bottom of their hearts, repent of their sins !   Doubtless Thou wouldst have received Judas, if he had done the penance that Peter did.   Blessed be Thy mercy, O Lord, by which I beseech Thee to make me worthy of the vision of Thy majesty, in the kingdom of Thy glory.   Amen.

(7) Rom. v. 20.
(8) Joan. xx. 19; vi. 20.   Luc. vii. 48; xxii. 82.

3. Consider St. Peter, with great joy and exultation of mind, returned to the place where his fellow apostles were, *to confirm them in their faith*, as Christ our Lord had commanded him; and his testimony was so powerful, that many believed upon it, as may be gathered from the very words which they spoke, saying,—" Surrexit Dominus vere, et apparuit Simoni." " The Lord is risen indeed, and hath appeared to Simon." As if they had said: " He is risen, not in figure, or appearance, but in all truth and certainty. And this we know, not because He appeared to Mary Magdalen, or to other women, but because He appeared to Simon, whose testimony is of great authority." Whence I will learn, by the example of this apostle, to show myself grateful for the benefits received from our Lord, and to make use of them to confirm my brethren in true virtue; which I am bound to perform so much the more diligently, as I have received greater talent to persuade others, and to be believed.

Colloquy.—O glorious apostle, with great reason art thou called *Simon*, that is to say, *obedient*, since thou art so truly obedient to the voice of thy master, in fulfilling that which He has commanded thee, doing the office of a *rock* as *Peter*, and of a *head* as *Cephas*, by confirming and strengthening the faith of thy fellow disciples, whose head thou art to be : confirm in like manner my feeble faith, and perfect my imperfect obedience, in order that I may believe with great firmness that which thou didst believe, and obey my Lord with great fervour as thou didst obey. Amen.

MEDITATION VII.

OF THE APPEARANCE MADE TO THE TWO DISCIPLES THAT WENT TO EMMAUS.

POINT I.

"And behold two of them," who had heard of the women what the angels had told unto them, "*went the same day to a town which was sixty furlongs from Jerusalem, named Emmaus.* And they talked together of all those things which had happened. And it came to pass that while they talked and reasoned with themselves, Jesus also drawing near, went with them. But their eyes were held that they should not know him."(1)

1. Consider, first, the *cause* why these two disciples went out of Jerusalem upon this occasion, which was in order that they might withdraw themselves from that place, which they considered dangerous, and take some refreshment in the town of Emmaus, in which one of them was born; but the mystical cause was, that we might understand how the passion of fear and sorrow is wont to be the cause that the soul departs out of *Jerusalem,* which is interpreted the *vision of peace,* and from the society and company of the disciples of Christ, who are the good and godly, to seek some bodily ease, and some indulgence of the flesh amongst carnal kindred, or worldly persons, represented by *Emmaus,* which is interpreted, *a people despised,* or a *timorous council;* taking indeed in this erroneous counsel, as making light of the comfort of heaven, to hearken to the counsel of the earth. I will, therefore, endeavour never to render myself subject to this passion, for unless the mercy of Almighty God hinder those counsels

(1) Luc. xxiv. 13. Marc. xvi. 2. S. Th. 3, p. q. lv. art. 4.
Vol. V.—5.

which it suggests, I shall come to lose myself by listening to them.

2. I will meditate on the *causes* for which *Christ our Lord vouchsafed to appear to these two disciples*, as they walked in this journey.

i. The first cause was the compassion with which He was touched towards them, desiring, like a good pastor, to bring back to the fold these two straying and wandering sheep, that so we may understand how vigilant He is in this His office, hastening towards us with His mercy when we are in the greatest necessity, and following us when we have departed far from Him, till at last He overtakes us.

Colloquy.—O blessed be so good a pastor, who watches so carefully over His flock : it plainly appears, dear Lord, that Thou hast exposed Thy life for this flock, and hast redeemed it with Thy precious blood, since Thou art so careful to gather it together within the fold of Thy Church, and from that fold to bring it to the fold of Thy glory.

ii. The *second cause* was, that those two disciples were *much perplexed and distressed* as they went along; and it belongs to Christ our Lord, and is very usual with Him, speedily to assist and succour such, to moderate their sadness, and to send them some refreshment under it, according to that which He Himself said by the kingly prophet, —" *I am with him in tribulation.*" (2)

Colloquy.—O my soul, if thou sawest Him, who is present with thee in thy tribulations, although veiled and disguised, doubtless thou wouldst be joyful in them, holding it for a great blessing to be afflicted in exchange for the blessings of His presence.

iii. The third *cause* was, *because they were discoursing of*

(2) Ps. xc. 15.

godly things by the way, and Christ our Lord is well pleased to be present at such sort of colloquies, and, therefore, in the midst of these discourses, He joined Himself to them, according to that which He Himself had said:—" Where there are two or three gathered in my name, there am I in the midst of them."(3)   Hence I will gather, how good a thing it is, always, and in all places, to speak of God, and to employ ourselves in such discourses with our companions, especially in the time of tribulation, since Christ our Lord comes with such great speed to comfort those who are thus engaged; and, on the contrary, how evil it is to talk of evil and profane things, because Christ our Lord does not join Himself to such as talk of these things, but retires and flies from them.

3. I will consider lastly, how *the eyes of these disciples were withheld from knowing Christ because of their little faith*, for which defect our Lord permitted this impediment, till such time as their faith was more perfect; for, as the prophet Isaiah says,—" Unless you believe, you shall not understand." (4)   Another cause was the great sadness and inward affliction which had seized upon them; here we are taught that Christ our Lord is often present with us in our temptations and tribulations, helping us to fight, and to suffer them with patience: though we neither see Him, nor observe that He is present with us, but suppose that He is absent, because we do not feel the favour of sensible consolation.

Colloquy.—O good Jesus, suffer not my offences to cause so great a dimness of sight in my soul, as to hinder me from seeing Thee, when Thou art present, and from knowing Thee when Thou speakest within my heart: but if, in Thy secret providence, Thou

---

(3) Mat. xviii. 20.   (4) Isa. vii. 9, juxta Septuag.

hidest Thyself from me, yet, let not the presence of Thy grace be wanting to me, lest I be wanting through my frailty, in that which I ought to perform for Thee. Amen.

POINT II.

And He said to them,—" What are these discourses that you hold one with another, as you walk, and are sad? And the one of them whose name was Cleophas, answering, said to Him, 'Art Thou only a stranger in Jerusalem, and hast not known the things that have been done there in these days?' To whom He said, 'What things?' And they said, 'Concerning Jesus of Nazareth, *who was a prophet, mighty in work and word, before God and all the people.* And how our chief priests and princes delivered Him to be condemned to death, and crucified Him. But we hoped that it was He that should have redeemed Israel.' " (5)

1. Consider first, *the sweetness of Christ our Lord*, in this discourse with His disciples, to induce them to discover the wound of their unbelief, and to cure it at the root; for which purpose He asked them what were the subjects of their discourse, making as if He did not know them, because He desired to hear them out of their own mouths; and, in particular, He takes delight in hearing us speak together of those things, which He has suffered for our sakes, not at all offended at the mention of them, although they were so ignominious. Whence I will gather, that it is the property of the Spirit of Christ to move us by His inspirations to speak, for two causes; first, to publish the greatness of Almighty God, and His glory; and next, to discover our own calamities, and to be cured of them.

(5) Luc. xxiv. 17.

2. With regard to the disciples, I will meditate on the high thoughts which they had of their master, although defective in regard to His divinity ; for they said of Him, first, that He was " *mighty in works,*" secondly, " *in words,*" thirdly, " *before God ;*" fourthly, " *before all the people.*"

Colloquy.—I rejoice, O King of Glory, that Thou art mighty in *works*, both in deeds of heroic sanctity and in stupendous miracles, in which Thou manifestest Thy infinite bounty and omnipotence.   I rejoice, likewise that Thou art mighty in *words*, teaching celestial doctrine, which illuminates the understanding, and inflames the will, and allures them to virtue and truth, in which Thou showest Thy infinite wisdom. I rejoice that Thou art so mighty *before God* as to appease His anger, and to obtain such abundant mercy for all men, in which Thou showest the equality that Thou hast with Him. I also rejoice that Thou art so mighty *before all people*, changing the hearts of men, and attracting them to Thy service, in which Thou discoverest the efficacy of Thy grace.   Manifest, O Almighty Lord, this Thy might in me, that, according to my strength, I may also be mighty both in words and works before God, and before men, working and speaking such things only as may be pleasing to Almighty God, and may edify my neighbour to Thy honour and glory.   Amen.

In these four things I ought to study to excel, in the same order as they are set down.   For, I shall not be mighty in *words*, if I am not mighty in *works ;* neither shall I be such, if I be not first such *before God :* and if I be mighty before God by means of prayer, and confidence in His omnipotence, I shall be much more mighty before men, as the angel said to the patriarch Jacob. (6)

3. The disciples discovered their *frailty and lack of*

____

(6) Gen. xxxii. 28.

faith, saying: "We hoped that it was He that should have redeemed Israel;" as if they had said, "but this His death happening, we have lost this hope." "*And now, besides all this*, to-day is the third day, since these things were done; yea, and certain women also of our company affrighted us, who, before it was light, were at the sepulchre, and not finding His body, came, saying that they had also seen a vision of angels, who say that He is alive."(7)   Where is represented the frailty and weakness of the imperfect, who are wont to lose, on a sudden, their great esteem for Almighty God, and His proceedings, in consequence of some adverse event falling out contrary to their own imperfect judgment, not knowing the ways which Almighty God takes to bring His purposes to pass; like these two disciples, who could not conceive that the death of Christ was a most fit means for the redemption of Israel, which they expected.

POINT III.

Jesus said to them:—"O foolish and slow of heart to believe in all things wnich the prophets have spoken. *O ught not Christ to have suffered these things, and so to enter into His glory?*   And, beginning at Moses and all the prophets, *He expounded to them in all the Scriptures* the things that were concerning Him." (8)

1. Here is to be considered, first, the *sharpness of the reproof* given by our Lord, which yet proceeded, not from indignation, but from zeal and commiseration, and was intended to stir up and quicken their faith, and to draw them out of the ignorance into which they had fallen. He called them "fools," or ignorant, because, having heard Him make mention so many times of this mystery, they did not yet understand it.   He l ewise called them "slow

<hr>

(7) Luc. xxiv. 22.   (8) Luc. xxiv. 25.

of heart," because, having sufficient reasons and motives to believe His Resurrection, yet they still stood in doubt of it.

Colloquy.—O sovereign master, with how much greater reason mayest Thou reprove me, and say to me : O foolish and slow of heart to believe all things which the prophets and Evangelists have spoken ; since there are many of these things which I do not know as I ought, and do not believe with a lively faith, so as to put them in practice. Take from me, dear Lord, this my folly and slowness of heart, that I may both know Thee and serve Thee as I am bound to do.   Amen.

2. Consider that *profound and admirable reason* which Christ our Lord added to this reproof :—" Ought not Christ to have suffered these things, and so to enter into His glory ?" —giving them to understand that their ignorance and hardness of heart proceeded from their not fully believing this truth.

Colloquy.—O my soul, open thine eyes, and consider, that if it were necessary that Christ should suffer such and so grievous afflictions, and so enter into His glory, which yet was His by title of inheritance, as being the Son of the Eternal Father by generation, much more necessary is it, that thou shouldst suffer something to enter into that glory which is none of thine, but only God's ; to which, through His only mercy, He has ordained thee. And if thou thinkest the same not necessary, thou art a fool, slow, and hard of heart, and worthy to be reproved ; but if thou believest this with a lively faith, work as thou believest, suffering such labours and afflictions as shall befall thee, since it is written—"All that will live godly in Christ Jesus, shall suffer persecution ;" (9) that is, for the love of Him.

(9) 2 Tim. iii. 12.

3. Consider *the efficacy with which Christ our Lord began to interpret to them the divine scriptures,* opening the interior of their soul, in order that they might understand them, and inflaming their hearts with a most ardent fire of love, that they might be affected to them, and to Him, who did interpret them, for so they said afterwards:—" Was not our heart burning within us, whilst He spoke in the way, and opened unto us the scriptures?" (10) This declaration they call, " to open the scriptures," which were before shut to them, since it drew the mysteries to light, which were hidden in them.

Colloquy.—O Heavenly master, who holdest in Thy hand the key of David, (11) to shut and open after Thine own will the divine scriptures, shutting them to the proud, and opening them to the humble: open them, O my Lord, to this Thine unworthy servant, so that my understanding may remain illustrated with the verity of the mysteries which lie hidden therein, and my will be inflamed with the charity Thou discoverest in them. Speak, Lord, to me, in the way of this life, that so my heart may burn within me, and my soul be melted with the sweetness of Thy voice.(12) O blessed disciples, which deserved to hear so divine a master, whose words are so many torches, which give light and burn to illuminate and inflame those that hear them : beseech Him to speak to me as He spake to you, taking compassion of my necessity, as He did of yours. Amen.

<h3 style="text-align:center">POINT IV.</h3>

" And they drew nigh to the town, whither they were going, and He made as though He would go farther. But they constrained Him, saying :—' Stay with us, be-

---

(10) Luc. xxiv. 82.   (11) Apoc. iii. 7.   (12) Cant. ii. 14.

cause it is towards evening, and the day is now far spent.' " (13)

1. Christ our Lord made as though He would leave these disciples and go farther, though, in truth, His desire was to stay with them. This was *to signify that in their opinion He was far from them ;* and also to provoke the fire to burst forth which burned within them, that thus they might invite and detain Him, and by this exterior work of harbouring a pilgrim, might make themselves worthy to harbour God within their souls, and to have Him manifested to them.

Colloquy.—O sweet Jesus, although Thou dost dissemble, yet certain it is that Thy " delights " are " to be with the children of men,"(14) and Thou much more desirest to be with them than they desire to be with Thee : indeed, if they desire to have Thee with them, it proceeds from this, that Thou dost first infuse this desire into them, so to accomplish Thine own. I give Thee thanks for this immense charity, which Thou bearest to Thine elect, by the which I humbly beseech Thee not to exclude me from my part in it. Amen.

2. The disciples not only invited Christ, but " constrained " Him to tarry with them: for Christ our Lord feels great delight when we constrain Him, with prayers, sighs, tears, penances, and importunate supplications, and allege titles, and reasons, which in a manner force Him to grant us what we crave of Him : yea, even when we come to use that importunate word, which Jacob used, saying :—" I will not let Thee go except Thou bless me,"(15) nor desist to wrestle with Thee, until Thou grant me what I ask. Yet in very truth, on such occasions we do not

(13) Luc. xxiv. 28.

(14) Prov. viii. 31.   (15) Gen. xxxii. 26.

force Him, but His bounty, charity, and mercy, force Him to favour us; for He Himself imprints and infuses that spirit into us by which we do Him violence. And, in a business of such importance as my salvation, I ought not to proceed coldly or slowly, but to use all diligence, yea, and violence as far as the same Lord will permit me.

3. To this effect it will be good to consider the prayer which these disciples made, saying:—"Stay with us, *O Lord, because it is towards evening, and the day is now far spent.*" Now they call Him " *Lord,*" whom before they called " *a stranger,*" because of the great reverence and love which they had conceived for Him; and alleged for a reason to detain Him, because it was towards night, and that the day was far spent.

Colloquy.—O good Jesus, stay with me, because in my soul, the light of faith begins to be darkened, the splendour of virtue, and the fervour of charity, begin to wax cold and decline; if Thou departest from me I shall be converted into an obscure and cold night: stay also with me, O Lord, because the day of my life draws towards night, and Thy presence is now more needful to me as the night of my death approaches nearer. Thou saidst, dear Lord, " If any one love me, he will keep my word, and my Father will love him, and we will come to him, and will make our abode with him." (16) I desire, O my Lord, to love Thee, and to obey Thee with the whole affection of my heart: stay, therefore, Lord, with me, that I may accomplish my desire, and attain to the life eternal; where I shall for ever abide with Thee. Amen.

This ejaculatory prayer, which the Church uses at this time, we may likewise often use with the same spirit, as has been put down in the preceding meditation.

<hr>

(16) Joan. xiv. 23.

POINT V.

"And it came to pass whilst He was at table with them He took bread, and blessed, and brake, and gave to them. And their eyes were opened, and they knew Him : and He vanished out of their sight." (17)

1. Here we are to consider the causes *why Christ our Lord would manifest Himself to these disciples,* while sitting with them at the table.

i. The first cause was, to make us understand *how greatly He esteemed hospitality and charity,* and how these works of mercy dispose us to receive Christ in His poor, and to obtain great favours ; for, as St. Gregory says, (18) these disciples were not illuminated when they heard the precepts of Christ, but when they accomplished them.

ii. The second cause was, to make us understand *that examples are much more powerful than words,* when any one would have himself known. For Christ our Lord, powerful in the one, and in the other, shewed them in the way, the sweetness and wisdom of His words; but at the table, the gravity and modesty with which He was accustomed to take the bread into His hands, the devotion with which He blessed it, the thanks He gave to His Father for it, and the charity with which He imparted it unto others. And, at the sight of these virtues, the eyes of their soul were opened so that they knew Him.

iii. The third cause was, *to signify the efficacy of the most holy Sacrament of the Eucharist,* figured by this bread, if it was not rather the Sacrament itself, as some say, which has virtue to illuminate the soul, and to enlighten the inward eyes much better than the honey which enlightened the eyes of Jonathan, son of Saul : for the taste of the sweetness which is received in this meat, discovers

(17) Luc. xiv. 30.   (18) Hom. xxiii. in Evang.

to us by experience, the excellency and sublimity of Christ our Lord whom it contains, and by means of whose presence it works such marvellous effects. From these three causes, I will conceive great desires to exercise the three things before specified, viz., the works of mercy—to give good examples to others,—and often to receive the Blessed Sacrament; beseeching this celestial master to help me so to exercise them, that my eyes may be opened to know and serve Him as He deserves.

2. Lastly, I will ponder the causes *why Christ our Lord presently disappeared, and left them at a time when they were principally to taste His presence.*—This He did to show the truth of that sentence of holy Job, where it is said :—" Thou visitest him early in the morning, and Thou provest him suddenly." (19) For, in this mortal life, the visitations of Almighty God are not of long continuance, nor of set purpose, but as in passing, so that, as soon as He appears He withdraws Himself, partly for our exercise,—partly that we may attend to the works of charity towards our neighbours. And so it happened in this present case: for, as soon as Christ our Lord had vanished out of their sight, the two disciples, replenished with unspeakable joy at having seen Him, and blaming their own slowness for not having known Him in the way, when they heard Him speak, and their hearts burned with His holy words, returned to Jerusalem, to declare this joyful news immediately to the apostles, publishing that they had seen Him, and knew Him in breaking of bread. So that those who, as they went to Emmaus, walked slowly, and, as we say, with feet of lead, for very sadness, returned with haste, being full of joy, and ran like harts.

Colloquy.—O mutation of the hand of the highest !

<hr>

(19) Job. vii. 18.

O infinite power of our Saviour Jesus!   In how short a space, O my God, didst Thou change the hearts of Thy disciples, and how many means didst Thou use to alter them!   Visit me, dear Lord, often in this manner, although Thou presently prove me, because the sight of Thee, even if it last no more than a moment, suffices to draw me out of all sadness, and to fill my soul with all celestial joy, dilating my heart, that I may "run the way of Thy commandments,"(20) until I come to see Thee, set in the throne of Thy glory, world without end.   Amen.

MEDITATION VIII.

OF THE APPEARANCE WHICH CHRIST MADE TO HIS APOSTLES ON THE DAY OF HIS RESURRECTION.

POINT I.

" When it was late, that same day" of the Resurrection... and the doors were shut where the disciples were gathered together for fear of the Jews, *Jesus came and stood in the midst* (1) *of them.*

1. I will consider first, the causes *why Christ our Lord deferred to visit His apostles until the evening,* there being many amongst them who greatly loved Him, and earnestly desired to see Him, as St. John, St. Andrew, and others.

i. The first cause was, because there were some amongst them slow to believe, and it was, therefore, needful to dispose them by little and little, that this apparition might be profitable to them.

ii.   The second was, to prove the patience of those He loved most, and with this delay to augment the desire

(20) Ps. cxviii. 32.   (1) Joan. xx. 19.   Luc. xxiv. 36.

they had to see Him, and to dispose them the better for the grace and favour which He meant to do them.

iii. The third was, because it is the custom of God our Lord, to come and comfort those that are His, at such times as they are most disconsolate, and past all hope of receiving Him. When the apostles, therefore, had shut themselves in the supper chamber, having lost all hope of seeing their master on that day, He suddenly entered to visit them. Whence I will learn patiently to expect the visitation and consolations of Almighty God, being persuaded that He will send them to me at such times as shall be most convenient for me, according to that which He said to Habacuc:—" If it will make any delay, wait for it, for it shall surely come, and it shall not be slack." (2) And of that which was said to Job:—" When thou shalt think thyself consumed, thou shalt rise as the day-star." (3)

2. I will consider, secondly, the causes *why He entered in, " the doors being shut."*

i. One was, to manifest to His disciples that His Body was truly glorified, and that, by the gift of subtilty, He could penetrate where He would, without any manner of impediment.—ii. Next, to show by this work the efficacy of His omnipotency, and that, as absolute Lord, He could enter and penetrate into the soul, and visit and comfort her with His inspirations, and change and alter her, as Himself would, without any obstacle being able to resist His efficacious will.(4)—iii. Moreover, to signify that it is grateful to Him when His servants shut the doors and windows of their hearts, their outward senses, that death may not enter by them.(5) These being shut, He Himself

(2) Hab. ii. 3. (3) Job xi. 17. (4) Rom. ix. 19.

(5) Jer. ix. 21.

enters as the Author of life, to replenish them with joy and gladness.

Colloquy.—O King of glory, Thine is my soul, with all her powers, for it is a house built with Thine omnipotence, to be Thine own habitation ; enter, therefore, into her as Lord and master, and do in her what Thou pleasest, for I desire in nothing to resist Thine holy ordinance : I desire to shut all her gates, so that nothing may enter, to displease Thy divine eyes; but if Thou, O my God, please to remain within her, they shall be shut much more assuredly by means of Thy presence.

3. I will consider, thirdly, *why He set Himself in the midst of them ;* which was, perchance, to manifest the truth of that which He said to them :—" Where there are two or three gathered in my name, *there am I in the midst*" (6) *of them,* as a sun to illumine them, as a master to instruct them, as a pastor to govern them, as a mediator betwixt God and man, to pacify them, and as a protector, defending and covering them under His wings; for all these offices does our Lord perform to those that are His, when He places Himself in the midst of them.

Colloquy.—O my soul, since Christ is there, where two or three are gathered together in His name, procure that thy three powers,—thy memory, understanding, and will—be gathered together in holy prayer, having the gate of thy senses shut, for then thy Lord will presently come, and set Himself in the midst of them, enlightening them as the sun; teaching them as master, governing them as pastor, and. lastly, uniting them with Himself, with the union of perfect love.

<hr>

(6) Mat. xviii. 20.

POINT II.

Jesus said to them:—"It is I; fear not. But they, being troubled and frightened, supposed that they saw a spirit. And He said to them, Why are you troubled? See my hands and feet, that it is I myself; handle, and see; for a spirit hath not flesh and bones, as you see me to have. And when He had said this, He showed them His hands and feet:" "the disciples, therefore, were glad when they saw the Lord."(7)

1. The words which Christ our Lord spake to His apostles when in the midst of them, are the effects and signs of a good spirit.

i. The first word was, " Peace be to you;" as if He had said, "Remember that I said to you, Peace I leave with you; my peace I give unto you;"(8) this peace have I now gained by my Passion and death, and now impart the same to you, and salute you with it."—ii. The word was, " It is I," which was to say, " I am the same I was wont to be in nature, person, and condition; I am your master, your Saviour, your protector, your brother, your Lord, and your God." And by these words, pronounced after so sweet a manner, He appeased and quieted them, and made Himself known to them.—iii. Then He addressed the third word, " Fear not," as if He had said, " Although fear assault you, yet do not admit it, nor give it leave to enter into you; fear not the fury of the Jews, nor the anger of the Gentiles, nor the rage of kings and princes, which have risen up against me, for I being in the midst of you, you are secure from all these troubles."

Colloquy.—O King of glory, vouchsafe to come into my soul, place Thyself in the midst of her powers, and say to them,—" Peace be to you." Give me,

(7) Luc. xxiv. 36. Joan. xx. 20.   (8) Joan. xiv. 27.

dear Lord, that peace which the world cannot give, place peace in my flesh, and in my spirit, in my powers, and in all my senses; give me peace with Thy Father, and with my brethren. Say, Lord, to my soul,—" It is I, fear not," for if I have this pledge, that Thou art with me, there is no cause why I should fear, having such a protector.

2. I will consider, secondly, the *great benignity of Christ our Lord;* for, not contented with assuring His disciples of His Resurrection by the sight and hearing, giving them His own body to behold, and speaking to them with His own voice, He would further assure them *by their touch,* giving them leave to touch and to handle His Blessed Body ; especially His feet, His hands, and His side, in which the marks of the wounds of the nails and lance remained. This was to heal the wounds of infidelity and pusillanimity, with which their hearts were wounded; for, to this end, amongst others, did He retain those sacred marks after His Resurrection. And so, indeed, it came to pass, that, approaching to those wounds with great reverence and love, they were illuminated by that touch, confirmed in faith, and filled with love and joy for the glory of their master.

Colloquy.—I give Thee thanks, O Sovereign master, for the favour which Thou hast done to Thy disciples, and in them to all of us. It is well seen, that Thou hast changed the law of fear into the law of love, since in old time Thou tookest life from them who beheld the ark of the Testament with curiosity, or rashly attempted to touch it:(9) but now Thou who art the true Ark of the New Testament, exhibitest Thyself to be seen and touched, communicating life and joy to Thy disciples, that see and touch Thee. Oh that I had been present in this blessed company and that I might have seen the beauty and

<hr>

(9) 1 Reg. vi. 19. 2 Reg. vi. 6.

glory of my Redeemer Jesus, have heard His sweet voice, and have touched His precious wounds! O most sweet Jesus, behold me placed, in spirit, before Thy venerable presence, adoring Thy sovereign majesty, and prostrate in heart, I approach to kiss Thy precious wounds, with great confidence, for, by means of them I shall be healed of my own.

POINT III.

Some of the disciples, not yet believing that it was the same Christ who had been crucified, and wondering "for joy, He said, 'Have you here anything to eat?' And they offered Him a piece of broiled fish, and a honeycomb. And when He had eaten before them, taking the remains, He gave to them."(10)

1. Here is first to be considered the *greatness of the love* of Christ our Lord, who, not contented with those things which He had said and done to assure His disciples of His Resurrection, added this other great sign of singular humanity and affability, *asking of them something to eat*, and eating with them, although it was a thing very remote from His glorious estate. From whence I will draw great motives of loving Him, who humbled Himself, and showed Himself so courteous for our advantage; I will also take an example to humble myself, that I may do good to my neighbours, although it be in something which does not altogether agree with the greatness of my estate, because it will not be against this greatness, being done for the good of my neighbour.

2. In the mystery of this eating, the broiled fish *was a figure of His Sacred Humanity*, which was broiled in the fire of tribulations upon the cross. And the honeycomb represented His Divinity, which is the fountain of all sweetness; both which are found conjoined in the Blessed

(10) Luc. xxiv. 41.

Sacrament, and both which Christ our Lord ate, in the night of·His Passion; both these we now offer in sacrifice to Him; and both these He gives us for the sustenance of our souls, to inflame us in the fire of His love, and to fill us with spiritual joy.

Colloquy.—O Beloved of my heart, if Thou askest ought of me to eat, what shall I offer Thee, agreeable to Thy taste, but this fish and this honey? That which Thou has given me, the same do I give again to Thee, and hope to receive it from Thy hand to eat of it, and to satisfy my necessity; and if Thou requirest ought else of me, behold me here, who like a fish swim in the tempestuous sea of this world, oppressed by the licence of my flesh, and the evil humours of my sensuality. Draw me, dear Lord, out of this sea, burn me with the fire of Thy divine love, dry up my abominable humours, and season me with the sweetness of Thy grace, that, like to a honey-comb, I may be delightful to Thy divine taste. Amen.

3. Finally, Christ our Lord, having showed these disciples by the aforesaid signs that it was Himself, brought to their memory that all which was come to pass had not happened by mere chance, but *"that all things must needs be fulfilled which are written in the law of Moses, and the Prophets, and in the Psalms,* concerning" Him.(11) " Then He opened their understanding, that they might understand the Scriptures," as He did to those who went to Emmaus. And it is to be believed that their hearts burned within them, when He declared the Holy Scriptures to them. With this favour He sealed the testimonies of His Resurrection, alleging and confirming the same with holy Scriptures, which none could ever understand, if the same

(11) Luc. xxiv. 44.

Christ did not open their senses to understand them; and if I understand them with the light which this Lord gives me, I shall not omit to believe and to embrace what they teach.

Colloquy.—O heavenly master, who saidst unto Thy apostles,—"to you it is given to know the mystery of the Kingdom of heaven, but to the rest in parables, that, seeing they may not see, and hearing may not understand,"(12) I confess that the sublimity of Thy sovereign mysteries are hid from me, and concealed from my understanding, because it is much obscured through my sins; but remember, O Lord, that through the merits of Thy Passion, Thou hast opened the book that was shut, and sealed with seven seals, (13) so that it may be read. Open, Lord, to me, I beseech Thee, the book of Thy sacred mysteries, that I may understand them, and be wholly inflamed with the fire of Thy love. Amen.

4. From what has been said in this meditation, we may learn the especial means which God uses in comforting His friends by interior feelings, of which mention has been made in the Introduction of this Book, chapter xi. For in this apparition Christ comforted His apostles, not only in their external senses, but proportionably in their internal;—for to their *sight* He showed Himself to them risen, and very beautiful;—to their *hearing*, He spoke to them with great sweetness and courtesy;—to their *touch*, permitting them to touch His most precious wounds;—to their *taste*, distributing to them the remains of the fish and honey;—and finally, opening and perfecting their *interior senses*, to the end they might understand the Scriptures, and the sacred mysteries contained in them. All which Christ our Lord works spiritually in those souls

(12) Luc. viii. 10.   Mat. xiii. 11.   (13) Apoc. v. 8.

which give themselves to contemplation, as has been showed in the aforesaid chapter, and will be further seen in the ensuing meditations.

MEDITATION IX.

ON CHRIST'S GIVING TO HIS APOSTLES THE HOLY GHOST, AND THE POWER TO REMIT SINS.

POINT I.

"He said, therefore, to them again:—*Peace be to you. As the Father hath sent me, I also send you.*"(1)

1. Christ our Lord, in this appearance, said twice to His apostles, "Peace be to you."—The first was *on entering:* in order to dispose and *make them capable of knowing the mystery of His Resurrection;* because when the heart is molested with remorse for sins, disordered passions, and a multitude of cares, or with a troop of imaginations, it is not sufficiently disposed to know Christ, and to contemplate His holy mysteries, whence it is needful that Christ our Lord should first appease and pacify it; yet not without our own concurrence and help to take away the four impediments of contemplation aforementioned, which St. Bernard calls,(2) "Culpa mordens, sensus egens, cura pungens, irruentia corporearum imaginum phantasmata— Sin gnawing, sense needing, care pricking, and the troop of corporal imaginations pressing and intruding." These impediments being removed, by means of the interior peace which Almighty God imparts to us, the soul, co-operating to that end, is made capable of the consolations which have been specified in the end of the preceding

(1) Joan. xx. 21.   (2) Ser. xxiii. in Cant.

meditation.　He said to them the *second time*,—"Peace be to you," the better to *dispose them for the office* He intended to impose upon them, viz., to go through the world, to converse with men, and to convert them; which cannot be done but by those who conserve peace in themselves, and are, as much as lies in them, strongly disposed to conserve it with one another, with others, and all with Almighty God.

Colloquy.—O King of peace, say twice unto my soul,—"Peace be to thee," that I, partaking both of the one and the other peace, may come to the knowledge of Thy celestial mysteries, and help others also to know them; so that we may all love Thee, and serve Thee with true peace, and with true charity. Amen.

2. Consider the words of Christ our Lord to His apostles:—"As the Father sent me, so I send you." In these words He committed to them the office for which He had chosen them, viz., of apostles, or "Sent." As if He had said:—"As my Father sent me into the world, that I might teach it the way of verity and virtue—even so do I send you, that you may finish what I have begun." Whence is to be seen the great dignity which Christ our Lord gave to His apostles, making them His legates and successors in the work of the conversion of the world, according to that of the apostle, saying:—"Christ hath placed in us the word of reconciliation. For Christ, therefore, we are ambassadors, God, as it were, exhorting by us. For Christ, we beseech you, be reconciled to God."(3) And in the same dignity others do, and succeed, even to the end of the world, so that there will never be wanting some who may attend to its conversion and perfection. And this word, *sicut*, "as," has great force and emphasis, for

<hr>

(3) 2 Cor. v. 20.

although it does not denote equality, yet it denotes great similitude.   As if He had said,—" I, who am equal to my Father, send you, as He sent me, granting you many of those graces and gifts which I have in myself, that you may perform the same office which I have performed." But, to the end we might not think that this office was one of ease and rest, in the same words He admonished them of the charge and burden of it, saying, " Like as my Father, although He loves me, sent me not to receive honours and contentments, but to suffer ignominies and disgraces, as my office requires, even so I, although I love you, send you to suffer great persecutions, that you may comply also with yours, as I suffered the like in satisfying mine ; for the servant or disciple ought not to be more privileged than he that sent him for his legate."(4)

Colloquy.—O Apostle and supreme Priest, Christ Jesus, to whom the name of Apostle pre-eminently belongs, since Thou wast sent by the eternal Father to save the world ; it is just that we should all conform ourselves to Thy life, and follow the steps of Thy holy mission, sustaining the labours which Thou sustainest, to accomplish the will of Him that sent Thee.   Behold here I offer myself, wholly in Thy service, send me where it pleases Thee, for I am ready to suffer what Thou shalt ordain ; for since it is Thou Who sendest me, Thy grace will also help me to accomplish what Thou commandest.

POINT II.

" When He had said this, *He breathed upon them, and He said to them, Receive ye the Holy Ghost.*"(5)   The greatness of this gift we will consider in Meditation XXII.   At present we will dwell upon the manner in which it is given, and *the mystery of this breathing.*

(4) Joan. xiii. 16.   (5) Joan. xx. 22.

1. First, He breathed to signify, that *the Holy Ghost* which He gave them, *proceeded from Him,* as the breath proceeds from one who breathes. So that Christ does not only give us His gifts, but gives the Holy Ghost also together with them, who, although distinct in person, is yet not so in substance. Blessed be such a giver, who, with such liberality and facility, gives us so great a gift, a gift as precious as Himself who gives it.

2. Secondly, He breathed to signify that *it was He who breathed into the face of Adam,* whom He had formed of the slime of the earth, "the breath of life," by which he became a " living soul ;"(6) and that this breath works the same effect in the soul, that the other did in the body, i.e., it quickens it, makes it beautiful, gives it motion and senses, and works proportionable to the supernatural life which He had communicated to it: and consequently such as the body is without the soul, such the soul is without the grace of the Holy Ghost to quicken it. I will, therefore, conceive a most inward desire of this Divine Spirit, craving the same of Christ our Lord, with exceeding fervour.

Colloquy.—O sweet Jesus, breathe into my soul this breath of the Holy Ghost, that she may live the new life of grace, and work the works worthy of life eternal, to Thy honour and glory. Amen.

3. Moreover, this breathing is an air, which we send with force out of the mouth, to blow away some dust or mote upon a garment, or other clean thing: and *in this manner the Holy Ghost is given to those that are already just,* as the apostles were, in form of breathing, that with an inward force they may be moved to that which is good, and be purified and cleansed from their faults and

<hr>

(6) Gen. ii. 7.

imperfections, although but light, so that nothing may remain in them that beseems not purity of spirit.

4. Finally, this gift was *as a pledge of that spirit, which He was to give them on the day of Pentecost*, in the form of a vehement wind, in much greater abundance, just as a vehement wind far exceeds a breath; for that which is given this day, was given for one effect only, viz., to pardon sins; that of the day of Pentecost for many other effects, as will be seen in the proper place.

POINT III.

Then Christ our Lord added;—" *Whose sins you shall forgive, they are forgiven them; and whose sins you shall retain, they are retained.*"(7)

1. In these words, Christ our Lord *granted to His apostles power to pardon sins*, a power which is proper to Almighty God, because it only appertains to Him that is injured, to pardon the injury that is done Him. As sin, therefore, is a most grievous injury against God, and against His law, it appertains only to God to pardon the same—or to those to whom He gives power to this end. This power He gave not to angels, but to men, for whom He made Himself man. Neither did He give it to men who went before His coming into the world, (8) that is, to the priests of the ancient law, who, as they could not heal the leprosy of the body, but only declare that it was healed, (9) so much less could they cleanse the leprosy of the soul. But to the priests of the new law, Christ our Lord gave full power by means of the sacraments, to cleanse souls really and truly from the leprosy of sin, in His name, and as His vicars; and so makes them participate in that infinite dignity of Saviour, which is signified by the name of Jesus, because in virtue of Him, they save and deliver

(7) Joan. xx. 23.   (8) Isa. xliii. 25.   (9) Luc. xvii. 14.

from sin, for which we ought to give Him innumerable thanks.

Colloquy.—O most liberal Jesus, how shall we repay Thee for so singular a benefit as this is ?   And since Thou wouldst give to others so great power, had it not been better to have given it to the angels, who were pure and clean from sin, zealous of Thy honour, and which they knew well how to defend ?   O immense liberality, O liberal mercy !   To sinful men Thou impartest Thy power to pardon sins, that they may pardon with more liberality the more they know their own necessity; and although it is most just that they should regard Thy honour, yet Thou art pleased also that they should have respect to their own profit.

2. This mercy and liberality are the more conspicuous, *since in many things He has put no bound nor limit to this power.*—i. For, first, it extends *to all men* in the world, of whatever estate or condition, without excluding any, as long as they live in this mortal life; so that unless the sinner himself neglects to seek pardon of his sins, by means of the sacrament, nothing can be wanting to him to obtain pardon from defect of power.—ii. Secondly, the same power extends *to all kinds of sins*, however grievous and enormous; so that, if they repent, there is power upon earth to pardon even those who commit the sin against the Holy Ghost; that sin of which Christ Himself said, that it should neither be forgiven in this world nor in the world to come,(10) because of the difficulty which they who have so sinned, place in the way of remission.—iii. Thirdly, it extends to *any number of sins committed during life,* so that not only seven times seven, but seventy times seven,(11) yea, seventy thousand times seven, and without number, may be pardoned to him who sins so often, and

(10) Mat. xii. 82.(11) Mat. xviii. 22.

this with wonderful sweetness. For, as Christ our Lord, with the breath which He breathed from His mouth, gave to His apostles the Holy Ghost; even so the confessors, with the words of absolution, which proceed out of their mouth, in the virtue of Christ, give it to penitents, and deliver them from their sins. And to the end, that this power might remain perpetually in the Church, Christ our Lord would that bishops, the successors of the apostles, should, with the same breathing, and speaking the same words which He pronounced, give the Holy Ghost, and ample power to pardon sins, to those priests whom they ordain.

Colloquy.—O most loving and most liberal Jesus, if it had cost Thee little to pardon sins, I should not so much wonder that Thou art so liberal in communicating such ample power to pardon them : but having cost Thee the price of Thy most precious blood, shed with such terrible pains, and contumelies, who can but wonder, and go forth out of himself to publish everywhere Thine infinite mercy. Seventy thousand times be blessed Thine infinite charity, by which I humbly beseech Thee, that Thou wouldest vouchsafe to help all sinners, to profit by it, and obtain the pardon which Thou on Thy part offerest them. Amen.

3. From what has been said, I will understand *with what spirit and fervour I am to approach the holy sacrament of Confession,* as he that goes to receive the Holy Ghost, by means of the word of absolution, which, like the breath of Christ, proceeds from the mouth of the priest. Of which matter something has been said in Meditation XXX. of the First Part.

MEDITATION X.

OF THE APPEARANCE MADE TO THE APOSTLES—ST. THOMAS BEING PRESENT—ON THE EIGHTH DAY AFTER THE RESURRECTION.

POINT I.

"Now Thomas, one of the twelve, who is called Didymus, was not with them when Jesus came. The other disciples, therefore, said to him, We have seen the Lord. But he said to them, Except I shall see in His hands the print of the nails, and put my finger into the place of the nails, and put my hand into His side, I will not believe."(1)

Here are to be considered *the defects* which were in this apostle, not to despise him, but for our own admonition, and to make more apparent the mercy of Christ our Lord in curing him, and how greatly he profited by the same cure.

i. The first defect and default was, that *he departed from the company of the other apostles*, perhaps because he was weary of them, or wished to attend to some other thing more agreeable to his taste. Thus he deprived himself of so great a good, as to see Christ our Lord, and enjoy the graces and favours which He imparted to His other companions. Whence I will learn how great an evil it is to separate myself from the company of the good; and if I be Religious how prejudicial it is to withdraw from the community of my brethren, and fall into the vice of singularity. For Christ our Lord abides in the midst of those who are united in love and charity, and abandons those who make themselves singular, to the detriment of brotherly charity.

ii. The second sin was, *incredulity*, together with hard-

(1) Joan. xx, 24.

ness of heart, and pertinacity of judgment; for he refused to believe that which all his fellow disciples testified as eye-witnesses; and preferred his own judgment by secret pride before the judgment of all the others.

iii. The third sin, *a certain kind of presumption* and curiosity, which arrived at such a pitch, as to prescribe to God Himself the manner in which he would be induced to believe; saying, that he would not be content with seeing with his eyes Christ alive, but must also put his fingers and his hand into His wounds. This temper truly is very pernicious to those who treat with God, for they ought not to presume on themselves, nor yet to pretend to especial favours, nor assign the means by which they will be induced to believe; neither ought they so to dedicate themselves to the divine service, as to reject the ordinary means which God has appointed.

iv. The fourth effect was a sort of *perverseness*, by which, for the space of eight days, he remained in his bad disposition, so as not to be softened by the saying of his fellow disciples, neither of Peter, nor of those who saw Him on the way to Emmaus. Perhaps, too, the Blessed Virgin our Lady told him the same, with the other devout women, to all of whom he lent a deaf ear, persisting in his hardness, in which he persevered many days, and would have persevered to the end of his life, if Christ our Lord had not come to cure him, All this succeeded, by the especial providence of Almighty God who permitted it; partly, that the hardness of Thomas in not believing might give greater stability and solidity to his testimony, after he had himself believed; partly, that we might see our own weakness if God withdraws His hand from us, and that none can come to Christ by faith, if it be not given him from above, and unless he be drawn by His Father.(2)

, (2) Joan. vi. 44.

Colloquy.—Son of the living God, since Thou knowest the substance of which I am made, shake me not off from Thy hand, lest I perish; deliver me from these four vices, which, like four winds, beat upon the house of Thomas, that they may not also beat upon mine, and overthrow it to the ground.

POINT II.

" After eight days, again His disciples were within, *and Thomas with them.* Jesus cometh, the doors being shut, and stood in the midst, and said: Peace be to you. Then He saith to Thomas, Put in thy finger hither, and see my hands, and bring hither thy hand, and put it into my side, and be not faithless, but believing."(3)

1. I will consider first, with what infinite *charity Christ* our Lord cares for His sheep: for, having waited eight days for Thomas's conversion, and seeing him persevere in his ;hardness of heart, He would no longer delay His remedy, but *came in person* to heal him, manifesting Himself to him and to the others, entering in, the doors being shut, and saluting them with these words,—" Peace be unto you," as He had done before, that thus He might move him to believe.

Colloquy.—O most loving pastor, who lovest one sheep as much as many, and dost willingly leave the ninety-and-nine in the desert, to come and seek that one which has gone astray, and fled from the flock, until Thou findest him; now I see that Thou art always the same, since the desire to save this sheep, Thine apostle, who had lost himself, caused Thee to come to seek him, take him by the hand, and desire to put him in Thy heart.

2. Although Christ our Lord could have appeared to St. Thomas alone, as He did to St. Peter, yet He would

(3) Joan xx. 26.

not, but *in the presence of the other apostles.*—First, that Thomas might understand that this grace was not vouchsafed to him for his own deserts, but because he was in the company of the other good and beloved disciples of our Lord:—Secondly, that the rest might more manifestly see the exceeding charity of their master, who, to do good to one, and that one incredulous, appeared to all, and with His presence comforted all, and also, that as all had been witnesses of the incredulity of Thomas, they might likewise be witnesses of his faith, and thus confirm themselves the more in their own. Whence is to be seen the sweet providence of our Lord, who not only turned the defect of one to his own good, but also to the good of the other elect, so disposing of His cure that all might gather its fruit.

3. I will consider, thirdly, the *mildness and affability* with which Christ our Lord spoke to Thomas, while He condescended to his weakness. For, that Thomas might understand that Christ knew his thoughts, and understood what he said, He would convince him by this very means, saying to him,—" Since thou hast said, that thou wilt not believe, except thou shalt see and touch the wounds of my hand and side, come hither, and put thy finger into the holes of my hands, put thy hand into my side, and be no more faithless, because I have not deserved this of thee, but be believing, to which thou art worthily invited by these wounds."

Colloquy.—O infinite mildness of the words of Jesus! Now I see, O my Saviour, how justly Thy apostle said, " the goodness and kindness " towards man, of our Saviour God, " appeared, not by the works of justice" which He did, " but according to His mercy He saved us."(4) Thy benignity and kind-

<hr>

(4) Tit. iii. 4.

ness, O my Saviour, appeared this day, when Thou appearedst to Thomas, saving him, not for his works, which did not merit it, but according to Thy great mercy, as a pledge of which Thou hast said, that it hides not itself from those that seek it, and also it plainly offers itself to those that seek it not, and discovers itself to those that ask it not.(5)

POINT III.

"Thomas answered and said to Him, My Lord and my God. Jesus saith to him; Because thou hast seen me, Thomas, thou hast believed; blessed are they that have not seen, and have believed." (6)

1. First, consider this illustrious confession of St. Thomas. For it does not appear by the holy Gospel whether he touched the wounds of Christ our Lord, or contented himself with having seen Him, and heard His words, He inviting him to touch them, yet it is to be believed, that for reverence sake, he abstained from touching them, casting himself at His feet.(7) But Christ our Lord *took him by the hand, and caused him to accomplish his first desire;* thus manifesting the greatness of His charity. Thomas having touched the wounds, became so illuminated, that with great affection of heart he confessed that Christ was his Lord and his God, clearly acknowledged his humanity and divinity, and entirely gave himself up to His holy service with most fervent love; as he declared by the words, "My Lord and my God," which are words of most tender love, and for this cause he said not our Lord and our God.

Colloquy.—With great reason, O Thomas, dost thou call thy master "my Lord, and my God," since He so greatly loved thee, that it was only for thy

(5) Isa. lxv. 1.   Rom. x. 20.   (6) Joan. xx. 28, 29.
(7) S. Th. 3, p. q. liv. art. 4, ad 2, et citat. S. Leonem.

good that He appeared to thy fellow disciples : and as if He were forgetful of them, He directs His words wholly to thee, to inflame thee in His love.   O sweet Jesus, I also with Thomas, freely confess that Thou art my Lord and my God, because Thy love is come to such a pass, that Thou art ready to do that for me alone, which Thou didst for him; for Thou hast already loved me, and hast delivered Thyself to death for me, (8) and now desirest to apply the fruit of Thy death to me, as if Thou hadst suffered for me alone.

2. Secondly, although He approved the confession of Thomas, yet *He would not praise him for it* by calling him blessed, as He did St. Peter, when he confessed Him to be the Son of the living God,(9) because he had been slower in believing than St. Peter: and that others should not take occasion by this example to require as much, craving the proof of the senses for believing the mysteries of God. He therefore rather conveyed a secret rebuke to him in the words :—" Because thou hast seen me, Thomas, thou hast believed :" as if He had said, It was needful for thee to see me and handle me, to believe that I am thy Lord and thy God.

3. Then our Lord presently added :—" Blessed are they that have not seen, and have believed."   This He said for the comfort of the faithful, who though they obtained not the grace to see Him in this mortal life, yet they believed without seeing, that which Thomas saw and handled. The same Lord also said at another time; " Blessed are the eyes that see the things which you see," for "amen I say to you, that many prophets and kings," and just men, "have desired to see the things that you see, and have not seen them,"(10) but now He says, " Blessed are they which

(8) Gal. ii. 20.   (9) Mat. xvi. 17.

(10) Mat. xiii. 16.   Luc. x. 23.

have not seen, and have believed:" for on the one side we enjoy all the goods and fruits which He purchased for us by His death, as of the sacraments which He instituted, the examples which He gave us throughout the whole course of His life, the sermons which He preached, and the perfect law which He taught us; and on the other side, our faith is more meritorious, inasmuch as we believe without either having seen or handled with our corporal senses, that which they both saw and handled. This faith is the beginning of all our beatitude, into which, if it be perfected by love and charity, it will finally bring us to enter.

Colloquy.—I give Thee thanks, O my Saviour, for the care which Thou hadst to comfort those who could not enjoy Thy blessed presence, and since I have not the blessedness of those who beheld Thee with their corporal eyes, I desire perfectly to attain that blessedness which those enjoy who behold Thee with their spiritual eyes. Illuminate them, O Lord, with Thy celestial light, that my faith being quickened, and my charity inflamed, I may always believe in Thee, and always love Thee, so that I may come at the last to be blessed with Thee, in Thy celestial kingdom. Amen.

MEDITATION XI.

THE CAUSES WHY OUR LORD BEING RISEN AGAIN, RETAINED IN HIS GLORIOUS BODY, THE SACRED WOUNDS IN HIS FEET, HANDS, AND SIDE.

Presupposing what has been said in the preceding meditations, we will collect in this the causes *why Christ our Lord* being risen again, *would retain in His glorious body,* the signs of the wounds of His feet, hands, and side, pondering the spirit which lies hid in each of them, and gathering the fruit which may be gathered from them. (1)

POINT I.

1. The first cause was, to *confirm His disciples* in the faith of His Resurrection, showing them, not only His body that they might feel it, but the very holes also, which the nails and lance had made, that so they might believe that it was the selfsame body which was fastened to the cross, and not another made anew. By this fact He confirms us also in the faith of our own resurrection, which will be with the selfsame bodies that we had in this mortal life, according to that of Job:—" For I know that my Redeemer liveth, and in the last day I shall rise out of the earth, and I shall be clothed again with my skin, and in my flesh I shall see God. Whom I myself shall see, and my eyes shall behold, and not another; this my hope is laid up in my bosom."(2)   After the example of this holy man, I also will lay up this hope in the depths of my heart, to comfort me in my calamities and infirmities, believing firmly that although my flesh should be wounded and full of worms, from the feet to the head, and like Job, lie on a dunghill, and be flayed, and bored in a thousand parts upon a cross, as was that of Christ our Saviour, yet it shall rise again to a new life ; and if there should remain in it some signs or wounds, this will not be because of the weakness of Him that raised it, but for the greater glory and beauty of the risen body. With this hope I ought to encourage my flesh willingly and patiently to support the labours which I suffer.

2. The second cause was, *that the same wounds might serve for signs and trophies of His victorious triumph ;* as also for arguments, to show how much He esteemed pains

<hr>

(1) S. Th. 3, p. q. liv. art. 4.   (2) Job. xix. 25.

and contumelies, honouring His wounds so far as to retain and place them in His glorified body, with a singular beauty and splendour. By this He intended to *encourage* us to suffer, to make very great account, and to hold it for a high honour, to bear the marks of any wounds in our body, that is to say, of any labours like those of Christ our Lord, which we have suffered for His love, according to that of the apostle St. Paul ;—"For I bear the marks of the Lord Jesus in my body." (3)

Colloquy.—O most sweet Jesus, Thou art my Lord and my Redeemer, and I Thine unworthy slave ; and since lords mark their slaves with certain marks, that they may be known to be the slaves of such a lord, and may not fly from his service, set and imprint upon me the marks and signs of Thy sacred wounds, that I may be always Thine, and never fly from Thy divine service. Amen.

POINT II.

3. The third cause was, that *they might serve as a memorial to put Him in mind of what we have cost Him*, and move Him to love us, pardon us, and evermore to do us good. And that He who as God, as the prophet Isaias says, is not forgetful of us, because He keeps us written in His hands,(4) may neither be so forgetful of us, as man, since He bears it within His hands, how deeply He bought us. And as they are open with the holes which the nails made, so does He hold them open and extended, to fill us with His benediction, and with the love which His open side discovers.

Colloquy.—O most sweet Redeemer, this it is which obliges me never more to be forgetful of Thee, but to set Thee " as a seal upon " my " heart, as a seal " upon my " arm," (5) that my works and my desires

<hr>

(3) Gal. vi. 17.　　(4) Isa. xlix. 16.　　(6) Cant. viii. 6.

may always be sealed with Thy infinite charity, and
fulfil in all things Thy holy law.   And seeing Thou
commandest the Hebrew people to bind as a sign
upon their hand the law given by the hands of angels,
that they might be mindful of it ;(6) how much more
reason is there, that I should do the like with the law
which has been given me by the hands of the Lord of
angels, pierced with nails for the love of me ?

4. The fourth cause was, that *He might show these wounds
to His Eternal Father,* and thus, exercising the office of our
perpetual advocate and mediator, (7) might appease the
wrath and indignation which He had conceived against
us for our sins.   For if the sight of the rainbow in the
heavens, beautiful with its three colours, so appeases the
anger of Almighty God, that for this sign He perpetually
remembers not to drown the world again with a deluge
of water, (8) how much more will He be appeased upon
beholding this rainbow of the empyreal heavens, Christ
Jesus our Lord, with those three sorts of wounds, in His
hands, feet, and side, and will serve Himself of this bow
as of a sign and motive not to chastise the world as its sins
deserve?   With this spirit ought I to show to the Eternal
Father the wounds of His Son, and to beseech Him, that
for them He would lay aside the anger He has conceived
against me, and against all men, saying to Him :

Colloquy.—" Behold, O God our protector ; and
look upon the face of Thy Christ ;" (9) look likewise
upon His blessed hands, feet, and side : and for the
wounds of His sacred hands, grant us that ours may
be always exercised in good works, and by those of
His feet, that ours may always walk in perfect ways,
and by the wound of His side, that ours may be

(6) Deut. vi. 8.   (7) 1 Joan. ii. 1.   (8) Gen. ix. 14.
(9) Ps. lxxxiii. 10.

always wounded with His love. O my soul, follow the counsel of the divine wisdom, and lifting up thine eyes to the empyreal heaven, "look upon the rainbow and bless Him that made it : it is very beautiful in its brightness, it encompasseth the heavens about with the circle of its glory, the hands of the most High have displayed it,"(10) and adorned it as thou seest. Blessed be the hands which have made this bow, by whose ordination He extended His hands upon the Cross, adorned with the variety of celestial virtues, in sign of peace to all the elect, and to encompass them with the circle of His protection, and place them afterwards on the throne of His glory. Amen.

5. The fifth cause was, *to provoke us with the sight of these wounds, to love and obey Him*, acknowledging by them how much He has loved us, and how much He has suffered for our sake; so that spiritual sight of these wounds, which remain at this present in the glorified body of Christ our Lord, is most effectual to awake in us the desire of employing all our powers in the service of our Lord. And by these wounds, as has been said, we may enter to dwell within Him, and to be united with Him, in the union of actual remembrance, knowledge, and love, imagining that He says to us from heaven;—"Arise, my love, my beautiful one, and come: My dove," return with a speedy flight into " the clifts of the rock," into " the hollow places of the wall ;"(11) " enter into the wounds of my body, not now defiled with blood, but beautiful and glorious.—If thou seest thyself chased by the legions of hell, fly to these wounds that they may defend thee from their temptations. —If thou art persecuted by the vanities of the world, and by the depraved passions of thy flesh, have recourse to these wounds, for in them thou shalt find a house of refuge

<hr>

(10) Eccles. xliii. 12.   (11) 4 p. Med. liii. p. 4. Cant. ii. 14.

against all fears.—If thou seest thyself molested with cares and business, retire from them, and enter into these wounds, in which thou shalt find quiet and repose for thy spirit.—If thou desirest to know me, and love me with all thy heart, come to these wounds, and enter into them, and there thou shalt see the great account which I make of thee, and how much I love thee, and such flames of love issue from my heart, as shall wholly set on fire thine, and unite it with and transform it into mine. Behold the wounds of my hands, and fortify thine to fight for my glory, as I have fought for thy salvation. Behold the hole of my side, and open thy side, giving me all thy love, as I have given thee mine. Behold the wounds of my feet, and direct thy steps to my holy service, imitating mine with perseverance until thou purchasest a crown of glory.

These considerations and affections, I ought to exercise, remembering the wounds of Christ our Lord, and that I may view them more narrowly, I will excite my faith to contemplate them in His glorious body, not only in heaven, but also in the holy Sacrament of the altar, where they are like five fountains of our Saviour, whence flow the waters of grace and of spiritual comforts, to all who approach them with fervour. (12)

POINT III.

6. To these causes is added a sixth, which is to *confound the damned in the day of judgment,* by showing them the wounds which He received from them, as witnesses of the great desire He had to save them, if they had not by their own default, put an impediment in the way. To whom, as St. Austin says, (13) He will speak in this manner;— "Behold here the Man whom you crucified, behold the

(12) Isa. xii. 30.　　　　(13) In libro de Symbolo.

wounds which you inflicted, acknowledge the side which you lanced, which for you, and by you was opened, yet, notwithstanding, you would not enter into it." Then will be made that most terrible lamentation foretold of these miserable men, when they see that they have neglected the opportunity they had of saving themselves, and the great reason why Christ our Lord has to condemn them. On the other hand, with the self-same wounds, Christ our Lord will make joyful His just, not only on that day, but for all eternity, for they shall clearly see in them so many motives to love Him, who received and suffered them for their sakes.

Colloquy.—O most loving Saviour, by these wounds I humbly beseech Thee to work in me the effects, for which Thou retainest them in Thy glorious body, permitting me to fly and enter into them with the wings of a dove, and to dwell in them, as in a nest and place of repose; for I desire nothing more in this life, than always to think upon those things which Thou hast done and suffered for me, loving Thee for them, and obeying Thee with perseverance, until I come to enjoy Thee in Thy glory, world without end. Amen.

MEDITATION XII.

OF THE APPEARANCE MADE TO THE ELEVEN DISCIPLES AS THEY FISHED IN THE SEA OF TIBERIAS.

POINT I.

" There were together Simon Peter, and Thomas, who is called Didymus, and Nathaniel, who was of Cana in Galilee, and the sons of Zebedee, and two other of His disciples. Simon Peter said to them, I go a fishing. They say to him, We also come with thee. And they went forth and entered into the ship ; and that night they caught nothing."(1)

1. Here is to be considered first, how these disciples went a fishing, *partly from poverty*, and that they might have something to eat ; *partly to avoid idleness*, for the time was not yet come when they were to employ themselves in fishing for men. As soon, therefore, as Peter said, " I go fishing," the others offered to bear him company, thus showing the concord and conformity of wills which they had in the works of virtue: Whence I will conceive a desire of imitating these holy disciples in the exercise of these three virtues, poverty, charity, and love of labour, against idleness.

2. All that night *they took no fish*, as it also happened to them at another time, when St. Peter said, " We have laboured all the night and have taken nothing:"(2) to signify how little human industry is able to do, if it alone be employed to fish for souls, and to draw them out of the sea of their sins. Peter, therefore, and Paul, and any other however learned and holy, and however great a preacher, will yet travail all in vain, if he wholly rely upon his own strength, and unless God Himself be present at the fishing ; and for this cause St. Paul said,—" Neither he that planteth is anything, nor he that watereth ; but God that giveth the increase."(3) For this reason the workmen of souls are to ground themselves in great humility, if they desire their labours to prove profitable, remembering that which Christ said, " without me you can do nothing."(4)

Neither is it void of mystery, that at both these times of fishing, the scripture says, it *was by night*, to signify the miserable estate in which the world was before the coming

(1) Joan. xxi. 2. (2) Luc. v. 8.

(3) 1 Cor. iii. 7. (4) Joan. xv. 5.

of Christ, the true Sun of justice, with whose light the fishing prospers, and without whom nothing is effected. Moreover, here is represented to us, that he who labours in the night of ignorance, and in the misty darkness of mortal sin, profits nothing, nor are his works meritorious of life eternal. And for this cause the kingly prophet, David, said,—" It is vain for you to rise before light ;"(5) as if he had said, Before you receive the light of divine grace, in vain will be all your labour, because, without it, you cannot work the works worthy of light. Whence, I will gather, the great misery of a sinner, who, though he labours much, yet profits not; he wearies himself with fishing during the whole night of his miserable state, and takes no fruit of merit for life eternal; for although he catches riches, honours, and contentments, yet all these are nothing, and his labour is wholly lost, since in time of his greatest need, they will undoubtedly fail him.

3. Ponder what these seven disciples did, when they saw they could take no fish. *Bearing their labour patiently they began to think upon their master*, and of the want they had of His holy presence; and it is to be believed, that they spoke amongst themselves of that which at other times had happened to them on that very sea, and concerning Christ our Lord, and that, sighing, they said:

Colloquy.—O sovereign master, where art Thou? Why dost Thou leave us in this labour? Why dost Thou not hasten to supply our poverty? What marvel is it, that the fishes do fly the fishers' nets, since Thou dost fly the fishers themselves? Come, Lord, and approach unto us, for with Thy coming will come the fishing which we desire.

These words, or the like, I am to speak in spirit, when I see my pains and labours are without profit, hoping that I

(5) Ps. cxxvi. 2.

shall be heard, because God hears "the desires of the poor."(6)

POINT II.

"But when morning was now come, Jesus stood on the shore, yet the disciples knew not that it was Jesus. Jesus therefore said to them; Children, have you any meat? They answered Him, No. He saith to them, Cast the net on the right side of the ship, and you shall find. They cast, therefore, and now they were not able to draw it for the multitude of fishes."(7)

1. Here is to be considered first, the charity of Christ our Lord, *in hasting to comfort His beloved disciples*, although He made Himself known to them by little and little, that His appearance might redound to their greater profit. For this cause He placed Himself upon the bank-side; He would not walk upon the waters, nor enter into that ship; to signify that the state of life which He retained after His Resurrection, was stable and remote from all mutability and alteration, and ordained to last for ever in the land of the living. And though He knew that they had taken no fish all that night, yet, making as if He knew it not, He asked them if they had any fish; by this means inducing them to acknowledge their own necessity, and how unable they were to fish of themselves without His assistance, which yet He desired presently to give them.

Colloquy.—O most liberal Jesus, how many times dost Thou come to our gates, asking and craving something of us, not so much because we have to give Thee, as because Thou desirest to give to us ? Thou didst ask of the Samaritan, that she would give Thee a little water to drink, because Thou desiredst to give to her the living water of Thy grace.(8) Thou requirest us to give alms to the poor, because Thou

(6) Ps. ix. 38.   (7) Joan. xxi. 4.   (8) Joan. iv. 7.

desirest to bestow abundant alms on those who shall do as Thou requirest. Would to God I might give Thee what Thou requirest of me by Thine inspiration, that so Thou mightest give me that which by that inspiration Thou desirest to give me. Amen.

2. I will consider, secondly, how He commanded them *to cast the net on the right side of the ship;* to signify the prosperous success and ending which that fishing should have, and how it was a figure of the fishing for souls, which were to be drawn out of the sea of this world for everlasting life, by the power of Christ, who is the right hand of Almighty God. The disciples obeying this commandment, caught a multitude of great fishes. In this is seen the efficacy of obedience, and with how great truth the wise man says—"An obedient man shall speak of victory,"(9) gaining many souls unto Almighty God; and it should be well considered, that in the other fishing, St. Peter knew that it was Christ who commanded him to cast the net, and he obediently said,—"In verbo tuo laxabo rete." "At Thy word, I will cast forth the net:" but this time he knew not that it was Christ that commanded him, yet nevertheless he submitted his judgment and obeyed, and drew a great multitude of fish: for Christ our Lord is greatly delighted that we obey every human creature for the love of Him, and that we deprive ourselves of our own judgment, and of our own will, to do the will of others, in things in which there is no sin. And so sometimes it happens, that Christ indeed is there, where we thought Him not to be, and obeying man, we obey indeed Christ, who speaks by his mouth, and assures us, that if we cast our net on the side pointed out by Him, we shall draw great store of fish. This virtue of obedience, therefore, ought to be very familiar to me, if I

<hr>

(9) Prov. xxi. 28.

desire to have prosperous success, as St. Peter had, who for this is called Simon, which is to say, obedient.

POINT III.

"That disciple, therefore, whom Jesus loved, saith to Peter,—It is the Lord: Simon Peter when he had heard that it was the Lord, girt his coat about him, for he was naked, and cast himself into the sea. But the other disciples came in the ship, for they were not far from the land, but, as it were, two hundred cubits, *drawing the net with fishes*. As soon as they came to land, *they saw hot coals lying, and fish laid thereon*, and bread.—Jesus saith to them: Bring hither of the fishes which you have now caught. Simon Peter went up, and drew the net to land, full of great fishes, one hundred and fifty-three. And although they were so many, the net was not broken."(10)

1. Here we must consider, first, in these two disciples, Peter and John, the effects which fervent love produces, as well in the contemplative, as in the active life. This love in contemplatives sharpens the interior sight of the soul, that like John, they may know Christ when others know Him not, and give notice of Him to others, and cause love in those who are fervent in things which belong to the active life, so that as soon as they know Him, they set themselves to follow Him. And as St. Peter, hearing that it was our Lord, forsook the net, the fishes, and the ship, and putting on his garment, out of reverence, cast himself into the sea, to go as soon as might be where his master was, (for it seemed to him too long a delay, to go no faster than the ship would go:) even so must I endeavour to follow Christ our Lord with greater fervour, and wish speedily to arrive at the land of eternity where He is, so that leaving for this cause whatever I have, I must expose

(10) Joan. xxi. 7.

myself to all the perils and labours of the tempestuous
sea of this world, and considering their pace to be too
slow who follow the course of a common life, I must
therefore endeavour to quicken mine with all the expedition possible.

2. Secondly, I am to consider *the mysterious excellence of
this present fishing*, compared with that other which St.
Peter made in his first vocation: for that was a figure of
the fishing for souls, which were to enter into the Church
and to believe in Christ our Lord, and to receive His law;
for which cause, Peter was not commanded to cast his net
on the right side of the ship, but on every side, on the
right hand and on the left, that, by gathering good and
evil fishes, great and little, with which the two ships
might be filled, should be figured the two people, Jews
and Gentiles, under one head, Christ, and His vicar Saint
Peter.(11)   And the net which gathered them began to
break, because in this life, the Church and gospel of Jesus
Christ sometimes suffers some rupture and schism.   But
the fishing of this day was only of the predestinate and
elect for everlasting life, and for this was made on the
right side of the ship, and not on the left, because the
elect are to be placed upon the right hand of the judge.
All these fishes are great in sanctity and purity of life, for
in heaven none are little.   The net is drawn to the land,
where Christ is, which is the land of the living, and is not
broken: because then there shall be no dissensions nor
schisms, nor anything else which may disturb them, for
the Angels shall separate the evil from the good, as our
Lord said in the parable of the net.(12)

Colloquy.—O blessed fish, which art caught with
this net! O blessed water of life, in which these fishes
are nourished and sustained, attaining that perfect

(11) Luc. v. 7. S. Aug. in Ps. xlix.   (12) Mat. xiii. 49.

health and life, which Christ has gained for them! O holy prophet Ezechiel, how well is thy prophecy fulfilled, by so great a multitude of great fish, which the fishermen of Jesus Christ have caught in these waters, which issue forth of the right side of the celestial temple.(13) Grant me, O most sweet Redeemer, that I may live in the lively waters of Thy grace, that so I may be drawn out of them, for life eternal. Amen.

3. Consider, finally, how the disciples, " as soon as they came to land, *saw hot coals lying, and a fish laid thereon*, and bread ; after which " Jesus saith to them, Come and dine,'' and taking bread He gave it to them, and the fish in like manner. In which shines forth the affability and liberality of our Redeemer towards His disciples, in preparing them this dinner : and inviting them to eat with bread made by His own hand miraculously, and other fishes, besides those which they had taken, to signify, first, how careful He is to give food and spiritual refection to those who labour for His love, and for obedience to Him, administering to them the meat of angels, and celestial bread to comfort them, casting by this means, coals upon their hearts, that they may be wholly inflamed with the love of Him. Secondly, to signify, that whilst we labour on earth, He prepares us a most delightful banquet above in heaven, to which He Himself will invite us, and will serve us at the table, giving us for food His sacred Divinity and Humanity.

Colloquy.—O blessed they who shall eat this bread in the Kingdom of God ! O happy those who shall sit with Christ at His table in the Kingdom of His Father!(14) O that I were one of those seven disciples, full of the seven gifts of the Holy Ghost, with

---

(13) Ezech. xlvii. 1.   (14) Luc. xiv. 15, et xxii. 30.

which I might worthily assist at this holy banquet! Accept, good Jesus, this my desire, and fortify the same with Thy holy grace, to the end I may come to enjoy Thee in Thy glory.   Amen.

MEDITATION XIII.

ON CHRIST'S INSTITUTION IN THIS APPEARANCE OF ST. PETER AS UNIVERSAL PASTOR OF HIS CHURCH, AND DELIVERY TO HIM OF ADMIRABLE INSTRUCTIONS OF PERFECTION.

POINT I.

" When, therefore, they had dined, Jesus saith to Simon Peter,—Simon son of John, *lovest thou me more than these?*   He saith to Him, Yea Lord: Thou knowest that I love Thee.   He saith to him: *Feed my lambs.*   He saith to him again; Simon, son of John, lovest thou me?   He saith to Him, Yea Lord, Thou knowest that I love Thee. He saith to him, *Feed my lambs.*   He saith to him the third time, Simon son of John, lovest thou me?   Peter was grieved, because He had said to him, the third time lovest thou me?   And he said to Him, Lord, Thou knowest all things: Thou knowest that I love Thee.   He said to him, *Feed my sheep.*"(1)

1. Christ our Lord, having promised to St. Peter, the keys of the kingdom of heaven, in recompense of that illustrious confession which he made of His Divinity: now willing to deliver them to him, together with the primacy over the universal Church, *first examined him touching his love,* asking him, if he loved Him more than the others did; by which He has given us to understand, that the prelates of the Church ought to excel in faith,

(1) Joan. xxi. 15.

and to be eminent above all others in love and charity. And He called him by the name of Simon, which signifies obedient, and by the name of John, which signifies grace, or Jonas, which signifies a dove; to denote, that with faith and charity, are to be united obedience, with the plenty of the grace of the Holy Ghost, to accomplish him perfectly in his office.

2. He examined him *three several times* concerning his love, to the end that with his triple answer, he might recompence the triple denial which he had made; and as these denials sprung from pride and presumption, preferring himself before his fellow disciples: so these three answers of love were accompanied with humility, not daring to say that he loved Christ more than the others, but only that he loved Him, and even in this also was he very fearful, not trusting to his own knowledge, but appealing to the knowledge of Christ our Lord, saying, —"Thou knowest that I love Thee:" and still more in his third answer was he sorrowful with humility, fearing lest Christ saw somewhat in him contrary to that which he thought of himself, and therefore said:—Thou, Lord, knowest all things, and knowest whether that be true or no which I do say. Whence I will gather, how pleasing humility is to Christ our Lord, and not to presume upon ourselves, and how secure it is always to fear oneself, remembering that which St. Paul says, "I am not conscious to myself of anything, yet I am not hereby justified; but He that judgeth me is the Lord,"(2) and it may be that He finds some fault in me, which I find not in myself.

3. Moreover, He examined him three several times *concerning love:* to signify, that he who was to be the pastor of His sheep, ought to be very *deeply rooted in*

(2) 1 Cor. iv. 4.

charity, and in the three degrees of it: for he ought to be perfect in the purgative way of beginners, in the illuminative way of proficients, and in the unitive way of those who have aspired to perfection.(3) Again, he ought to excel in purity and cleanness of heart, exempt from all sins and imperfections, and trained in the exercise of virtues, and in the union of love with the three Divine Persons. And, finally, he ought to be perfect in charity towards God, towards his neighbours, and towards himself.

Colloquy.—O beloved of my soul, grant me that I may cast very deep roots in humility and charity, so that I may attain to the end of Thy commandments, which is, to love Thee with "a pure heart, and a good conscience, and an unfeigned faith,"(4) persevering even to death in the loyalty of true love.

4. I will ponder, fourthly, how Christ our Lord, having said twice to St. Peter:—"Feed my *lambs*," said to him the third time,—"Feed my *sheep*:" to signify that He made him *universal pastor of His flock*, not only of the *ordinary or common faithful* signified by the lambs, but also of those which are *the spiritual mothers of others*, figured by the "sheep," such as are confessors, preachers, masters, and all the other inferior prelates of the Church, in order that the whole Church might be "unum ovile, et unus pastor," "one fold, and one shepherd." But He said not to him, "feed thy lambs," or "thy sheep," but *my* lambs, and *my* sheep; to give him to understand that he was not Lord of the flock, but only His substitute or vicar, and that therefore he was to look unto the flock of the faithful as to the flock of Christ, Prince of pastors, to whom he was to render an account of his office, as St. Peter likewise understood Him, and afterwards left the

(3) S. Th. 2, 2, q. xxiv. art. 9.   (4) 1 Tim i. 5.

same in writing. In which the charity of our Saviour towards us greatly shines forth, in sign of the love which we bear unto Him, and in recompence of the innumerable benefits which He has bestowed upon us, He exacts of St. Peter that he feed His sheep, and that he declare in this the love which he bears Him, in loving and having a tender care over His sheep.

Colloquy.—O sovereign pastor, how great is. the love which Thou bearest Thy sheep, and how greatly Thou desirest that the pastors, Thy servants, love them, and feed them for the love of Thee ! I, Lord, desire to show the love, which I have to feed the sheep, which Thou hast given me, and which I have within me, which are my powers, and senses, governing them according to the order of Thy divine will : and in the same manner, to feed those without me, which Thou hast likewise committed to my charge, because they likewise are Thy sheep. For in this alone that they are Thine, this ought more to move me to be careful of them, than if they were mine.

5. I will consider, lastly, how He said to Peter, *three several times,*—" Feed my lambs" and " sheep" to signify, three sorts of food with which he was to feed them ;— that is, with the spirit, praying for them; with the tongue, teaching and instructing them,—and with works, giving good example to them. (5) To feed them with doctrine, with sacraments, and with the examples of good life, assisting them with all the works of mercy, as well spiritual as corporal, feeding not only the spirit, but the body also in time convenient; all this did Christ our Lord impose upon pastors, threatening by the prophet Ezekiel, (6) very terribly, those who fed themselves, and not the

(5) S. Ber. ser. ii. de Resur.   (6) Ezech. xxxiv. 8.

sheep, seeking in their office their own honour and emolument, and not the utility and good of souls.

POINT II.

Immediately our Lord added:—"Amen, amen I say to thee, when thou wast younger, thou didst gird thyself, and didst walk where thou wouldest. But when thou shalt be old, thou shalt stretch forth thy hand, *and another shall gird thee, and lead thee whither thou wouldst not.* And this He said, signifying by what death he should glorify God."(7)

1. Christ our Lord, under this parable, *discovered to St. Peter, the infallible sign of the true love which He bore to him,* and of the right use of the pastoral office, which He imposed upon him, which was to undergo the death of the cross, as the same Lord had done before him, in confirmation of which He said,—"The good shepherd giveth His life for His sheep."—And " greater love than this no man hath, that a man lay down his life for his friends."(8) Wherefore, to the end that Peter might well understand what he offered himself, when he answered Christ—" Thou knowest that I love Thee :" and what Christ imposed upon him, when He said to him, " Feed my sheep :" He added this foregoing parable, ` by which He signified that he should undergo the death of the cross.

2. The second shall be to consider the *spirit of these words,* in which Christ our Lord touches two kinds of labours and mortifications.

i. The one which a man undertakes *of his own choice,* denying his own appetites, chastising his flesh with penances and austerities, and offering himself to undergo great labours, in which a man doth gird and bind himself: and although he may contradict his own inclinations,

(7) Joan. xxi. 18.(8) Joan. x. 11; et xv. 13.

yet walks he nevertheless where he will: for, as none enforces him, so he undertakes those labours when and how he will, led thereto by his reasonable will: in which there is at times some intermixture of self will, because self love is wont t nourish itself with spiritual meats. (9) This manner of mortification is proper to those who are beginners in virtue, but yet fervent, and of a strong constitution: and therefore novices in virtue are to begin from hence.

ii. There are other labours, which *come to us* by the hands of others, whether of men persecuting us, or of devils tempting or tormenting us, or of God Himself, who so disposes for our mortification, as are infirmities, pains, dishonours, poverty, false witnesses, and other persecutions, which we suffer for justice sake, like as the blessed martyrs suffered. In these a man extends his own hands, embracing them, because it is the good will of Almighty God. But yet it is another which girds him, nails him, crucifies him, and leads him whither he would not, if he followed his own natural inclination. These kinds of labours are rather proper to those that are old, long inured, and perfect in virtue, and God grants them to them whom He desires to make very perfect, for by this means a man is wholly purged from self-will, and rests only on the will of God, who is He that principally girds us in these tribulations.

Colloquy.—O most sweet Jesus, if Thou be He who girdest me in this manner, ordaining or permitting the pressure of the labours which I suffer, gird me as Thou wilt with Thine own hand, because though it seems austere to me, yet will it be most gentle to me. And as Thou girdest Thyself, embracing things so exceedingly austere, and extendest Thy hands

(9) S. Aug. in illud Ps. xlix. Med. li. ad finem in 4. p.

upon the cross, where they girded Thee with most hard nails, leading Thee whither Thy natural will refused to go, it is not much, that I Thy servant do bind and gird myself, and go whither my flesh and my own will would refuse to go.

These two manners of mortification *am I to embrace in all kinds of things,*—First, I myself seek for some mortification, according to that which David says,—"I met with trouble and sorrow."—Secondly, embracing the same, when it comes from others, according to that which the same prophet says, " Trouble and anguish have found me."(10)

3. Thirdly, I will consider those words of the Evangelist,—that St. Peter, by this kind of death, "should glorify God;" for Almighty God is greatly glorified by us, when we gladly suffer for the love of Him.

Colloquy.—Oh happy were I, if I had been worthy to extend my hands as Peter did, and that another might bind me, glorifying God, by such a manner of mortification.　O blessed self-mortification, by which the glory of God is so dilated and increased !　" Let my soul die the death of the just, and my last end be like to them," (11) and let no other death befal me, but that by which Almighty God may be most glorified.　Amen.

POINT III.

" And when He had said this, He said to him,—*Follow me.* Peter turning about, *saw that disciple whom Jesus loved, following,* who also leaned on His breast at supper, and said,—Lord, who is he that shall betray Thee? Him, therefore, when Peter had seen, he said to Jesus, Lord, and what shall this man do ?　Jesus said to

(10) Ps. cxiv. 3; et cxviii. 143.　　(11) Num. xxiii. 10.

him ;—So I will have him to remain till I come, *what is it to thee?* follow thou me."(12)

1. Christ our Lord arose from the place where He was set, and beginning to walk, said to Peter, " Follow me ;" *to confirm by this fact that which He had said*, giving him to understand that he was to follow Him, after a different manner from the other disciples, not only in the Evangelical and perfect life which all embrace, but also in the office of supreme pastor, and in that kind of dying on the cross, as Himself died on the cross.

Colloquy.—O most sweet master, say to my soul, follow me in this kind of death of the cross: that dying with Thee on earth, I may come to reign with Thee in heaven.   Amen.

2. Although Christ our Lord said nothing to St. John, *yet he began also to follow Him:* for, the force of love which he bore to Christ carried him after Him, and consented not that he should be separated from His company ; the holy envy, to see St. Peter follow Him, forced Him likewise to follow Him.   Here we have proposed to us a manner of vocation, or calling to follow Christ, without the help of exterior words, which proceeds partly from a love and desire to remain always in His company ; partly to see the good example of others who follow Him, especially when they are our friends and acquaintance, whose conversion and change of life aids much to the change of ours ; this manner is also greatly pleasing to Christ our Lord, as it was pleasing to Him that John did follow Him upon this occasion, and the same Lord likewise called him interiorly, and drew him after Him, saying to his heart, " Follow me," although He did not call him with His mouth.

(12) Joan. xxi. 19.

3. Although St. Peter, through the zeal of friendship, (because he loved St. John,) desired to know what should become of him, and whether he were to endure the death of the cross or no; Christ, notwithstanding this, *reprehended him,* because this desire was accompanied with overmuch curiosity, pretending to know that which did not concern him, and which was known to God alone, nor could be known of any other, unless He revealed the same to them, and therefore He said,—" If I will have him to remain until I come, (that is, to the end of the world, when I shall come to judgment,) what is that to thee? Follow thou me." That is to say, this care appertains not to thee, but to *me,* who love him, and have a provident oversight of all that which concerns him; that which touches thee is, that thou follow me after the manner that I have told thee. In this He gives us three advices:— i. That we do not busy or entangle ourselves to know those things which do not concern us, not even under any title or pretext of human friendship.—ii. That in such cases we wholly refer unto the divine providence the care of that which concerns our kinsfolks, and our familiars, trusting in this that God Himself will provide for them.— iii. That, leaving the care concerning others, we attend unto that which touches ourselves, which is, that we follow Christ in that kind of life, for which He has ordained us, since this care suffices for every man, and to this the others are reduced. For, if I be careful to follow Christ, He will be careful over me, until He bring me to the rest of His eternal glory. Amen.

MEDITATION XIV.

OF THE APPEARANCE MADE TO ALL THE DISCIPLES, IN THE MOUNT OF
GALILEE, AND THE THINGS HE COMMANDED THEM, AND PROMISED
THEM.

POINT I.

"And the eleven disciples went into Galilee, *unto the mountain where Jesus had appointed them*, and seeing Him, they adored Him ; but some doubted." (1)

1. The eleven apostles going to Galilee, by the commandment of Christ our Lord, went that way *with exceeding joy of mind*, hoping to enjoy the sight of Him for a longer time; and, by inspiration of the same Lord, they went and gave notice of His Resurrection to all the disciples that were dispersed through Galilee, who gathered themselves together, " more than five hundred brethren," (2) and they ascended the mountain which was appointed them, (which is believed to be the mount of Thabor) expecting there the appearance of their master. Here is represented to us the charity and zeal of the apostles, in calling together their fellow disciples, that they also might enjoy this blessed sight; the fervour, likewise, with which that multitude united in charity, ascended that mountain, instructing us, that if we desire to see Christ with the sight of contemplation, and to know His mysteries with celestial light, we ought to endeavour to ascend the mountain of a perfect life, and to aspire to the summit of charity, and of fraternal unity, for this is that which most disposes to attain the same.

2. *How liberally Christ our Lord performed the promise* which He made to His apostles, that they should see Him in the mount of Galilee; and it is to be believed that He

(1) Mat. xxviii. 16.   (2) 1 Cor. xv. 6.

discovered to them some part of His glory, and of His splendour, as He discovered to the three disciples in the self-same mountain, when He was transfigured before them. Oh, how contented and how fully satisfied did those holy men remain, and how gladly did they repeat those words which St. Peter spoke in the transfiguration, saying,—" Domine, bonum est nos hic esse," " Lord, it is good for us to be here" with Thee, unless Thou dispose otherwise of us. All the apostles adored Him, and acknowledged Him for their God ; and if any doubted, they were some of the residue of the imperfect disciples, who, though they doubted at the first, yet Christ, with His presence, took away their doubt, and filled them most full of joy.

POINT II.

" And Jesus, coming, spoke to them, saying :—*All power is given to me in heaven and in earth;* going, therefore, teach ye all nations," and preach the gospel to all creatures.(3)

1. Christ our Lord obtained by the merits of His Passion and death, inasmuch as He was man, *all power in heaven and earth.* For, although it were His, as He was God, and due to Him, for many other titles by reason of the hypostatical union, and for that He was head of angels and men, yet would He also gain it by the point of the spear, and for this cause said now to His disciples, " All power is given me in heaven and earth." Power in heaven is to open the gates, and to admit men to enter into it, to distribute unto them celestial seats, and to command angels whatever He will, for the good of His elect. Power in earth is to remit sins, to change the hearts of men, and to impart His graces and spiritual gifts amongst us, and both of these He fulfilled when He ascended to heaven, according as David said—" Thou hast ascended on

(3) Mat. xxviii. 18.

high, Thou hast led captivity captive, Thou hast received gifts in men.''(4)

Colloquy.—I rejoice, O my Saviour, for this Thy sovereign power, and render many thanks to the eternal Father, that He did give the same to Thee, because with so great right Thou hast deserved the same. Rejoice, O my soul, for that thou hast so powerful a Redeemer, nor do thou doubt to serve Him, who can do all He will, both in heaven and earth. O my Saviour, "what have I in heaven? and besides Thee what do I desire upon earth?"(5) Thou sufficest me for all things, for in Thee, who canst do all, I have them all.

2. Christ our Lord making use of this power, command-ed His apostles *that they should go through the whole world*, and should *teach all nations* not only Jews, but also Gen-tiles, and not only noble and powerful persons, but also however vile and base they were, preaching the Gospel to all creatures, instructing all in the articles of our faith, as well those which appertain to the Divinity and Trinity of God, as those which appertain to the Humanity of Jesus Christ, in which appear how it is the will of Christ our Lord, as St. Paul says, that all men " be saved, and come to the knowledge of the truth :" (6) for, as the bounty of the celestial Father appears in this, that He makes the natural sun to " rise upon good and evil, and raineth upon the just and the unjust sinner ;" (7) so the charity of His Son is seen in this, that the sun of His gospel shines to all men in the world, and the rain of His divine doctrine waters the hearts of men through the whole earth, without mak-·ing difference of one or other, or without any exception of persons, because all are His own creatures.

(4) Ps. lxvii. 19.   (5) Ps. lxxii. 25.   (6) 1 Tim. ii. 5.
(7) Mat. v. 45.

Colloquy.—O most loving Father, since I am Thy creature, illuminate this little world which is within me, which Thou createdst; enlighten all my powers, and water them with the dew of Thy sovereign doctrine, that I "may know Thee, the only true God, and Jesus Christ" (8) whom Thou hast sent, Thy Only Son, that working according to this knowledge, I may obtain the life eternal.   Amen.

POINT III.

" Baptizing them in the name of the Father, and of the Son, and of the Holy Ghost; teaching them to observe all things, whatsoever I have commanded you." (9)

1. Christ our Lord, after He had commanded His apostles to teach those things which concerned faith, to all men, catechising them as it were, and disposing them to receive baptism, He commanded them *two other things.*— The first was, to *baptize them in the name of the Father, and of the Son, and of the Holy Ghost,* by which He changed the rigour and hardness of circumcision, into the softness of baptism, as also the laws, to which they were an entrance. For circumcision was a gate, and entrance to the ancient law, which was a law of fear, and of servitude, and, therefore, did cauterize and sign them with an exterior sign, both painful and shameful, cutting away parts of the flesh, with the effusion of blood. But baptism is a gate and entry to the new law, which is a law of grace, and of love, a law of sons, written principally in their hearts, and, therefore, signs them only with an easy ablution of water, in sign of the interior ablution of the soul, by which it imprints the character or sign of Christianity, and communicates to them the grace and charity proper to sons.

Hence it is that baptism is conferred *in the name of the most Blessed Trinity,* because all the three Divine Persons

(8) Joan. xvii. 3.   (9) Mat. xxviii. 19.

work wonderful effects in him that is baptized. The Father adopts the person baptised for His son, and makes him heir of heaven, and, therefore, receives him also under His protection.—The Son of God takes him for His brother, and co-partner of His inheritance, and admits him to the participation of the merits and fruits of His holy Passion, receiving him for His disciple, and for His dearly beloved friend.—The Holy Ghost takes that soul for His spouse, adorning it with the dowries of supernatural virtues, disposing it unto Him in faith and charity, and in most abundant mercy. (10)   And all the most Holy Trinity takes her for His temple and habitation, entering into her with desire to remain for ever within her, and to unite her with Him with an union of love, like to that union which the three Divine Persons have in their divine essence. These are those glorious names which Isaias calls the *new names*,(11) and which God imposes on the baptized, and on that Christian who is united with Jesus Christ, and is His son, His friend, His companion, His disciple, and whose soul is the spouse of this infinite God.

Colloquy.—Let all the Hierarchies and Angels praise Thee, O Lord, for the innumerable benefits which Thou hast imparted unto men, and bestowest upon them by the means of this sovereign sacrament. What shall we render unto Thee for that singular sweetness which Thou usest towards us, whom Thou hast bought with Thy most precious blood? Thy body was cauterized with most terrible wounds, that Thou mightest anoint my soul in Baptism with most excellent gifts, and mightest clothe the same with the garments of Thy grace. What say I of Thy grace? since Thou Thyself art made her garment, as Thine Apostle says,—" As many of you as have been bap-

(10) Ose. ii. 19.   (11) Isa. lxii. 2.

tized in Christ, have put on Christ." And "all we who are baptized in Christ Jesus, are baptized in His death. For we are buried together with Him by baptism unto death; that, as Christ is risen from the dead, by the glory of the Father, so we also may walk in newness of life."(12) Confirm in me, O Lord, what Thou hast begun, renewing the dignity which Thou gavest me in Baptism, that I may come to the full fruition and glory thereof. Amen.

2. The second thing which He commanded them was, that they should *teach the baptized to observe all things whatsoever He had commanded them;* as if He had said to them, " They ought not to content themselves only to be baptized, but also to lead a life worthy of the faith and grace which I impart to them in holy baptism, observing not the precepts and ceremonies, which Moses commanded to be kept in his written law, because all those are now annulled; but all these things which I commanded you when I published my Evangelical law."

By this commandment, therefore, Christ our Lord took from our necks the heavy yoke of the ancient law, whereof St. Peter said, in the name of all the apostles:—" Neither our fathers nor we have been able to bear," (13) and has imposed the sweet yoke and the light burden of the Evangelical law, with the obligation of accomplishing all His commandments, of which we may not break so much as one.

Colloquy.—I give Thee thanks, O most sweet master, for having changed the most heavy yoke of Moses, into the most sweet yoke of Thy Gospel, to the great ease and solace of our souls. It is most just, O Lord, that I accomplish all Thy commandments, since they are few, and sweet, and proposed by Thee, to

(12) Gal. iii. 27. Rom. vi. 3.   (13) Act. xv. 10.

whom I owe so much, for all that Thou hast done and suffered for me.   Dear Lord, I desire to keep them, and to teach others also how to keep them, for Thou hast said, " he that shall do and teach, shall be called great in the Kingdom of heaven." (14)   Help me, Lord, with the liberal gift of Thy Spirit, exactly to accomplish both these things which Thou here commandest.   Amen.

POINT IV.

" He that believeth and is baptised shall be saved ; but he that believeth not shall be condemned."(15)

1. This promise and threatening Christ our Lord added *to encourage us to the accomplishment of what He commanded,* neither does He promise nor threaten corporal or temporal goods or evil, as He did in the ancient law, but spiritual and eternal goods or evils; which are, to enjoy the salvation which He has gained us by His Passion and death, or to be deprived of it everlastingly, that is to say :—"He that shall believe and shall be baptised and accomplish those things which I have commanded you, shall obtain pardon of his sins, and the spiritual health of his soul, by means of my grace, and afterwards life eternal ; but he that shall not believe, will be deprived of all this ; and the like shall happen to him who believes by faith, but denies God by his works ; (16) because he conforms not his life to that which he believes, nor accomplishes in work that which he promised in holy baptism."

Colloquy.—O God of my soul, discover to me the innumerable treasures which are inclosed in these words, " shall be saved," that the love of them may incite me to accomplish all that is necessary to save me.   Discover also to me, the abyss of my miseries, which are inclosed in these words, " shall be con-

(14) Mat. v. 19.   (15) Mar. xvi. 16.   (16) Tit. i. 16.

demned," to the end, that the fear of such terrible evils may urge me, when the love of celestial goods do not awake me.

2. I will likewise consider the infinite charity and liberality of Christ our Lord, which shines in this, that He said not, "he that believeth not, *nor shall be baptised,*" shall be condemned, but only *he that believeth not;* to teach us that although it be true that whoso shall omit baptism by contempt or notable negligence shall be condemned, because "unless a man be born again of water and the Holy Ghost he cannot enter into the Kingdom of God;"(17) still when a man has a desire to receive the same, and yet cannot, without his own fault, he shall not be condemned, if he have a lively faith, and true sorrow for his sins, for he is now spiritually engendered and incorporated with Christ, in virtue of his contrition and desire of baptism; nor would this Lord restrain the entrance into heaven, that a man capable of reason should be excluded from it for not having received that, which, without any fault of his he could not receive.(18)

POINT V.

"And these signs shall follow them that believe. In my name they shall cast out devils; they shall speak with new tongues; they shall take up serpents, and if they shall drink any deadly thing, it shall not hurt them; they shall lay their hands upon the sick, and they shall recover."(19)

This promise may be considered in three senses.

1. The first is, *according to the letter* by which Christ our Lord gave power to the faithful to work these miracles, *when it was expedient for the propagation of the faith,*

(17) Joan. iii. 5.   (18) S. Th. 3, p. q. lxviii. art. 2.
(19) Marc. xvi. 17.

and conversion of souls, which power shone wonderfully in the primitive Church, and now likewise He grants the same when it is needful for His glory ; and it is very necessary that this faith and confidence be lively in us, since it is the infallible word of our Lord, who says:—" If you have faith as a grain of mustard-seed, you shall say to this mountain, 'Remove from hence thither,' and it shall remove, and nothing shall be impossible to you."(20) The second sense is of the power *which at this day also these preachers, priests, and confessors have* to work the wonders spiritually in the souls of the faithful; for, as St. Gregory says, they cast devils out of them, when they absolve them, and deliver them from their sins.(21) They " speak with new tongues," when, with the spirit of Christ and with celestial language, they preach unto them the doctrine of truth ; they take up " serpents" when they take from them enmities, rancours, and dissolve the subtleties of Satan ; they " drink some deadly thing," which does not hurt them, when they converse amongst the wicked, and hear their wickedness, and yet no part of it cleaves to them ; they " lay their hands on the sick and heal them," when, with their admonitions and examples, they strengthen such as are feeble and languish in virtue, to amendment of life.

Colloquy.—O Saviour of souls, send many workmen into this world, who may work these wonders worthily, by which faith may be enlarged, charity quickened, and the glory of Thy heavenly Father in all augmented. Amen.

3. The third meaning of Christ's promise is, to understand it of the power which every faithful Christian has, *to work these signs and wonders in himself,* through the

(20) Mat. xvii. 19. Med. xlix. 8. p.
(21) Hom. xxix. in Evang.

virtue of Jesus Christ. For, as St. Bernard says:(22)—
" We cast devils forth of ourselves, when we have contrition
of heart, and perfect sorrow for our sins ;—we speak with
' new tongues,' when we leave the tongue of the old earthly
Adam, and speak the language of the new celestial Adam,
occupying ourselves in thanksgiving, and in divine praises,
and in discoursing always of things pleasing to Almighty
God ;—we ' take up serpents,' when we take away the
occasions of returning to sin, and all whatever may infect
or poison our heart ;—we ' drink some deadly thing' without detriment, when we feel evil suggestions and fleshly
temptations, but yet consent not to them :—we lay our
' hands upon the sick,' and heal them when we heal the
sicknesses of our soul and her passions, with exercises of
good works, of penances, and of mortifications. These are
the signs of those that believe, as they ought to believe,
which yet they cannot work in their own name, but in the
name and virtue of Christ.

Colloquy.—O most powerful and most faithful
Christ, I believe in Thee, I hope in Thee, and there-
fore in Thy name resolve to begin to work these
wonders, trusting in Thy mercy, that according to
Thy promise, Thou wilt help me to perform them.
Amen.

MEDITATION XV.

OF ANOTHER PROMISE WHICH CHRIST OUR LORD MADE TO HIS DISCIPLES
TO REMAIN WITH THEM TO THE CONSUMMATION OF THE WORLD.

After those things which we have related, Christ our
Lord added :—" Behold I am with you all days, even to
the consummation of the world."(1) This promise is one

(22) Serm. de Ascens.   (1) Mat. xxviii. 20.

of the most comfortable and most glorious that Christ our Lord made to His Apostles, and in every word of it there is much to be considered. Considering *who the Person is that* makes this promise. *What reasons move Him* to make it. *How He accomplishes* what He promised. *To what persons,* — *With what continuation,* and *for what time;* for all this is expressed in the words proposed, of which the first word " Behold," invites us to consider the whole attentively.

POINT I.

1. Consider first, *the reasons which moved Christ our Lord* to say to His disciples that He would remain with them.—i. The first was, to *comfort them in the absence* which He was to make, ascending to Heaven; as also for the absence which He made, seeing them but seldom, and after some intervals during the forty days He remained in this world after His Resurrection. As if He had said,— " Although I ascend to heaven, and shall now see you but seldom, yet know and hold for certain that I am with you invisibly; I will not leave you fatherless and without a comforter; for although you see me not corporally, yet am I always as present with you as if you saw me."—ii. The second was *to encourage them to the expedition which He had committed to them,* sending them through the whole world to preach, baptize, and to work miracles, assuring them that He would always be with them, to help them; as if He had said, " Dismay not yourselves, thinking that you are too unfit and feeble for so high a commission; for I myself am always with you, fortifying your weakness; and I myself it is who am to work these works in you, and to accompany you wherever you go, without departing from your side."—iii. The third was *to help them in the execution of all that He commanded them ;* for knowing that He was present with them, and beheld them how they

behaved themselves in their function, the thought of this should make them the more careful and diligent in performing it not only without default or imperfection, but with all the perfection that was possible for them, as those who were in the sight of their Lord and master, and whom they greatly endeavoured to please.

2. These three reasons will I apply to myself, imagining that Christ says unto me in respect of them:—Behold, I am present with thee, as *comforter*, as *helper*, and as *witness* of what thou doest; wherefore never be forgetful of me, but always remember that I am with thee; in thy labours to comfort thee; in thy functions and ministry to assist thee: and in all thy works to judge thee and reward thee.

Colloquy.—O most sweet Lord, if Thou be with me, what can be wanting to me? O invisible God, grant me to live, as if I always saw Thee; leave me not fatherless, for Thou art my Father; leave me not comfortless, for Thou art my comforter; be Thou always with me, for Thou knowest I can do nothing without Thee, and that I can do all things with Thee; and knowing that Thou seest me, my slothfulness may be quickened by the presence of Thee. Amen.

POINT II.

Secondly is to be considered *the greatness of this promise,* which is comprehended in these four words, " I am with you."

1. I will ponder first *who Ile is that says,* "I," not as to Moses, " My angel shall go before thee, and shall keep thee in the way, and shall bring thee into the land of the Canaanites ;"(2) but I myself am with you, and will accompany you in this your journey, and will keep you, and cause you to enter into the land of the Gentiles. I am

<hr>

(2) Exod. xxiii. 20. et xxxii. 34.

God omnipotent, infinite and eternal, whose will no creature can resist.—I am your Saviour, who have vanquished the Devil, despoiled hell, destroyed the kingdom of sin, and triumphed over death, to whom all power is given, both in heaven and earth. I it is that send you throughout the world as my Father sent me, assisting you as He assisted me. I am your master and protector, whose power, liberality and love you have experienced and am still the same I was wont to be. I am with you, and am your invisible and inseparable companion, as until now I have visibly been with you.

2. Secondly in saying,—"I am with you," *He comprehends all the ways He can be with them.*—i. The first is common to all creatures, to whom He is most present, giving them the whole being, life, and motion which they have.—ii. The second is common to all the just with whom He is present by His grace, giving them supernatural life and virtues.—iii. The third is special to the elect alone, with whom He is present with particular providence, careful of them, and working by them great and wonderful works.—iv. The fourth is by the most Blessed Sacrament of the altar, in which He is really and truly, as He is God, and as He is man, to be our meat and spiritual nourishment. After all these manners is Christ our Lord in His holy Church, careful of her, and governing her as a king in his kingdom,—as a pilot in his ship,—as a father of a family in his house,—and as a master in his school, and all this He promises when He says—" I am with you," that is, with you who represent my universal Church, with you who are my dear beloved disciples, and with all those who shall follow and imitate you.

Colloquy.—I give Thee thanks, O most sweet Jesus,

for so liberal and so noble a promise which Thou makest to Thy Church, and to the disciples of Thy school; happy are they with whom Thou art after so delightful and pleasant a manner of presence. Oh that Thou mightest always be with me after this manner, that so I might always be with Thee, serving Thee, and loving Thee, without being ever separated from Thee, for all eternity. Amen.

POINT III.

Thirdly is to be considered the *continuation and duration of this presence,* which is declared in these last words, " all days, even to the consummation of the world." So that Christ our Lord is with us, not partially, one day present and another absent, but all days, all hours, and all moments of the day; not for a limited time of a thousand or two thousand years, but to the end of the world. In which words He assures us that His Church shall last until the end of the world, and consequently, her laws, sacraments, and sacrifices; and that, therefore, He is with us to-day, and will be also to-morrow, even until the last day; and this world being ended, He will be with His in a much better and much more excellent manner, which shall endure for all eternity. For all these favours I am to render thanks to our Lord, and humbly to beseech Him to make me partaker of this benefit of His remaining with me always, in all times, and in all places, without forsaking me so much as a moment unto the ending of my life, purposing also not to forsake Him, and doing my utmost endeavours not to forget Him; remembering that which St. Bernard says :—" As there is no moment wherein a man does not use or enjoy the goodness of Almighty God; so ought there to be no moment in which he has Him not present in his memory."(3)

(3) S. Ber. de Interiori Domo, c. 9.

Colloquy.—It is great reason, O my God, for that Thou art always with me, and hast me present before Thee, I also should be with Thee, and have Thee always present before me ; but because this exceeds my feeble forces, grant me by Thy grace, that which I desire, by which that shall be most easy to me, which without the same I cannot do.   Amen.

MEDITATION XVI.

OF THE DIVERS APPEARANCES WHICH CHRIST OUR LORD MADE TO HIS DISCIPLES DURING THE FORTY DAYS HE REMAINED WITH THEM, AND THE MANNER IN WHICH HE VISITED SOULS SPIRITUALLY FIGURED BY THOSE APPEARANCES.

Besides the appearances which have been related, it is certain that He made many others, as may be gathered from that which St. Luke says, that He showed Himself to His disciples *" after His Passion by many proofs, for forty days appearing to them, and speaking of the Kingdom of God."*(1)   In which words certain things are to be considered which appertain to these appearances, pondering at the same time the spirit that is contained in them, inasmuch as they represent the spiritual visitations wherewith Christ our Lord visited souls invisibly.(2)

POINT I.

1. Although Christ our Lord, for the space of forty days, was always with His disciples invisibly, after the manner we have declared, yet sometimes for their greater consolation *He showed Himself to them alive*, risen again, and glorious, proving to them by sundry very effectual arguments, *that He was the same that had been dead;* sometimes suffering them to touch His wounds, other times

(1) Act. i. 3.   (2) S. Th. 3, p. q. iv. art. 5 et 6.

eating with them, other times working miracles, such as was to enter in to them, the gates being shut, that they should take a multitude of great fishes at an instant upon His word, and finally alleging other reasons and testimonies out of the divine Scriptures, which spoke of His resurrection; and after this manner did He encourage and comfort them, as often as He appeared to them.

2. *The same thing Christ our Lord performs towards the souls of His elect*, with whom He remained in the manner aforesaid, invisibly all the time of their life, figured (3) by these forty days, to whom He sometimes appears, that is, visits them interiorly, and encourages and comforts them, giving them some signs and testimonies of His presence, with most especial inspirations and affections of love, with sweetness and sensible devotion, which is the refection of the spirit, with very wonderful changes which He works within their hearts, and with the illustration and understanding of the verities of holy Scripture which He imparts to them. With these arguments He "shows Himself alive" to those who know that He who is within them is the living God, and who, as He lives, works in them those works of life. Also, when they communicate, He shows Himself in the same manner alive unto them, giving them assured signs that they have received the bread of life which descended from heaven; for He communicates unto them some light, or love, or desires, and purposes of a new life, sorrow for sins, and inflamed affections of devotion; whereby they understand that He whom they have received, is not bread alone, is not a dead, but a living thing.

Colloquy.—O invisible God, most present and most absent, Who sometimes hidest Thyself, that so Thou mayest seem to be far absent, and sometimes showest

(3) Lib. de Consen. Evang. c. 4.   S. Th. 3, p. q. xxv, art. 31.

Thyself, that so we may see Thee to be verily present, come, Lord, to my soul, and visit her with Thy most sweet presence, show Thyself to me, as my true and living God, working in me such works, as may bear witness who Thou art. O beloved of my heart, grant me so to receive Thee in the Blessed Sacrament, that I may presently see that I have received living bread, and the bread of life. " My soul hath thirsted after the strong and living God,"(4) leave her not, O Lord I beseech Thee, hungry and thirsty, leave her not dry and withered, as if she had received some dead thing. Amen.

3. Hence *I will gather these instructions*,—i. First, that although God is present in every place, and also within me, yet *through my fault He shows not Himself to me alive*, nor do I feel the effects of His presence, nor no more remember Him than if I were absent, or that He were some dead thing; for which cause I will endeavour to remove all those faults and anxious cares, which deprive me of so great a good.—ii. That communicating oftentimes I feel not that I have received within me the living God, but so remain, as if I had received some dead thing; *because my bad disposition deserves not that Christ our Lord comfort me*, nor work in me the signs of His living presence.—iii. That the arguments which Almighty God gives of His presence *are arguments of the true and living God*, different from others, which the evil spirit is wont to counterfeit, transfigured into an angel of light, and with the mask of Almighty God, being a false and feigned god. I am therefore humbly to beseech Him that when He shall vouchsafe me such favour as to visit me, that the same be with arguments and effects properly His, delivering me from the deceits of Satan, and from those which are wont to draw after them my own erring and sick judgment.

(4) Ps. xli. 3.

POINT II.

1. In these appearances Christ our Lord *spake to His disciples of the Kingdom of God;* sometimes bringing to their remembrance those things which He had said to them before His death; at other times discovering to them new mysteries and secrets, pertaining to the sacraments and sacrifices, and the order of the divine worship, of which many are preserved unto the present time by tradition;— at other times as master He expounded unto them the holy Scriptures, infusing light into them to understand them. Finally, He never spake to them of things vain, curious, or impertinent, but only of those which appertained to the Kingdom of God, that is, of "justice, and peace, and joy in the Holy Ghost,"(5) for the good of the Catholic Church. In these words sometimes He reprehended them for their incredulity and hardness; at other times He cheered, encouraged, and inflamed their hearts with His holy love, but always left them with peace and comfort, so that they were never weary of hearing Him.

2. The same does Christ our Lord perform *when spiritually He visits souls,* to whom always in these visitations He speaks somewhat to their hearts, according to that which David said: "I will hear what the Lord God will speak in me; for He will speak peace upon His people."(6) And to that which He says by the prophet Osee. I "will lead her into the wilderness, and will speak to her heart."(7) These speeches are by inward inspirations, in which no things are spoken that are vain, curious, or impertinent, but only those which appertain to the Kingdom of God, justice, sanctity, exercise of good works, peace of conscience with God and with one's neighbours, pure joy in the Holy Ghost, and expelling all sensual and worldly joy.—Some-

(5) Rom. xiv. 17.   (6) Ps. lxxxiv. 9.

(7) Ose. ii. 14.

times He brings to their remembrance the things they have read or heard, giving them a lively feeling of them:—at other times He discovers to them new affections, which they never had nor felt before; sometimes He rebukes them for their faults and lukewarmness: at other times He exhorts them, and encourages them to perfection. And by these words also is discovered that it is Christ that speaks, because the words of the spirit of the Devil, of the world, and of the flesh, are very contrary to these.

Colloquy.—O my loving Saviour, come unto the soul of Thy servant, and visit it, and speak unto my heart as Thou wert wont of the Kingdom of God, that she may conceive every day a new estimation of this Kingdom, and never cease to seek it until she obtain it, with perfection in this life, and afterwards see it and enjoy it clearly in the other. Amen.

POINT III.

Thirdly are to be considered, *certain properties of these visitations* of Christ, which shine in these appearances which He made to His apostles.

1. The first is, that these appearances were not continual, *but now and then*, and with interruption, to some, indeed, more frequent than to others,—because of their better disposition, and for their more vehement desire of seeing Christ. And it may piously be believed, that He appeared to our Blessed Lady every day, or at the least very often: to St. Peter also, more often than to others, for his greater fervour and love to Him. Even so the visitations of Christ our Lord, and manifestations made unto devout souls, are likewise interrupted, and more or less frequent, according to the will of the same Lord who visits them, and the dignity and fervour of the soul that is visited. Wherefore it behoves me, always to have, as

the apostles had, a burning desire to see Christ our Lord, and to enjoy His presence and His interior visitation, not for my own sensible pleasure or consolation, but because I love Him, and desire to be always with Him, in respect of the great good that from thence results, and like to the spouse, I may say to the angels and to the souls of the blessed: —" I adjure you, O daughters of Jerusalem, if you find my Beloved, that you tell Him that I languish with love,"(8) desiring His sweet presence, by which my great weakness may be strengthened.

2. The second property is, that these visitations were made *upon a sudden*, and when the apostles themselves thought least about them, for they lasted but a little while:—and sometimes He *vanished suddenly* from their sight, as it chanced to the two disciples of Emmaus, leaving them, as the proverb says, with the honey about their teeth. And even so, internal visitations are wont to come upon a sudden, and when we least expect them; and to last but a little while, and upon a sudden to depart: for Christ our Lord wills that we walk in this continual change, and depend upon His mercy, and as Himself says, —" A little while, and you shall not see me, and again a little while, and you shall see me,"(9) that so we be a little rejoiced with His presence, and again a little sad, because of His absence, desirous of His return; upon which St. Bernard says :(10)—" that, in this life, joyfulness may be had by the presence of the spouse, but not fulness, because, although indeed His visitation rejoices us, yet the vicissitude or change molests us: and when He comes, " Est rara hora, brevis mora ; a rare, hour, and a short stay :" for this sweet silence, which is made in the heaven of the just soul, scarcely lasts half an hour :(11)

(8) Cant. v. 8.　　(9) Joan. xvi. 17.

(10) Ser. xxxii. in Cant.　　(11) Apoc. viii. 1.

—in this we ought to conform ourselves to the divine will, and to believe for certain that all is done for our greater profit.(12)

3. The third property is, that these appearances were *not always in one time or place, or in one self-same exercise, but in different,* for to Mary Magdalen He appeared in the garden nigh to the sepulchre, to the disciples walking to Emmaus, to the eleven apostles in the supper-chamber, and to other seven upon the seaside, and to others on the mount of Galilee : so also *interior visitations have no certain place, time, or employment,* for sometimes they happen in prayer, in spiritual reading, in time of refection, or in the exercise of some good work : sometimes in the recollection of the soul, and on a solemn feast, sometimes in the fields, and on a day of labour, for our Lord wills. that in all time, places, and occupations, we be so prepared, that we put no impediment in the way of His visitation and consolation, and that we always depend upon His divine providence, " for the Spirit breatheth where He will :"(13) visiting us with His inspirations, in such time, place, and occasion, as Himself judges most convenient.

4. The fourth property is, that in these appearances sometimes *the visitation of Angels went before ;* at other times Christ our Lord showed Himself in *divers figures, and manifested Himself by little and little :* at other times He showed Himself wholly *upon a sudden,* and with *great splendour;* like as He did to the Virgin our Lady, and sometimes with little, according to the disposition of the persons to whom He appeared. In the same manner in the spiritual visitation of souls, Christ our Lord communicates the light and knowledge of His divine presence, and other internal favours, in proportions which are conformable to the ordination of His eternal wisdom, and to

(12) S. Greg. 1. xxx. mor. c. 12.

(13) Joan. iii. 8.

the disposition of those souls which He doth visit. That which we are to procure on our behalf is, a generous and confident mind, expecting and desiring of our Lord, no less than His own self, begging always that which is best, and that which is most pleasing to Him; for this great and 'excellent kind of confidence, and this generosity of heart, obtains, as St. Bernard says, (14) great things of Almighty God, after the imitation of that great Moses, who said unto God, " Shew me Thy glory." And he received an answer, " I will show thee all good."(15)   And of David, who said, " My heart hath said to Thee, my face hath sought Thee, Thy face, O Lord, will I seek," (16) and with this determination he aspired to so great highness, that he came to say, "For what have I in heaven, and besides Thee, what do I desire upon earth?"   These and the like affections am I to awake within my heart, saying to Christ our Lord, sometimes with St. Philip,— ' Lord, shew us the Father, and it is enough for us:' (17) other times with the spouse,

Colloquy.—" O beloved of my soul, show me where Thou feedest and where Thou reposest at noon-day;" show me by this celestial light, the place where at noon-day Thou sleepest with most fervent love the sleep of death, and where with most clear light like to the noon-time of the day, Thou dost manifest to the Blessed Thy sovereign glory; show me also the ways of fervour, to the end that I may profit and increase in Thy service without any delay, until I come to the light of the perfect day.   Amen.

(14) Ser. xxxii. in Cant.   (15) Exod. xxxiii. 18.
(16) Ps. xxvi. 8.   : (17) Joan. xiv. 8.

MEDITATION XVII.

ON THE APPEARANCE OF CHRIST TO HIS APOSTLES ON THE DAY OF HIS ASCENSION.

POINT I.

The day being come in which Christ our Lord had decreed to ascend to heaven, as He had loved His which were in the world, so in the end He gave them greater signs and arguments of His love, and to this end, *He appeared that day to His disciples in the supping chamber, as they were eating,* and also ate with them, amiably with great signs and tokens of love, and then said to them, that day He was to depart to His Father: and it may be believed, that to comfort them in the sorrow which this news caused them, He repeated some of those reasons which before He had delivered them in the sermon He made after supper.

1. First, He said to them,—" I go to *prepare you a place,* and if I shall go and prepare a place for you, *I will come again and will take you to myself, that where I am you also may be :*"(1)—as if He had said, I ascend to heaven to open the gates, and to give entrance to such just persons as have deserved the same, to the end that they may enjoy the mansions which are prepared for them in the house of my Father: rejoice ye, for I will come again to fetch you in the hour of your death, and will lead you with me, placing you in that place which my Father has designed.

Colloquy.—O my beloved, ascend in good time up to heaven, since it is Thine and was principally created

---

(1) Joan. xiv. 2.

for Thee ; but forget not to return for me, that I also may come where Thou art, assisting me with Thy grace, to the end I may be worthy to be admitted into Thy glory. Amen.

2. Then immediately, He added another reason, saying, —" If you loved me, you would indeed be glad because I go to the Father, for the Father is greater than I :" (2) that is to say—If you love me, you ought to rejoice at my honour, and my contentment, because I ascend to my Father which is in heaven, who is greater than I, as I am man, and is to honour and glorify me, setting me upon His right Hand, where I shall enjoy with quiet that eternal Kingdom, which I have conquered by my Passion.

Colloquy.—I rejoice, O most sweet Jesus, that Thou ascendest to Thy Father, because I love Thee more than myself, and desire thine honour more than mine own ; and since Thy Father is also mine, I have great hope, that Thou wilt hereafter bring me to enjoy His divine presence.

3. Thirdly, He further added : " *It is expedient to you that I go ;* for if I go not, the Paraclete will not come to you : but if I go, I will send Him to you :"(3) as if He had said : It does not only affect my honour, that I ascend to heaven, but also *your profit*, to the end your faith may be perfected, your hope erected, you charity purified, and that the plenitude of the Holy Ghost may come down from heaven, for if I ascend not the Holy Ghost will not come to you: as well because it is decreed that I ascend first, and send Him from thence to you, as also for that yourselves are not well prepared to receive Him, because you adhere with a certain kind of carnal love to my cor-

<hr>

(2) Joan. xiv. 28.   (3) Joan. xvi. 7.

poral presence, which manner of love it is necessary for you to cast off, that you may be capable to receive so sovereign a gift. Wherefore, O my soul, consider attentively that thy God is a spirit, and that He will be loved with a spiritual love, quite exempt from all savour of self-love: for, if to love the corporal presence of Christ with a love less pure, and with some self-interest, hinder the coming of the Holy Ghost, how much more will the inordinate love of thyself, or of any other creature, hinder the same.

Colloquy.— O sweet Saviour, govern my soul as seems best to Thee and if it be expedient for her spiritual profit, that Thou absent Thyself from her, and withdraw all sensible consolation, Thy will be done, for I know for certain, that Thou wilt send the Holy Ghost the Comforter in due season, with that plenitude that is requisite for her, to persevere in Thy love.

POINT II.

After that Christ our Lord had comforted His disciples, He said to them,—"*Stay you in the city, till you be indued with power from on high.*"(4) In which words He promises to them the coming of the Holy Ghost, but in a manner very mysterious, as will appear, pondering each word apart by itself.

1. First, therefore, He says to them, "*Sedete.*" "*Sit ye,*" or "*tarry,*" that is to say, be quiet; to teach them that the quietude of the body and of the soul, with the calmness and stillness of the heart, is of great importance to receive this celestial Gift. Moreover, to admonish them, that they should expect with patience and longanimity, without hastening more than was expedient, referring the care hereof to Almighty God: and for this

(4) Luc. xxiv. 49.

cause He would not assign a certain day, wherein He intended to send the Holy Ghost, that so they might daily expect Him, daily ask Him, and daily prepare themselves to receive Him, but only said to them, that they should be baptized with the Holy Ghost, " not many days hence," (5) to the end that they should take comfort hereby, that the delay of His coming should not be long. Hence I will learn to expect with quietness and patience, the coming of the Divine Spirit, with that plenitude which I desire, referring the day of His coming to the Divine Providence, according to that of Isaiah, saying; " He that believeth, let him not hasten." (6)

2. Secondly, He said to them, that they should tarry " *in the city*," that is of Jerusalem. And although it might have seemed more to the purpose, that they should have gone to the desert, or else to some mountain, separate and apart, there to expect with quietness the coming of the Holy Ghost, yet He willed that they should expect the same in the city, as in a place frequented by many people, because the Holy Ghost was not sent for them alone, but for the good of all men, and therefore it was desirable He should be given in a public place, from whence they might presently issue forth to preach the law of Jesus Christ, conformably to the saying of the prophet Isaiah—" The law shall come forth from Sion, and the word of the Lord from Jerusalem."(7) Moreover, God our Lord much more esteems the solitude of the heart, than the solitude of the body: and to show, that in the midst of the noise of the people, there may be had a heart quiet, peaceable, and apt to see and receive God. And, it may be, for this cause not without mystery, this city, though very populous, was called " Jerusalem," as much as to say, " vision of peace."

(5) Act. i. 5.   (6) Isa. xxviii. 16.   (7) Isa. ii. 3.

Colloquy.—O Prince of Peace, pacify my heart, and quiet my spirit, that in all places and times, I may pray to Thee, lifting up pure hands to heaven, expecting the gift which Thou hast promised me. Amen.

3. Thirdly, He willed them that they should tarry in the city, adding, " *till you be indued with power from on high :*" that is to say, with the power of the Holy Ghost. By which He gave them to understand, that of themselves they were naked, and disarmed, feeble, weak, and void of that spirit, and power, which was needful to go into the world to preach the Gospel: and that, therefore, they were to stay until the Holy Ghost should come on them, who should clothe them with His grace, arm them with His gifts, and fortify them with His celestial virtues, giving them force, virtue, and power for this mission. And this virtue, as the Lord says, comes from on high, because it is most high, and far surpassing all human power: so also for that " every best gift, and every perfect gift, is from above, descending from the Father of lights," (8) whose dwelling and habitation is on high. Hence I will draw two admonitions.—i. The first, that it is of great importance, *to ground myself in true humility,* confessing my nakedness, and my weakness, for of myself, neither have I garments, nor sufficient weapons, nor can clothe myself with them, unless some others clothe me like a child: and for this cause Christ our Lord said not, tarry until you indue or clothe yourselves, but until you be indued.— ii. The second admonition is, that *it is a rash presumption to issue forth to these weighty expeditions before we have the means,* and be indued with power from on high, for he that goes forth to fight without weapons against strong enemies, will be easily vanquished by them.

(8) Jac. i. 17.

Colloquy.—O Father of lights, from whom all good and celestial gifts descend, behold how poor I am in Thy presence, and so little a child, that I neither have garments in which to clothe me, nor yet can clothe myself unless Thy mercy perform both the one and the other in my behalf. Clothe me, Lord, with virtue from on high, by which I may take in hand such commissions as concern Thy service; and permit not that without such virtue, I rashly expose myself to that I am not able to perform; for if I seek to fly without wings, instead of ascending on high, pride will cast me down into the profoundest depths.

4. Christ our Lord in saying to them, that they should tarry in the city till they were indued with power from on high;—gave them to understand, that as soon as they had received this power, they were to issue forth upon His business: for as it had been rashness to have gone forth before they had received this power, so should it be pusillanimity not to issue forth having received the same; the apostles, therefore, presently issued forth, as will be seen in Meditation XXIV.

POINT III.

This said, "*He led them out as far as Bethania,*" to "*the mount that is called Olivet.*" (9)

1. Christ our Lord commanded all His disciples, who were in that feast chamber, *that they should presently go to Bethany,* to the mount of Olivet, for that from thence He would ascend to heaven. It is not certain that He Himself brought them forth and accompanied them for some time, suffering Himself to be seen of them, and not of other men who passed by the way; or whether He vanished from them and the disciples went alone: however, they presently obeyed the commandment of Christ our Lord.

(9) Luc. xxiv. 50.　Act. i. 12.

And it may be believed, that at their going from the feast chamber, they called to mind that former going forth to the garden of Gethsemane (which was seated upon the one side of the mount of Olivet) full of sorrow and anxiéty, trembling for fear of the troubles which they foresaw would befal them by the death of their beloved master; but now they go forth with great anxiety, mingled with sadness and joy, expecting this glorious ascending up to heaven. And with this fervour they walked speedily to the place which was assigned them.

2. Christ *chose the mountain of Olivet whence to ascend to heaven,* on which He had prayed to His Father with great agony, and with a bloody sweat,—on which He was forsaken of His disciples,—delivered by Judas to His enemies,—taken of the Jews,—bound with cords, and trampled under their feet;—and finally, from whence He issued forth to suffer the ignominies of the cross, He would ascend to enjoy the greatness of His glory: that so we may understand that by such travails He gained heaven, which He went to possess: and that if I have patience, the same which was the beginning of my humiliation, shall likewise be the beginning of my exaltation, and that from these temporal labours I shall ascend to everlasting repose. Moreover, Christ therefore designed for the place of His Ascension Bethania, which is interpreted, house of obedience, and the mount of Olivet, which signifies the top of mercy and of charity; to signfy to us, that all things whatever He did, from His Incarnation to His Ascension up to heaven, were done to obey His Father with most perfect obedience; in whose house of obedience He so lived, that He never departed from the same; all these things likewise which He did, He directed to that supreme and high end, of charity and mercy, for the good of men, for their love, and to deliver them from their miseries. And withal

teaches us, that the way to ascend to Heaven, is from Bethany, and the mount of Olives, that is, by the house of obedience, and height of charity and mercy, " purifying," as St. Peter says, our "souls in the obedience of charity."(10)

Colloquy.—O Only begotten Son of the Father, who by the ways of obedience and charity, ascendest to sit upon His right Hand, assist me, I beseech Thee, that during my whole life I may dwell in the house of obedience, never departing in the least point from Thy holy will, endeavouring always to ascend to the highest degree of charity and mercy, till I come to arrive with Thee to the highest of Thy glory, where I shall see Thee, and enjoy Thee for all eternity. Amen.

II.—MEDITATIONS ON OUR LORD'S ASCENSION INTO HEAVEN; AND THE CONDUCT OF THE APOSTLES AND DISCIPLES FROM THE TIME OF HIS DEPARTURE UNTIL THE COMING OF THE HOLY GHOST.

MEDITATION XVIII.

OF THE ASCENSION OF CHRIST.

POINT I.

1. The disciples, and the most holy Virgin, being in the mount of Olivet, Christ appeared to them (1) with a countenance more bright and pleasant than at other times; and instead of embraces, which those who love are wont to give one another at their departure, He suffered all of them to kiss ⸲His sacred feet and hands, whence issued forth a

(10) 1 Pet. i. 22.
(1) S. Th. 3, p. q. lvii. Marc. xvi. 19. Luc. xxiv. 51.

most odoriferous smell, which incredibly comforted their hearts. First of all, without doubt, His most blessed Mother our Lady approached, who with the title of a mother, sweetly kissed the wounds of His Side, desiring to enter within her Son, to ascend to heaven together with Him, if it might have been granted to her ; but as she was most resigned to the divine will, so would she will no other thing than what Almighty God would will. Next followed St. Peter, St. John, and the other apostles and disciples, all of them with great reverence and devotion, touching and kissing those sacred wounds.

2. "*And lifting up His hands,*" as *St. Luke says,* "*He blessed them.*" (2) Two things did our Lord here do.

i. The first was, to *lift up His hands on high*, to signify that the benediction which He would give them, was not in earthly, but in heavenly goods, which He had obtained by His Passion and death, lifting up His hands upon the cross. And He lifted up both of His hands, because both of them were nailed to it, as also to signify the abundant largeness of His benediction, offering us with full hands the goods of grace and of glory. Whence I will conceive great affections of praise and gratitude, saying with the apostle;—" Blessed be the God and Father of our Lord Jesus Christ, who hath blessed us with spiritual blessings in heavenly places in Christ."(3)

Colloquy.—O most blessed Christ, by the love and excessive sorrow with which Thou liftest up Thy hands upon the cross, to gain for me celestial benedictions ; I do beseech Thee that Thou wouldst lift them up at this present, to impart to me Thine abundant benediction ; grant me likewise, O Lord, that I may lift up mine with prayers and works so perfect,

(2) Luc. xxiv. 50.　　　　(3) Ephes. i. 3.

that I may deserve that Thou lift up Thine to bless me. Amen.

ii. Secondly, St. Luke says; that "He *blessed them*," declaring by words those good things which He desired, and asked for them. And although we know not the words which He spake, nor the goods He desired, and asked for them, yet it may be, that He used those words with which Almighty God commanded that the sons of Israel should be blessed, saying, "The Lord bless" you, "and keep" you; "the Lord show His face to" you, "and have mercy on" you :(4) Our Lord turn His countenance unto you, and give you peace. Or else, perhaps, He repeated part of that prayer which He made in the sermon after supper, which was the highest benediction that He could give to them, saying to 'His Eternal Father: " Holy Father, keep them in Thy name," and protect them with Thy power, " whom Thou hast given me, that they may be one, as we also are;"(5) and may afterwards ascend whither I ascend, that they may see the glory which Thou hast given me, and the love Thou borest me before the creation of the world. And as the benediction of our Lord consists not in words alone, but also in works, doing what He says, so, together with that benediction, He replenished them with those celestial goods which He then demanded for them.

Colloquy.—O most sweet Jesus, to whom were present even those who were absent in that hour ; make me partaker, I beseech Thee, of this Thy blessing, whereon depends all my good. Let me not be like to reprobate Esau, who did not obtain the full benediction of his father Isaac. Bless me, O my Father, in this Thy farewell, not with an earthly, but with a heavenly

(4) Num. vi. 24.   (5) Joan. xvii. 11.

benediction, for earthly goods will ,in no way fill nor satisfy me, but heavenly goods will do both.

POINT II.

The benediction being given, our Lord began by *little and little to lift Himself up from the earth,* (6) and they beheld Him going into Heaven, not as Elias, carried in a chariot of fire, (7) but with *His own virtue* lifted up with the fire of His infinite divinity and majesty which aspires on high as to its proper place. Moreover, there accompanied Him all the souls of the just, and many choirs of angels which descended from heaven to ascend with Him. All the disciples had their eyes, both of soul and body, fixed on their master, elevated with three most inflamed affections.—i. The first affection was of *admiration,* to see a thing so new, as for a man to ascend into the air with so great pleasure and facility, and with signs of so great excellency and majesty.—ii. The second affection was of *exceeding joy,* rejoicing in the glory of their master, and in the Divinity which shone in Him. Neither did they rend their vestments for sorrow, as Eliseus did his, when he saw his master Elias ascend to heaven, but exulted from joy and contentment, to see Him mount with so great majesty.—iii. The third affection was, a very sincere *desire to follow Him,* and to ascend together with Him, because their hearts were wholly rapt after their Beloved, fulfilling here that which had been prophecied :—" Thou hast ascended on high, thou hast led captivity captive." (8) For two sorts of captives did Christ our Lord lead with Him, some really and in their proper persons,—such were the just whom He drew forth out of Limbo, who followed Him even to the empyreal heaven ; but besides these He led captive the hearts of His mother and disciples, who all in

(6) Luc. xxiv. 51. Act. i. 9.

(7) 4 Reg. ii. 11.   (8) Ps. lxvii. 19. Ephes. iv. 8.

desire followed Him, fettered with the chains of love, nor could they possibly depart from Him.

Colloquy.—Oh that it were granted me, that I might be one of these captives of Jesus Christ! O most sweet Jesus, carry my heart captive with Thee unto heaven, that so it may be always in Thy company. I rejoice that Thou ascendest through the air, flying as a swift eagle, and provoking Thy sons and little ones to fly up with Thee. Give me, dear Lord, the wings of an eagle, with which I may fly in following Thee, placing all my thoughts and my desires in ascending after Thee, for nothing besides Thee will I upon earth, nor desire anything more than to enjoy Thee in heaven.

POINT III.

The disciples beholding Christ our Lord as He ascended, "a cloud received Him out of their sight."(9)

1. Here is to be considered the mystery of this cloud, which, when Christ our Lord ascended through the region of the air, received Him within it in the sight of His apostles. And it may be believed that it was wonderfully beautiful and resplendent, *such as was fit to declare the majesty of that Lord* who ascended thereon, and the beauty of that celestial place to which He tended ; fulfilling that which was foretold, saying,—" Who makest the clouds thy chariot, who walkest upon the wings of the winds ;"(10)—that is to say, makes use of the clouds, as of triumphant chariots with which to ascend, flying with great pomp and majesty amidst the air. Oh what joy did the apostles feel, beholding that glorious Chariot in which their Lord and master went up to heaven ! although they cried not as Eliseus, when he saw Elias ascend in a chariot of fire ; for the suspension of spirit had taken from them

(9) Act. i. 9.   (10) Ps. ciii. 3.

the use of their tongue, yet each one it may be,   said in his heart that which Elias said ;—" My Father, my Father, the chariot of Israel and the driver thereof."

Colloquy.—O my loving Father, the fortitude and defence of the true Israelites, who were steadfast in Thy service, and careful to contemplate in Thee : whither goest Thou and leavest me ? O my most sweet Father, governor and protector of those who trust in Thee, admit me into this triumphant chariot, give me entrance into this bright shining cloud, that I may follow Thee in spirit, and enter to contemplate the glory of Thy sovereign majesty.   Amen.

2. Christ our Lord having entered a little within that cloud, He *was so covered with it, that He was taken from the eyes of His disciples*, which cloud represents to us all that which hinders us from seeing Christ our Lord, and causes us to lose the sight of Almighty God, which happens in two manners — i. Sometimes it happens through our own fault, and then our faults are the clouds which we put betwixt God and us, and are a great impediment of prayer and contemplation, according to that of the prophet Jeremiah, saying,—" Thou hast set a cloud before Thee, that our prayer may not pass through" (11) to heaven; since I put this cloud, it behoves me with the help of divine grace, to remove it from me, by the means of penance and mortification, examining in particular, if it be a cloud of pride, of covetousness, or of other inordinate love to any creature, and applying effectual means to dissolve that which hinders me from so great a good.—ii. Sometimes this cloud interposes itself without our fault, by the sole permission of Almighty God, who, as sometimes He shows Himself to us, so sometimes likewise He hides Himself from us, not willing that we see Him by the

(11) Thren. iii. 44.

sweet contemplation of His presence, to the end that we attend to other things appertaining to His divine service. And generally the feebleness of our flesh and the dulness of our understanding, and the multitude of cares and necessities which we suffer in this mortal life, are like clouds which hinder us from contemplating Him with that clearness and continuation which we desire, in the same manner as the clouds which pass frequently through the air, take away from us the sight of the sun.

Colloquy.—O infinite God, " who inhabitest light inaccessible"(12) to mortal men, take from my soul the clouds of sin which I have put, and dissolve the mist of temptations and molestations which I suffer, to the end I may contemplate Thy glory in this mortal life, until I come to see Thee " face to face," (13) without impediment of any cloud, in the life eternal. Amen.

POINT IV.

After the apostles had lost the sight of Christ our Lord they stood admiring and amazed, still *" looking up to heaven,"*(14) and would have remained a long time in that extasy, that is, if our Lord had not sent some one to them to awake them. " Behold," therefore, " two men" (that is two angels) " stood by them in white garments, who also said, Ye men of Galilee, why stand you looking up to heaven? This Jesus who is taken up from you into heaven, shall so come, as you have seen Him going into heaven."

1. In these words the angels gave two admirable instructions to the disciples, and to us in them.

i. The first that suspension, admiration, and other effects of divine contemplation in this life, *are to be taken with a certain measure* and limitation, because they are not

(12) 1 Tim. vi. 16.   (13) 1 Cor. xiii. 12.   (14) Act. i. 11.

our last end, but a means to accomplish so much the better the will of God and the obligation of our office ; and so, by way of reprehension, the angels said to them :—" Why stand you looking up to heaven ?" as if they had said :— " Cease, you have looked long enough ; go and accomplish that which is commanded you."—ii. The second instruction was, that together with the memory of this ascending of Christ into heaven, they should conjoin His coming to judgment, to the end that the sight of the former might confirm the faith of the latter, and that they might jointly preach them both to men, so that if they should grow careless to live well, saying, that their Lord is absent, and that He has ascended into heaven, they should correct themselves, remembering that He is to return again to judge them. Nor did they tell when He was to return, but only that He was to return ; to the end that they should be daily in readiness for His return, and should fear the reckoning they are to render Him. And although it be true that He shall come again as He ascended, as touching the majesty and greatness which He showed in His ascension ; yet He that ascended gentle and meek, with signs and tokens of great love, shall return terrible and fearful, with signs of great rigour, and shall exact an account of all things which He committed to us at His departure, without pardoning any that shall be found guilty.

Colloquy.—Wherefore, O my soul, " in the day of good things, be not unmindful of evils," (15) and in the day wherein thy advocate ascended to heaven, be mindful of the day, wherein He shall return to judge thee ; consider diligently what He commanded thee, and take care to accomplish the same, that when He shall return, He may take thee with Him, to reign with Him in the Kingdom of heaven. Amen.

(15) Ecclus. xi. 27.

2. The disciples, after hearing this charge of the angels— *adoring, went back into Jerusalem with great joy.*"(16) For understanding that their master was now on the throne of heaven, prostrate on the earth, they adored Him with great reverence, supplying with the sight of faith, that which they could not attain to with the sight of the body. And they returned with great joy, for although they returned without their Master, yet did they return as men more perfect, who rejoice more in that which God wills, than in what their own flesh desires, and more in the glory of Christ, than in their own satisfaction. The causes of this joy were chiefly three.—i. *Confirmation of faith* which remained in them, seeing so glorious a concl usion in the affairs of their Master ; and by what was past they remained fully assured of all which was to come— ii. Secondly, *great hope* which they conceived, that He would send to them the Holy Ghost which He had promised them, and that the time would come when they should ascend with Him, to be there where He was, according to what He Himself had said.—iii. Great and fervent *love* which they bore unto Him, of whose glory they so rejoiced, as if the same had been their own; and although their bodies walked upon the ground from the Mount of Olivet to Jerusalem, yet were their hearts above in heaven, contemplating the glory of their Lord. And from these causes so great a joy arose to them.

3. These three causes ought likewise to work great joy in my soul, quickening my faith, hope, and charity, in Christ our Lord, rejoicing in His glory and comforting myself with the hope of ascending where He is ; for which purpose I ought to take care to remove from myself all which may hinder this ascending, such are sins, vices, and inordinate affections to earthly things, and also to dis-

(16) Luc. xxiv. 52.

charge and rid myself of the superfluity of such things, that I may fly more lightly whither Christ Jesus is, because He Himself said :—" Wheresoever the body shall be, shall the eagles also be gathered together ;" (17) that is to say, where the glorified body of Christ our Lord is, there shall they be gathered together, which are renewed like eagles," (18) and with confidence in God, have changed their fortitude, and taken the wings of an eagle, (19) to ascend to contemplate and fly with swiftness to all those things which belong to His holy service.

Colloquy.—O King of heaven, who, like a kingly eagle, soarest in the air, and placest Thy nest in the height of heaven, (20) provoke me that I may follow Thee with desire, renew my youth like that of the eagle, to the end I may recover a new strength and a new fortitude, and with the same fly after Thee, following Thy steps, imitating Thy virtues, and transferring my heart thither, where Thy glorified body is, to the end that I may so live here on earth, that I may have my conversation above in heaven, where Thou livest and reignest, world without end.   Amen.

MEDITATION XIX.

OF CHRIST'S ENTRY INTO THE EMPYREAL HEAVEN AND OF HIS SITTING UPON THE RIGHT HAND OF HIS FATHER.

POINT I.

The first shall be to consider the *glorious triumph with which Christ our Lord entered the empyreal heaven,* where is to be pondered the company He led with Him, the exultation and heavenly harmony with which He entered,

(17) Mat. xxiv. 28.   (18) Ps. cii. 5.   (19) Isa. xl. 31.
(20) Job. xxxix. 27.

and the discourses and speeches which were used on His entrance.

1. First, the company was (1) *all those souls which He brought out of Limbo*, with certain just ones already glorified in their bodies, (if it be true that those who rose again with Christ, did not return again to die,) according to that which was written: that ascending on high, He "led captivity captive," that is to say, He led with Him the souls which had been captive in the lake of Limbo, taking them for His prisoners, and binding them with the fetters of love and charity, leading them with Him to their own unspeakable delight and consolation; forasmuch as it is worse and more miserable to be captive of the Devil, so much it is better and more glorious to be a captive of Jesus Christ.

i. *O how joyfully did this company of noble captives and prisoners ascend*, following their captain, desiring to see Him placed on the throne of His glory, where they should enjoy perfect liberty! They called to mind the straitness and darkness of Limbo, from whence they were delivered, and compared the same with the spaciousness and brightness of the empyreal heaven which they had entered, and admiring the beauty of the place, every one repeated that of the psalm:—" How lovely are Thy tabernacles, O Lord of hosts ; my soul longeth and fainteth for the courts of the Lord."(2)

ii. At this sight presently *began that heavenly music*, of which the prophet David said :—" God is ascended with jubilee, and the Lord with the sound of trumpet."(3) Oh, what jubilees of joy did those souls feel, marching in the company of their captain ! What voices of praise (resounding louder than trumpets) did their hearts send forth, glorifying their Sovereign Lord ! One, doubtless

(1) Meditat. ii. p. 4.   (2) Ps. lxxxiii. 1.   (3) Ps. xlvi. 6.

provoked another to sing such songs of praises, using those words of the self-same David:—" Sing praises to our God, sing ye: sing praises to our king, sing ye. For God is king of all the earth: sing ye wisely. God shall reign over the nations: God sitteth on His holy throne."(4) They likewise sung that of the other psalm:—"Sing ye to God, who mounteth above the heaven of heavens,"(5) and there dwelleth in a light inaccessible, to illuminate His elect with the light of His glory.

2. Together with the choir of souls, entered also a *choir of innumerable angels* who came to accompany Christ our Lord, who were, as David said, the triumphant " chariot of God," and were in number " ten thousand."(6)   All with great joy singing the triumphs of His victory, making between themselves dialogues and colloquies whereby to discover His wonderful greatness.   One said to another, " Lift up your gates, O ye princes, and be ye lifted up, O eternal gates, and the King of glory shall enter in!" others answered them by way of admiration: " Who is this King of glory?" who will enter by these gates?   And answer was made them :—" The Lord, who is strong and mighty; the Lord, mighty in battle,—the Lord of hosts, He is the King of glory."(7)   Others asked by way of exulting, " Who is this that cometh from Edom, with dyed garments from Bosra, this beautiful one in His robe, walking in the greatness of His strength?"(8)   Which is to say :—" Who is this who ascendeth from the world, all bloody and as · from a place of battle, invested with an humanity, bordered with the signs of wounds, but marvellously beautiful, and with arguments of great virtue and fortitude?" " I," says He, " that speak justice, and am a defender to save." " I have done justice in the world, satisfying for the sins

(4) Ps. xlvi. 7.   (5) Ps. lxvii. 34.   (6) Ibid. 18.
       (7) Ps. xxiii. 7. et seq.   (8) Isa. lxiii. 1.

of men, fighting against the Devil to save thee, and now do justice, myself ascending, and bringing them also with me up to heaven, which I have won for them." Then all with one voice said that of the Apocalypse:—" The Lamb that was slain, is worthy to receive power, and divinity, and wisdom, and strength, and honour, and glory, and benediction, for ever and ever."(9)

Colloquy.—O Saviour of the world, I rejoice at this so glorious a triumph, which Thou hast so well deserved. "Arise, O Lord, into Thy resting-place, Thou and the ark which Thou hast sanctified," since Thou hast so well laboured for the love of us. "Be Thou exalted above the heavens," ascend "upon the Cherubim," and fly "upon the wings of the wind," and place Thyself on high above all creatures, because Thou art better and superior to them all. Give me leave that I may enter with these angelic choirs, that joining my voice together with theirs, I may praise Thee and bless Thee, saying with them:—"Holy, holy, holy, Lord God Almighty, who was, who is, and who is to come,"(10) the heavens are full of Thy glory, by means of this glorious entrance which Thou makest into them.

3. But above all is to be pondered, *the unspeakable joy of Christ our Lord in this glorious triumph*, for of Him is fitly said,—" God is ascended with jubilee," His most holy soul exulting with ineffable joy, to see the happy ending of His labours ; and as the pastor, who had recovered the lost sheep, and carried him with Him into heaven, (whence He descended to seek him,) He said to the angels, " Rejoice with me, because I have found my sheep that was lost."(11)

(9) Apoc. v. 12 et 13.
(10) Ps. cxxxi. 8.　Ps. cvii. 6.　Ps. xvii. 11.　Apoc. iv. 8.
(11) Luc. xv. 5.

Colloquy.—O sovereign pastor, who at Thy so great expense, soughtest and foundest the lost sheep of mankind: I joy in this joy, which Thou hast, and with which Thou ascendest triumphantly above all the heavens. I congratulate Thy glory in this triumph, by the which I beseech Thee to make me also partaker of it, seeking me, and finding me in this life, and bringing me afterwards to enjoy Thee in the life to come. Amen.

POINT II.

1. Christ our Lord, having entered after this manner, and, " passing," as the apostle says, " into the heavens,''(12) He came to the top of the empyreal heaven, and *presented to His eternal Father those happy captives whom He brought with Him ;* and rendering, as it were, an account of those things which He had done in the world in His service, it may be He repeated that which He had said before to Him, in the sermon after supper :—" Father, I have glorified Thee on the earth; I have finished the work which Thou gavest me to do : and now glorify me, O Father, with Thyself, with the glory which I had before the world was, with Thee."(13) Oh what content did the eternal Father receive with that present which His Son made to Him, and with what signs of joy did He command Him to sit " on His right hand," and that so might be fulfilled that which David had foretold, saying:—" The Lord said to my Lord, Sit Thou at my right hand,"(14) He wills Him to sit ; to signify His quiet and peaceable dominion, and the infinite dignity of His person. He says, upon His right hand ; to give to understand that He imparted to Him the best and most principal of His glory, appointing Him a throne above all the Angels, and Archangels, above the powers and

(12) Heb. iv. 14.   (13) Joan. xvii. 4.

(14) Marc. xvi. 19. Ps. cix. 1.

Dominations, above the Cherubim and Seraphim, as head and Lord over them all; for to none of the angels did He ever say:—" Sit on my right hand,''(15) but would that all should be servants, and ministering spirits of His government.

2. Here I am to ponder how well the eternal Father recompensed the service of His Son, *exalting Him above all who had humbled Himself more than all.*—For the throne of the cross He gave to Him the throne of His majesty;— for the crown of thorns, the crown of glory;—for the company of thieves, the hierarchies of angels;—for the ignominies and blasphemies of the Jews, the honours and praises of the blessed spirits;—and because He descended into the profoundest parts of the earth, He made Him to ascend to the highest of the empyreal heaven, and gave to Him a name above all names, that in the name of Jesus every knee bow, and every tongue confess that Jesus Christ is in the glory of God the Father. Learn, therefore, O my soul, to humble thee for Christ, and thou shalt doubtless be exalted with Christ; for the same fidelity which the eternal Father performed towards His Only-begotten Son, the same will He perform towards His adoptive sons, for the love which He bears to His natural Son, in whose reward ours also is contained; for as the apostle says:— " God, who is rich in mercy for His exceeding charity, wherewith He loved us, even when we were dead in sins, quickened us together in Christ, by whose grace we are saved, and hath raised us up together, and hath made us sit together in the heavenly places, through Christ Jesus." (16)

3. Hence *will I draw great affections of confidence,* hoping to ascend with Christ to heaven, trusting in the mercy and charity of the Father, and in the great and abundant

(15) Heb. i. 13.   (16) Ephes ii. 4.

merits of the Son.   I will also conceive firm purposes, not to seek any other thing than Christ our Lord, and the accomplishment of His Holy will, always mindful of that which St. Paul says ;—" Seek the things that are above, where Christ is sitting on the right hand of God."(17)

Colloquy.—O most sweet Jesus, if where my treasure be there is my heart, then where Thou art, that shall always be, because Thou art my treasure, and besides Thee I repute nothing precious.   O my soul, consider that Thou art a pilgrim, and a stranger upon earth, that thy Father and thy Redeemer, now is, and sits above in heaven, make haste therefore to go where He is ; now are the gates of heaven open, which before were shut so many thousand of years, comfort thyself with this joyful news, run with the swiftness of a hart, fly with the wings of an eagle, ascend in spirit to the throne of thy Lord, and abide always close by His celestial bed, for if now thou dwellest there in spirit, thou shalt hereafter dwell there, glorified also in body, for ever and ever. Amen.

POINT III.

1. Consider, thirdly, how Christ our Lord, being set upon the right hand of His Father, *began presently to exercise His office, distributing the seats of Heaven* amongst those souls which ascended with Him :—some He placed amongst the Angels, others amongst the Archangels, and Principalities, and others amongst the Cherubim and Seraphim, giving to every one a place and seat according to his merits.   Concerning which I may discourse and ponder what seats He gave to the Patriarchs, to the Prophets, to the glorious St. Joseph, the spouse of His most holy Mother, as also to His precursor, St. John Baptist,

(17) Colos. iii. 1.

what place likewise He gave to them which ascended with Him in glorified bodies. Oh how great was the content of those souls when they saw themselves seated on such thrones, and in so glorious a company ! O how joyful were the angels, beholding those seats filled which their fellows through their pride, had left empty !—"God," as the prophet David says, "filling up" with men " the ruins" and falls of the wicked angels. (18) Oh how abundantly did the eternal Father accomplish the promise which He had made to His Son when He said :—Because He " hath delivered His soul to death, I will distribute to Him very many," which shall serve Him, and " He shall divide the spoils of the strong,"(19)

Colloquy.—I rejoice, O most sweet Jesus, that Thou hast this office to divide the spoils of Thy glory amongst those which have served Thee with true fortitude; make me, dear Lord, strong and constant in Thy service, that I may merit to be partaker of Thy spoils.

2. Christ our Lord sitting at the right hand of His Father, *began presently to perform the office of an advocate,* for men whom He had left below on earth, showing Him the wounds He had received to redeem them, and in accomplishing His commandment, in which office He still perseveres to this day. Hence I will conceive great affections of love and confidence, mindful of that which St. Paul says :—" Having a great high priest that hath passed into the heavens, Jesus, the Son of God, let us hold fast our confession" (20) of our hope, not fainting in the confession of that which we believe, nor in procuring that which we hope for; especially when I see myself fallen into any sin I ought to remember that saying of St. John :—" My little

(18) Ps. cix. 6.　　　(19) Isa. liii. 12.　　　(20) Heb. iv. 14.

children, these things I write to you, that you may not sin. But and if any man sin, we have an advocate with the Father, Jesus Christ, the just: and He is the propitiation for our sins; and not for ours only, but also for those of the whole world."(21) Being therefore, so just as He is, and having wrought so copious a redemption, He will not omit to be an advocate for me, and to apply to me the pardon He has obtained for me. And having opened the gates of heaven for me, He will not shut them against me, but will admit me to have part with Him in His kingdom, to the glory of His Father, with whom He lives and reigns, world without end. Amen.

MEDITATION XX.

ON THE RECOLLECTION AND PRAYER OF THE APOSTLES, FROM THE ASCENSION UNTIL THE COMING OF THE HOLY GHOST.

POINT I.

The disciples returning from Jerusalem, "went up into an upper room, where abode Peter, and John," and the other apostles, and " all these *were persevering with one mind in prayer with the women, and Mary the Mother of Jesus, and with his brethren.*"(1)

1. The apostles, moved by the spirit of Jesus Christ, *recollected themselves in that chamber* for the space of those ten days, retiring from the noise and tumult of the people, exercising themselves in fervent prayer to obtain the coming of the Holy Ghost; for, notwithstanding that Christ, our Lord had promised the same to them, yet knew they well that divine promises are accomplished by the means

(21) 1 Joan. ii. 1.   (1) Act. i. 13.

of prayer, especially this of which He Himself had said to them :—" If you, then, being evil, know how to give good gifts to your children, how much more will your Father from heaven give the good Spirit to them that ask Him?"(2)

2. *This prayer they accompanied with other excellent virtues*, which are set down in the words ensuing.

i. For St. Luke says that *they were greatly united*, and agreed, *having one heart and one will*, all praying and asking one and the same thing, for they knew the prayer of many, united with love, to be most efficacious before God, according to that their master had said :—" I say to you that if two of you shall consent upon earth, concerning anything whatsoever they shall ask, it shall be done to them by my Father, who is in heaven ; for where there are two or three gathered together in my name, there am I in the midst of them."(3)   As if He had said :—" They shall be heard of my Father, because I am with them, helping them to pray, exercising the office of an advocate and orator for them." And because Christ our Lord had so seriously recommended to them to love one another, they endeavoured to excel in that conformity of wills, which is the cause of mutual love.

ii. They were not only united with one another, *but every one with himself;* whence it proceeds that prayer is most recollected when the powers of the soul are conjoined and united together to pray. "For in this sense also," says St. Ambrose,(4) "is to be understood that which Christ our Lord said, ' That prayer shall be heard in the which two are gathered and accord,' that is to say, the exterior and interior man, the body and the soul, that is when the body by true mortification and subjection is

<hr>

(2) Luc. xi. 13.   (3) Mat. xviii. 19.
(4) De Instit. ad Virg. cap ii.

brought to agree with the soul; and both of them with another third, which the apostle calls the 'spirit,' so that to pray as we ought, the body must agree with the senses the soul with the imagination and inferior appetites, and the spirit with the superior faculties of memory, understanding and will, and then will Christ be present in the midst of these two or three united in His name, helping them to pray."

iii. *They remained with great perseverance in their exercise of prayer* not, from lukewarmness, leaving it, mindful of that which their master had said:—" We ought always to pray, and not to faint."(5)   And because Christ our Lord had not signified to them the time when He would give to them the Holy Ghost, therefore they prayed daily, asking the same, and multiplying their prayers with so great fervour, as though they were to receive Him that very day, importuning Almighty God to give Him to them, to the end that, although they merited not to obtain this gift as friends of God, yet that they might obtain the same " because of their importunity," as their master Himself had a dmonished them.(6)

iv. *They prayed in the company of the most sacred Virgin,* the mother of Jesus, whom, without doubt, they took for a patroness and intercessor for them, knowing full well that she alone could do much more with her Son and with the eternal Father, than all of them together.   The holy Virgin, therefore, prayed most fervently, and with her example moved and animated all the rest to pray with fervour and perseverance, and her prayer was so effectual, that we may say of her, that like as she obtained by her prayers the hastening of the Incarnation of the Son of God, so also she obtained the hastening of the coming of

<hr>

(5) Luc. xviii. 1.   (6) Luc. xi. 14.

the Holy Ghost, for the good of the apostles and of the whole world.

3. In these four virtues and circumstances of holy prayer, I ought to endeavour to imitate the apostles for obtaining the coming of the Holy Ghost; that is to say, by recollected prayer, with union of my powers and senses: union of charity with all persons: perseverance with importunity in demanding; and devotion to the Virgin, our Blessed Lady, humbly beseeching her as Mother, that she pray for me, and solicit for me before her Father and her Son, that they may grant me the fulness of the Holy Ghost.

4. Hence also I will learn that as the chamber in which the apostles remained is a figure of the Church, which is the house of prayer and union; so ought I to procure *that my soul become like to this chamber*, adorned with these virtues, to the end the Holy Ghost may descend into it, and enrich it with His gifts. Moreover, I will render great thanks to our Lord for having placed me in His Church, where I never pray alone, because she always prays for all, and many just, one for another; and so in virtue of the communion of saints, which is in the Church, my prayer is conjoined with the prayers of many just, if I unite myself with them.

POINT II.

1. Ponder secondly the *causes and motives* which the apostles had for this recollection and exercise of prayer, applying them to myself, that so they may work the same in me.

i. The first motive was that Christ our Lord had commanded them at His departure *that they should remain quiet in the city* till they were endowed with power from on high; in accomplishment whereof they withdrew themselves into that chamber, making it a house of prayer and place of refuge, calling to mind the mysteries which had been celebrated in the same, and those so high and divine discourses, which there they had heard from their holy master; and even as Christ our Lord, before He issued forth to preach in public, was forty days recollected in the desert: so would He that His apostles should remain at the least recollected for ten days, procuring the coming of that Spirit which first they were to receive, before they were to preach the Gospel publicly.

ii. The second cause was the *knowledge of their own weakness and insufficiency*, of which they had experienced on preceding occasions, especially in the time of His Passion; and because that they saw themselves now deprived of the presence of their master, who was wont to instruct and comfort them; both which things urged them and enkindled in them a fervent desire of the coming of the Holy Ghost, who might teach them and fortify them with His power; and so they ceased not to pray, to sigh, and to groan for His coming. Sometimes they demanded Him of the eternal Father, by the merits of His only-begotten Son, Jesus Christ, who in His name had promised Him; at other times they asked Him of Jesus Christ Himself, their Lord and master, beseeching Him to fulfil the promise which He had made them, to send Him to them; at other times they besought the same Holy Ghost that He would vouchsafe to come to visit them, instruct and comfort them, alleging for a just reason the great necessity which they had of His presence to discharge the office which was imposed upon them. And it is credible that sometimes all of them together, lifting up their hands to heaven, with great clamour of heart, prayed, saying:—" Come, O Holy Spirit, fill the hearts of Thy faithful, and enkindle in them the fire of Thy love;"(7) " come, O Spirit, our Creator and our comforter, visit the souls of Thy servants, replenish them with Thy celestial grace, comfort them with the sweetness of Thy love, and with the power of Thy virtue strengthen them."

But she who, amongst all the rest, prayed with greatest fervour, and most solicited the Three Divine Persons, was our Blessed Lady the Virgin, who craved the same with greater charity than all the rest, yet not for herself alone, but for the apostles ; for if at the marriage when wine was wanting, moved with compassion, she presently ran to her Son to ask it, with how much greater fervour is it to be thought she did ask now that precious wine of love and fervour, which proceeds from the Holy Ghost, for that assembly, which stood in so great necessity of it ?

2. In imitation of these holy persons I will excite in my soul the like desires, since it is clear to me how great necessity and want I have of this divine wine, endeavouring to make frequent colloquies with the Three divine Persons, humbly asking Him of either of them, making use of the hymns and psalms, which make mention of Him. Speaking with the eternal Father, or with His Son, Christ our Lord, I may say that of the prophet David:— " Create a clean heart in me, O God, and renew a right spirit within my bowels ; restore to me the joy of Thy salvation, and strengthen me with a perfect spirit." " Send forth Thy Spirit," and I shall be renewed, as Thou renewest by Him " the face of the earth."(8) Speaking with the Holy Ghost, the hymn, " Veni Creator Spiritus," and the Sequence or Prose, which is repeated in His Mass, is admirably proper, if it be recited with fervour, as

<hr>

(7) Offic. S. Spir.   (8) Ps. l. 12. Ps. ciii. 30.

> " Oh, come, Thou Father of the poor,
> Oh, come, Thou source of all our store,
> Come fill our hearts with love."

Oh most clear light, O burning fire, come and penetrate the interior of my heart, purify, temperate, illustrate, and inflame it with the flames of Thy divine love.

3. The Holy Ghost, whose property it is, as St. Paul says, to ask for the just " with unspeakable groanings,"(9) *did by little and little enkindle these desires in the hearts of the apostles*, because, desires are as precursors and fore-messengers of Almighty God in the soul, into which He is to enter.   And although He enkindled them in all these ten days, yet in the latter days, He enkindled them a great deal more ; for which cause I will beseech Him, that He would vouchsafe to forestall me with the like desires, which may dispose me worthily to receive Him.

Colloquy.—O Divine Spirit and eternal God, of whom it is written :— "Fire shall go before Him,"(10) enkindle in my soul the fire of these desires, that it may burn, and quite consume all that which may oppose Thy entry.   O sacred apostles, to whom this divine Spirit communicated such desires, beseech Him to communicate the like to me, that so I may be fit and capable to receive Him as you received Him, since my necessity is nothing less than that of yours. O glorious Virgin, behold in me the want of this wine, with which the Holy Ghost inebriated the apostles, and with great fervour represent to Him my necessity, that by thy intercession He inebriate me, as He did them.   Amen.

POINT III.

Consider, thirdly, *why Christ our Lord deferred His promise*, and the coming of the Holy Ghost *till after ten days*.

(9) Rom. viii. 26.   (10) Ps. xcvi. 3.

1. The first was, *to teach us the longanimity with which we ought to await and expect so sovereign a gift*, for in Holy Scripture the number ten signifies a multitude of days, like as the angels said in the Apocalypse:—"You shall have tribulation ten days," (11) that is to say, many days, for so our Lord would have us to understand, that the coming of the Holy Ghost is so great a benefit, that we ought to demand it, and to expect it many days, without being wearied or desisting, because all the time is but little, and afterwards He pays abundantly with the gift which He gives, even in one only day. Moreover, that which is soon got, is wont to be as soon lost, as it came to pass with Solomon, who quickly obtained the spirit of wisdom, and because it cost him little, he was not careful in keeping the same. Whence I will resolve to crave this celestial gift with great constancy, although it be needful to persevere long in this petition, applying to this purpose that which the prophet Habacuc said,—" If He shall make any delay, wait, for lo, He shall surely come," and He " shall not be slack :"(12) and, although He tarry contrary to thy desire, yet will He " not tarry," conformably to that which is agreeable to His greatness, that so His coming may turn to thy advantage.

2. The second cause was, *to signify with what perfection we ought to seek and look for this gift*, for the number ten signifies perfection, according to the saying of the prophet Baruch :—" For, as it was your mind to go astray from God, so when you return again you shall seek Him ten times as much."(13) Wherefore, who even desires to receive the plenitude of the Holy Ghost, ought to convert himself to Him with great fervour and

(11) Apoc. ii. 10.
(12) Hab. ii. 3.   S. Basil. de Const. Monast. cap. ii. ad finem.
(13) Baruch. iv. 28.

perfection, animating himself to keep the ten commandments of His divine law, and to persevere most instantly in the observation of them; for prayer and obedience obtain of God all whatever we ask of Him.

Colloquy.—O most sweet Jesus, who saidst to Thine apostles:—"If you abide in me, and my words abide in you, you shall ask whatsoever you will, and it shall be done unto you."(14)   Grant me to abide in Thee by true love, and that Thy words abide in me by entire obedience, that, asking what I desire, namely, Thy divine Spirit, Thou mayest give me the same in great plenty and abundance.   Amen.

3. Some suppose that in those nine days after the Ascension, *the nine choirs of angels* made an especial feast and adoration to Christ our Lord, every choir on his day ; (15) and that for this cause the Holy Ghost descended the tenth day. Whence I will conceive a great desire to imitate these nine choirs of angels in these nine days, each day craving of each choir that they would negotiate the coming of the Holy Ghost to me.

MEDITATION XXI.

OF THE ELECTION OF S. MATHIAS TO THE APOSTLESHIP, WHICH WAS PERFORMED DURING THIS TIME.

POINT I.

" In those days, Peter, rising up in the midst of the brethren (now the number of persons together was about a hundred and twenty) treated of the election of an apostle in the place of Judas, who might be a witness of the resurrection of Christ with the other apostles. And they appointed two, Joseph who was called Barsabas, who was

(14) Joan. xv. 7.   (15) Niceph. l. 1, cap. xxxvii.

surnamed Justus, and Mathias, and praying, they said:—
Thou, Lord, who knowest the hearts of all men, show
whether of these two Thou hast chosen to take the place
of this ministry and apostleship, from which Judas has, by
transgression fallen. *And they gave them lots, and the
lot fell upon Mathias*."(1)

1. First is to be considered *the providence which Christ
our Lord has that the number of His elect be never wanting*
to supply the offices and dignities of the Church militant;
for, as Judas failing, He would that Mathias should be
chosen to fill the number which He had designed of twelve
apostles; even so when any one fail in faith and Christianity, or in Religion, or in any degree which he holds in the
Church, He calls and chooses others in his place; and,
therefore, said to a certain bishop in the Apocalypse:—
" Hold fast that which thou hast, that no man take thy
crown."(2) Whence I will conceive two affections of great
importance. One of fear and humility, seeing the peril I
am in of losing what I have, and that another enter into
my place, as it happened to unhappy Judas, of whom the
Psalmist says:—" His bishoprick let another take,"(3) as
we have already pondered in the fourth part, Meditation
xvi. and xxi. The other is of great confidence in the providence of God towards His Church, and Religious states,
and towards all communities dedicated to His service, inspiring many to succeed in the place of those who either fall
from the faith, or depart this life.

2. Christ our Lord sweetly *governs His Church by means
of pastors*, which He places in it. For being able during
those forty days which He remained in the world after
His Resurrection, to choose another apostle in the place of
Judas, as He had chosen and named the rest before His

(1) Act. i. 15—23.

(2) Apoc. iii. 11.   (3) Ps. cviii. 8.

Passion, (this principally appertaining to Him by reason of His dignity and excellence,) yet would He not, but remitted the same to St. Peter, and to the college of the apostles, that they should name him, and the election be made by them, His Majesty invisibly assisting; which He so ordained for the greater honour of His vicars and ministers, and to teach us that what they do is done by His providence, and that they are to be obeyed in Him, as if He Himself ordained the same, since for this purpose He said:—" *He that heareth you heareth me.*"(4)

POINT II.

1. Consider secondly what in this case the apostles did on their part; and first is to be pondered, *the care that St. Peter had as head of that congregation in discharging the obligations of his office,* God inspiring into him what he was to do, and he in order to perform the same, applying the light which He had given him, when "He opened" his understanding, that he "might understand the Scriptures," so that he therefore now clearly understood what they foretold concerning Judas;—" his bishopric let another take." And it may be thought, that in this and such like cases which occurred, he consulted with the Blessed Virgin what he should do, as the mistress of them all, and more enlightened than all of them in the mysteries of holy faith, and in the understanding of the divine Scriptures. Hence I will learn that prelates, and all others, who sometimes apply themselves to recollection and prayer, ought not for this to fail in the obligation of their office; for by prayer, and by the accomplishment of the will of God, they dispose themselves to receive that which they desire by this recollection.

2. Secondly are to be pondered, *certain heroic virtues,*

(4) Luc. x. 16.

which that holy congregation then exercised, as true signs and tokens of that which the Holy Ghost was to work a little after in them.

i. The first was great *obedience and subjection* to the opinion and judgment of St. Peter, not any one either replying or contradicting, although some one might have said that it had been better to defer the same until the coming of the Holy Ghost, by whose presence and assistance they might be more assured in this election; but no such thing was alleged by any, all submitting their judgment to that of their pastor, and assenting to that which he proposed; teaching us by this after what manner we are to obey our prelates, that is, promptly, and with entire resignation of our own judgment, which I therefore will labour to imitate with great care, disposing myself by this obedience to receive the Holy Ghost, which is given to the obedient and is denied to the disobedient.

ii. The second virtue was *great union* and *concord,* in naming those two persons whom they had designed for the apostleship, without there being amongst them any ambitious pretension concerning his dignity, or discords, or contrariety of judgments and opinions, whether two should be named or more, or who they were that should be named; for all with great humility and submission of mind, held themselves unworthy of that apostolic dignity, upon which, with peace and concord, and with great assurance, they named two, who, in their judgment, were the worthiest in all that congregation, and the fittest for that office; after whose example I will ever procure, as far as lies in me, concord and humility, wherewith ambitions and factions in communities are prevented, and so are disposed to receive within them the Holy Ghost.

iii. The third virtue was *prayer and recourse to Almighty God,* who knows the hearts of men, that He might declare which of those two He had designed for that dignity. In which fact they confessed that men might easily err in such elections, because they know not their hearts, wherein the good or evil is enclosed, and therefore easily. suppose evil for good, or a less good for a better. They also confessed that God, in His eternity, had elected and designed some for the dignities and offices of His Church: this, therefore, ought to be our desire—to choose such as, that our election may be conformable to the election of God; which, above all, fervent prayer greatly furthers, made in union and in charity.

Colloquy.—O most Holy Spirit, by whose providence that sacred congregation of the disciples of Christ was directed and governed, impart to all the congregations of the Church these sovereign virtues of obedience and humility, of concord and prayer, that, being grounded in them, as in-four immoveable pillars, they may always persevere in the spirit of their holy vocation. And because without them I cannot persevere in mine, infuse them into me with great abundance of Thy grace, for the greater manifestation of Thy glory Amen.

POINT III.

1. Consider, thirdly, the causes *why our Lord chose St. Matthew for the apostleship, leaving Barsabas,* surnamed Justus.

i. The first was, because God would honour all His servants, and forasmuch as Barsabas was already greatly honoured, and in authority amongst the disciples, for the great opinion they had of his holiness,—in respect of which he was surnamed Just and was so called by all,— He would also honour Mathias, who had no such surname, giving him another name much more glorious, of His apostle, to the end, that all might likewise honour him with this name.

ii. To this we may add, that Mathias being otherwise a most holy man, was very humble, and carefully endeavoured to hide his holiness, the more to ground himself in true humility, and, therefore, had not yet obtained so honourable a name as that of " Just ;" and as it was the custom of Christ our Lord, to exalt the humble, (5) to " raise the needy from the earth, and to lift up the poor out of the dunghill," to " place him with princes, with the princes of His people ;"(6) so would He exalt and honour St. Mathias with the dignity of prince of His holy Church, which seems so to think of him,—reading on the feast of this saint the Gospel in which Christ our Lord gave thanks to His Father, that He had hid the mysteries of faith " from the wise and prudent," and " had revealed them to little ones," and invites them that they learn of Him to be " meek and humble of heart." (7)

Colloquy.—O most high God, who delightest to behold from the height of heaven, the little and humble ones who live on earth ; behold me with the eyes of Thy mercy, and make me humble of heart, as Thy beloved Son was ; that imitating Him in humility here on earth, I may be worthy to obtain part of His greatness in heaven.　Amen.

iii. The third cause was, that *we may learn to submit our judgment to the judgments of God*, which proceed by far different ways from those of ours.　For in this nomination, as is to be gathered by the text, they proposed in the first place Barsabas, and in the second Mathias ; but God our Lord crossed His hands like Jacob, to bless these two sons, choosing the last and leaving the first, not that

(5) Luc. i. 52.　　　(6) Ps. cxii. 7.　　　(7) Mat. xi. 29.

Barsabas was unworthy, but to give to understand, that in these gifts of graces, God does what He will, because He wills, and because it is His pleasure, and, therefore, oftentimes " the first are last, and the last first;" " Ita Pater, quia sic placitum fuit ante Te." " Yea, Father, for so it hath seemed good in Thy sight."(8)   Nor can any one for this complain, for God gives to all that which is necessary for their salvation ; but in other extraordinary and superabundant favours He may do what He pleases, without injury to any one.

2. Hence I will gather ; that as just Barsabas was not offended, nor complained, nor envied his companion, but as a just man, conformed himself in all things to the divine will, and as St. Mathias was not proud of the dignity he received, nor yet despised his companion, but with humility of mind held himself inferior to him in justice and sanctity, so should I, when I shall see myself neglected and accounted less than others, do that which Barsabas did: and if I shall see myself preferred before others, I am to do that which Mathias did, *conforming myself to the will of God*, in whose " hands my lots are,"(9) and by whose providence it happens to us, as well to be neglected, as to be elected, and to be reputed more or less than other men, persuading myself, that when Almighty God vouchsafes me these favours, it is not because I am more holy than others, but that I may earnestly endeavour to be so ; and perhaps it is because I am more weak than others, and therefore stand in need of extraordinary succours.   But chiefly I ought to rejoice in all those things which God does, even though they turn to my contempt, for nothing ought to bring me greater consolation than the divine and eternal ordination. And this is one of the most excellent dispositions we can

(8) Mat. xx. 16.   Luc. x. 21.   (9) Ps. xxx. 15.

have, to receive the plenitude of the Holy Ghost, as these two holy men received it.

Colloquy.—I give Thee thanks, O Sovereign Father, for the secret and hidden providence with which Thou distributest Thy gifts to Thy elect, honouring and enriching all, though some more, some less. I humbly reverence Thy hidden judgments, believing them to be most just. I rejoice in the favours which Thou dost to all Thy servants, and that others receive far greater than myself, and this because it pleases Thee. That which I humbly beseech Thee is, that my sins do not bind Thy liberal hands, I refer all the rest to Thy divine providence, since whatever Thou shalt give me, how little or small soever it be, is much greater than my merit. It suffices me to hold it for great, only because it comes from Thy holy hand, and with this alone, to animate myself to glorify Thee for ever and ever. Amen.

---

(3) MEDITATIONS ON THE COMING OF THE HOLY GHOST, AND HIS GIFTS.

MEDITATION XXII.

OF THE GREAT BENEFIT WHICH ALMIGHTY GOD DID TO THE WORLD, IN GIVING THE HOLY GHOST; AND OF THE MOTIVES AND ENDS FOR WHICH HE GAVE HIM.

I have desired to place this meditation before that which concerns those things recounted of the Holy Ghost by Saint Luke, that the wonderful greatness of this gift, and the circumstances with which it was given may be the better understood; considering who it is that gives us the Holy Ghost—to whom He is given—for what motives—and for what effects and ends.

POINT I.

Consider first how the eternal Father, when the day appointed for this purpose had arrived, *determined to send to the world the Person of the Holy Ghost.*(1)

1. *This He did for three reasons:*

i. The first was *His infinite bounty and charity*, which, as it moved Him to give us His Son for Redeemer, so also it moved Him to give us *the Holy Ghost for sanctifier*, and this merely of grace and of pure love, without any merit of ours, but many demerits in a thousand respects; for the world having so evilly treated the Son, it deserved not to receive the Holy Ghost. Wherefore as Christ our Lord said to Nicodemus:—"God so loved the world as to give His Only-begotten Son;"(2) so we likewise may say that, He so loved the world as to give it His own Spirit, who is equally good with the Father and the Son, since He is one God with both persons.—ii. The second motive was, the merits of Jesus Christ our Lord, Who by His Passion and death merited this gift for us, and sitting on the right hand of His Father pleads the cause of men, shewing Him His wounds and craving the accomplishment of that promise, which He made them, to give them this divine Paraclete; and this petition was so effectual, that it was presently heard and accepted by the Eternal Father, thereby to reward the labours with which He had so well served Him.—iii. The third motive was, our own necessity and excessive misery, which moved the bowels of this Father of mercy to compassion, to send us the Holy Ghost, the last repairer of all our evils, so that "truth and mercy have met each other," (3) to negotiate and obtain this happy coming. "Truth," on the part of Christ our Lord, who

(1) Joan. xiv. 26.   (2) Joan. iii. 16.   (3) Ps. lxxxiv. 11.

had merited all justice; "mercy," on the part of the goodness of God, who regarded our misery.

Colloquy.—I give Thee thanks, O supreme Father, for the infinite charity, which moved Thee to give us so infinite a gift, giving to us all that good which proceeds from Thee. Thou hast given us Thy Son, who proceeds from Thy understanding as Thy Word; and Thou givest us in like manner the Holy Ghost, who proceeds from Thy will as Thy love. What shall I give Thee for so precious gifts? Take, O Lord, my understanding and my will; with all the works which proceed from them, that all may redound to Thy greater glory, world without end. Amen.

2. The Holy Ghost is likewise sent and given to *us by Jesus Christ our Lord*, the Son of the living God, from whom jointly with the Father the same Holy Ghost proceeds. (4) He, so fulfilling that which long before was prophecied saying, " Thou hast ascended on high, Thou hast led captivity captive, and hast given gifts to men: (5) that is, by sending the Holy Ghost, in whom all celestial gifts are contained. And the motive which He had, besides His bounty and His mercy, and besides our misery and necessity, was, that the Holy Ghost should conclude and effectually perfect the redemption of the world, and advance the work which God the Son had first begun: as our Lord signified in the sermon after the supper, as we shall see hereafter. With this affection I will crave of Christ our Lord to send into me the Holy Ghost, saying,

Colloquy.—O Redeemer of the world, who, in the desire that all Thy actions might be most perfect, didst thus provide for the consummation of the work Thou hadst begun; give me, I beseech Thee, Thy divine Spirit, to consummate the same in me, applying

(4) Joan. xv. 26; et xvi. 7.   (5) Ps. lxvii. 19.   Ephes. iv. 8.

to me effectually the copious fruits of Thy redemption. Amen.

3. Consider lastly, that although the Father and the Son, send us the Holy Ghost, yet *He likewise gives Himself to us* : for He is both the Giver and the Gift, because of the singular love which He bears to us ; and because He proceeds from the Father and the Son as Love, giving unto us His love, He likewise gives Himself to us, and therefore we may beg of Him that He would communicate and vouchsafe to give us Himself.

Colloquy.—O divine Spirit, vouchsafe to give Thyself to me, for without Thee no gift at all can satisfy me.   O giver of gifts, give me the greatest gift of all gifts, which is Thyself, for with Thyself Thou wilt also give me all that is Thine.   And because it is Thy property to be a gift, show Thyself a gift to me, giving me what Thou art, that I may give Thee what I am.   Amen.

POINT II.

Secondly, we are to consider *the ends for which* the Father and the Son sent the Holy Ghost to us : collecting them from those words which Christ our Lord spoke in the sermon after the last supper.

1. First the Holy Ghost came *to succeed Christ our Lord in the office of protector, advocate, and comforter* : and thus He did that in an invisible manner towards the apostles, which Christ Himself was visibly wont to do : and so He said to them, " I will ask the Father, and He will give you another Paraclete, that He may abide with you for ever," (6) who shall have care of you, and shall be your patron and protector in your troubles, your comforter in your sorrows, your advocate and intercessor in your neces-

(6) Joan. xiv. 16.

sities, asking for you, " with unspeakable groaning,"(7) by which He impels and excites you to pray, and to ask for that which is expedient for you. And this Paraclete, as He is to come invisible, shall never depart from you, as I depart by my corporal presence, but He will abide with you for ever.

Colloquy.—I give Thee thanks, O Redeemer of the world, for having given us such a successor in Thy absence, who shall be to us a strong protector, a sweet comforter, and a careful advocate and solicitor. O most Holy Spirit, come to Thy servant, who sighs to have Thee with him; be to me in battles, a buckler, in perils, a protector, in afflictions, a comforter, and in all my necessities a faithful procurator, impelling me to pray so fervently, that I may obtain the remedy for them. Amen.

2. Secondly, Christ our Lord gave us the Holy Ghost, who might succeed Him *in the office of Master*, teaching us and repeating within our hearts, the doctrine which He preached by word of mouth, and so He said to His apostles:—" When the Paraclete, the Holy Ghost," shall come, " whom the Father will send in my name," (that is in my place, and for my sake,) "He shall teach you all things, and bring all things to your mind," (8) which I have hitherto said, and shall hereafter say to you; He shall teach you all things proper for you to know, in order to work out your salvation and perfection, and the accomplishment of your office, many points of which at present exceed your capacity. Moreover, whatever you have heard, read, or learned of my doctrine, He shall suggest to your memory, when it shall be needful for you, and shall repeat and speak it within your spirit, to the end that neither by ignorance, nor by forgetfulness, you fail in any

(7) Rom. viii. 26.   (8) Joan. xiv. 26.

thing suitable to your calling. Nor shall this teaching be dry, or of pure speculation, but substantial and full of devotion:—and therefore St. John said, that His "unction" doth teach us all things."(9)

Colloquy.—O celestial master, who, without the noise of words, fillest the memory with truths, and so illustrates the understanding to know them, that the will is likewise affected to them ; come and visit my rude, ignorant, and forgetful soul, and since Thou art the Spirit of verity, teach her all truth, repelling from her all lies and falsity, and so assist her, that she may know all that which she should know, nor forget it when it is to be put in execution.   Amen.

3. Thirdly, the Holy Ghost was given to the apostles, to the end that He might interiorly *give them testimony of Christ*, and of what He was in the same manner that our Lord gave testimony of Himself while on earth, that being so instructed, they might afterwards declare the same publicly to the world, offering themselves to martyrdom as witnesses of this truth, and, if needful, to die in testimony thereof. The Holy Ghost, therefore, whose office is to give testimony to what Jesus Christ our Lord is, entering into the heart of the just, so enlightens him that he may believe our Lord to be both God and man, his Saviour, and only remedy, and enables him to conceive a great esteem of Him, and love Him with all his heart, and be excited to imitate Him ; He incites him also to exercise works so holy, and sometimes so miraculous, that they themselves give testimony of that Christ, whom he imitates.

Colloquy.—O my Saviour, send on me the " Spirit of truth," who proceeds from Thee and from Thy

(9) 1 Joan. ii. 27.

Father, that with the abundance of His interior light, He may make me know who Thou art, in such a manner that I may love Thee, and may do works whereby Thy Father may be glorified, and Thou known and honoured. Amen.

4. Fourthly, the Holy Ghost *came to reprehend and correct the vices of the world and to convince it of them*, and of the victory which our Saviour gained over the Devil, and this He did in the same manner that Christ our Lord performed this office when He preached; and with regard to which He said :—" When the Paraclete is come He will convince the world of sin, and of justice, and of judgment," (10) that is to say, clothing Himself in your persons, by means of you; He will convince the world of its sins and infidelities; He will convince it that it has done wickedly in not believing in me, and for not having kept my law; moreover, He will convince it with reasons and testimonies of justice and sanctity of life, and of my holy law and doctrine: and lastly, will make it understand the judgment which I have given against sin, condemning the Devil, casting him forth of the world, reproving wickedness, and approving justice. All this the Holy Ghost does interiorly in the little world of every man, because His office is to reprehend the evil which every one does, to exhort him to the justice which he ought to do, and to discover to him the judgment, which, in reason, he ought to make between good and evil, and between Christ and the Devil, that embracing the good, and following Christ, they may abhor evil and fly the Devil.

Colloquy.— O most Holy Spirit, come into this abridged world of my soul, convice and cleanse her of her sins, enlighten her on Thy justice, and teach her how to make true judgment: for Thou no less

(10) Joan. xvi. 8.

showest Thyself my true comforter and advocate, when Thou reprehendest my vices, than when Thou cherishest me with Thy consolations.

POINT III.

1. The third shall be to consider *the infinite greatness of this gift* which Almighty God gives us in giving us the Holy Ghost, who by excellence, is called "gift of the most high," (11) because He is the chiefest of all gifts, and the spring and fountain of them all. So that God our Lord, not content with giving us grace and charity, the supernatural virtues, and the seven gifts of the Holy Ghost, would also give us the beginning and cause of all the rest, to the end that He might preserve, govern, augment and perfect them: as He who having a fountain, is not contented to give of the water, but will needs give the fountain also from whence the water floweth perpetually. (12) And for this cause Christ our Lord speaking of the Holy Ghost whom they were to receive who should believe in Him, said:—"He that believeth in me,—out of his belly shall flow rivers of living water." (13) And to give them to understand, that these rivers should be perpetual, He said:—"The water that I will give him, shall become in him a fountain of water, springing up into life everlasting." (14)

Colloquy. — O most Holy Spirit, Crystal river of "living water," "proceeding from the seat of God, and of the Lamb," and waterest the city of our Lord, and "the tree of life, bearing twelve fruits, yielding its fruits every month," whose "leaves" are "for the healing of the nations;" (15) come to this little city of my soul, water it with Thy abundant

(11) Hymn. Eccles.

(12) S. Th. 1, p. q. xxxiii.   (13) Joan. vii. 39.

(14) Joan. iv. 14.   (15) Apoc. xxii. 2.

graces, and produce in it Thy " twelve fruits," communicating unto it " charity, joy, peace, patience, benignity, goodness, longanimity, mildness, faith, modesty, continency, and chastity ;"(16) and to the end that these fruits may not dry and whither away, assist me always to conserve them in their greenness, and to augment their perfection to the attaining of life everlasting. Amen.

2. From the consideration of the greatness of the Holy Ghost I am to conceive *a great confidence*, that God will give me all that I shall ask of Him; for He who gives that which is more, will doubtless give me that which is less, according to the saying of St. Paul:—"He that spareth not even His own Son, but delivered Him up for us all, how hath He not also, with Him given us all things?" (17) And so I may also say, that He who hath given us His divine Spirit, how shall He not give us also all things with Him, which proceed from Him, demanding them in the virtue of the same Spirit, and by the merits of the Son, by whom He is given. To this confidence I will join an internal desire that the Holy Ghost produce within me these " twelve fruits," weighing what each one is, and asking each one of them with a peculiar petition. And first I will ask " charity," saying :—

Colloquy.—O divine Spirit, Thou art charity itself, and he that is in charity, is in Thee, and Thou in him ; engender this charity within my soul, that with it I may love Thee, and produce abundant fruits of Thy love. Amen.

In this manner I will demand the other fruits, as also His seven gifts, of which we shall by and by make an especial meditation.

(16) Gal. v. 22.   (17) Rom. viii. 32.

POINT IV.

Fourthly, we are to consider *to whom this sovereign gift of the Holy Ghost is given*, to discover so much the more the greatness of the divine liberality.

1. Although it was a great liberality on the part of Almighty God to impart this gift to poor fishermen, ignorant and pusillanimous, and to a multitude of other men of less moment, yet that it is a greater wonder that He should offer the same *to all people of the world*, Jews Gentiles, and barbarous nations, excluding no man, how vile or despicable soever he be, and how great a sinner soever he has been, so that he would only dispose himself to receive Him. For, as St. Peter said, "God is not a respecter of persons, but in every nation he that feareth Him, and worketh justice is acceptable to Him," (18) and shall receive from Him the Holy Ghost; for so indeed He gave Him to many of those who were partakers in the death of His Son, and to innumerable other persons, who worshipped for gods the beasts and serpents of the earth; in such a manner that he who before was a dwelling of the devils, and a den of lions and of dragons, the same is now the temple of the living God, and the dwelling of the Holy Ghost, in whom He rests with His gifts, fulfilling that which He promised by the prophet Joel,—" I will pour out my Spirit upon all flesh."(19)

2. *O infinite liberality of our God:* whither could His most liberal mercy aspire further, than to pour forth in so great abundance, a spirit so precious as His own, upon vessels so vile as these of ours! Is it not Thou, O Lord, who sometimes says, "My Spirit shall not remain in man for ever," (20) "because He is flesh?" how then sayest Thou now that Thou wilt "pour out" Thy "Spirit upon

(18) Acts x. 34.   (19) Joel ii. 28.   (20) Gen. vi. 3.

all flesh?" If Thou speakest only of Thine own flesh, united with Thy divine Person, it is but reason that Thou pour Thy Spirit upon it, for such a Spirit well beseems such flesh: but Thou sayest that Thou wilt pour it forth upon " all flesh," which knows nothing but how to war and rebel against Thy Spirit: why, therefore wilt Thou join a Spirit so heavenly to flesh so earthly? O immense charity, O incomprehensible liberality ! God will not give His Spirit to him who is flesh, and who covets to live according to the laws of flesh, rejecting the laws of the spirit, but if he who is flesh endeavour to change his fleshly life, bewailing the time that he has spent in it, God will pour forth His Spirit upon him, with which He will quicken his flesh to live a spiritual life worthy of such a spirit.

Colloquy.—I give Thee thanks, O Father of mercies, for the infinite bounty which Thou showest, in giving so precious a gift to so vile a creature as man, and in joining Thy divine Spirit with our miserable flesh; if Thou wilt that Thy mercy should manifestly shine in these Thy gifts, behold here a man who is wholly flesh, but desires to be quickened with Thy Spirit. Give Him graciously to me, O Lord, that He may dwell in me, and that my soul may glorify Thee for the sovereign benefit which Thou dost to me who am so unworthy to receive it. Amen.

MEDITATION XXIII.

POINT I.

" *And when the days of Pentecost were accomplished, they were altogether in one place.*"(1)

Upon these words we are to consider the mysteries contained in the *place, time, and day*, in which the Holy Ghost came, and in the assembly of persons on whom He descended.

1. We are to consider it was by the inspiration of the same Holy Ghost, *on the day of Pentecost, that all the disciples of Christ* assembled together,—*with the Blessed Virgin our Lady,—in the house and chamber wherein they were wont to assemble at other times.*—They were in number at least, *a hundred and twenty,*—as St. Luke reports a little before. " All these were persevering with one mind in prayer," beseeching the Eternal Father, by the merits of His Son, and the Son also, to send to them the Holy Ghost whom He had promised them, whose prayers were presented before Almighty God, by the holy angels: which being joined with the prayers of Christ our Lord, as Man, it was decreed that on the same day He would give them what they asked, because there is no term of time so long to which he does not at length come, who perseveres in asking, and expects with patience the coming of our Lord.

2. This house and chamber, as has been said elsewhere, (2)*represents the universal Church,* in which all those assemble who are the disciples of Jesus Christ,—united together

(1) Act. ii. 1.   (2) Med. xxvi. et 4 p. Med. x.
Vol. V —13.

in the same faith, in the worship of the same God, and in the observation of the same law. And, as on this day the Holy Ghost was given to them only that were in the house, and not to those who were out of it; so He is given to those only who remain within the Church, disposing themselves to receive Him, nor shall any ever receive Him who do not live within the Church. For, as the dove found no place out of the ark of Noe where her foot' might rest, (3) so the Holy Ghost, figured by that dove, finds none on whom to rest out of the Church, which is represented by the ark :(4) and therefore Christ our Lord said, that the world could not receive the Holy Ghost, (5) calling the world the congregation of those who have made shipwreck of His faith, reprove His doctrine, and resist His holy law. This ought to move me to render exceeding great thanks to Almighty God, for having brought me to this house of His holy Church, in which if I be not in fault, myself, I may receive the Holy Ghost, disposing myself by prayer and union to receive Him, as the apostles did.

3. Ponder, thirdly, the cause why the Holy Ghost came on *the day of Pentecost,*—which was a feast of the Jews, instituted in memory of the law, which God had given them on Mount Sinai, and which was celebrated fifty days after the feast of the Paschal lamb. The cause was, to signify that the Holy Ghost came principally *to imprint on the souls of men the law of grace,* which Christ had preached, and to put an end to the ancient law, which was a figure of the new, therefore the one was given on the same day that the other was published, although in a different manner, for the ancient law was a law of fear, and was therefore given when " thunders,—lightnings,— and the noise of the trumpet sounded exceeding loud," (6)

(3) Gen. viii. 9.   (4) 1. Pet. iii. 20.   (5) Joan. xiv. 17.
.(6) Exod. xix. 16.

and with threatenings of death, on Mount Sinai. It was also written on " tables of stone :"(7) because it was most heavy, and was given to men of a stiff neck, and of a stony heart : but the new law is a law of love, and therefore with great sweetness the same Holy Ghost has written it in the bowels of men, (8) and in the tables of their hearts, taking from them their stony hearts, and giving them " a heart of flesh,"(9) as He had promised by His prophets.

Colloquy.—O Sovereign Father, whose hand is Thy Son, who proceeds from Thee, by whom Thou createdst all things, and whose finger is the Holy Ghost, who proceeds from both, by whom Thou hast renewed the face of the earth, writing by Him Thy holy law in the hearts of men : write it in mine with this finger of Thy right hand, with such great force that it may never more be blotted out. And since Thou commandest me likewise to write it in the tables of my heart, co-operating by love to its accomplishment, grant what Thou commandest, that so I may accomplish what Thou willest. Amen.(10)

4. The Holy Ghost also came *fifty days after the Passion and Resurrection of Christ;* to signify, that with His abundant coming, He gave a plenary jubilee, signified by the number of fifty, giving a full pardon of all debts and sins, in virtue of the Passion of our Redeemer. (11) And for this cause the Church says of the Holy Ghost, that He is " Remissio peccatorum." " The forgiveness of sins."

Colloquy.—O most Holy Spirit, come with plenitude into my soul, and grant her this plenary jubilee, pardoning all her sins, which being discharged, she may in great jubilee, ascend to the joys of Thy eternal glory. Amen.

(7) Exod. xxiv. 12.
(8) Jer. xxxi. 33. Heb. x. 16.   (9) Ezech. xxxvi. 23.
(10) Prov. iii. 3. et vii. 3.   (11) Lev. xxv. 10.

POINT II.

" And suddenly there came a sound from heaven, as of a mighty wind coming."(12)

In every word of these there is declared some mystery, or property, of the coming of the Holy Ghost into the soul, by means of the inspirations which go before His entrance. These are certain sudden motions which we feel within our soul, and which like lightnings discover to us some truth of faith, and as certain sparkles of fire, affect and inflame us to that which is good and holy.

1. This sound came *" suddenly;"* to signify that the inspiration of the divine Spirit, and His visitation, has no certain day nor hour assigned and determined, but cometh when a man least expects it, and when and how the same Holy Ghost wills, because " Spiritus ubi vult spirat," " The Spirit breatheth where He will." (13) For, as we shall say by and by, (14) He inspires by His mercy alone, and therefore I ought to beseech Him at all times to come, and I should expect His coming, leaving to His paternal Providence whatever day and hour shall be pleasing to Him: for He will come when it shall be most expedient for me, although, whensoever He comes, His coming will be sudden to me.

2. This wind came *" from heaven,"* not from the east or west, nor from the north or south of the earth; to signify that the inspiration of the Holy Ghost is not from the earth, and that there is no power in it to raise this wind, but that it is to come from heaven: for, as St. James saith: " Every best gift, and every perfect gift, is from above, coming down from the Father of lights;"(15) The " gift," by excellency " good," is the Son: and the " gift" by excellency " perfect," is the Holy Ghost, and all the

(12) Act. ii. 2.
(13) Joan. iii. 8.   (14) Med. xxvi.   (15) Jac. i. 17.

gifts and presents which proceed from these two, descend from heaven, from the eternal Father, from whom the Son and the Holy Ghost proceed.

Colloquy.—O Father of Lights, send from high, this so good and perfect gift. Let the wind of Thy divine Spirit come from heaven, that it may take me away, and carry me with it to the place whence it came. Amen.

3. This sound was of air, or of "wind," to signify that the Holy Ghost by His inspiration works in us certain wonderful effects, signified by the "wind." For, by His inspiration He gives and preserves in us the spiritual life of grace: by this we breathe, and mortify the heat of our concupiscence: it both cleanses and purifies us, separating in our souls the precious from the vile, "the wheat from the cockle," and the good and perfect from the evil and imperfect; it also impels and moves us to fly vice and to follow virtue. We live, therefore, and breathe by the air, and cannot subsist without it: so in this divine Spirit, and in virtue of Him:—"Vivimus, movemur, et sumus," "we live, move, and are"(16) in the being of grace, and, without the Spirit, we can neither have nor preserve this being and life.

Colloquy.—O Spirit of life, who, breathing upon the dead that Ezekiel saw, didst instantly revive them, (17) come and breathe upon such souls as are dead by sin, that Thou mayest revive them by Thy grace. O "south wind" of heaven, blow through the "garden" (18) of my soul, that by this Thy breath, the trees of virtues, which are planted therein, may bud forth their odoriferous fruits to the glory of Almighty God, and the edification of my neighbour. O Eternal God

(16) Act. xvii. 28.　　　　　(17) Ezech. xxxvii. 10.
(18) Cant. iv. 16.

who, with a refreshing wind, didst recreate the three children in the fiery furnace of Babylon, (19) send upon me this refreshing wind of Thy divine Spirit, to temper the flames which burn in the furnace of my sensuality, and that all the powers and faculties of my soul may be provoked, to give to Thee perpetual prayers. Amen.

4. This wind was "mighty:" to signify the force and fervour with which the Holy Ghost impels us, enabling us to do the works of virtue, with a certain sweet and loving force, not against our will, but enabling us to do them with great alacrity and delight, for He is an enemy of all sloth and lukewarmness ; and, as St. Ambrose says:— "Nescit tarda molimina,' Spiritus Sancti gratia:" "the grace of the Holy Ghost does not approve slowness or sluggishness in the works of virtue :" (20) for when He enters into the soul, He leads it like a ship that sails with the wind in her stern, without labour, and with great swiftness, for He is the pilot that governs and conducts her to the port and harbour to which she is to go. And of such St. Paul says :—" Whosoever are led by the Spirit of God, they are the sons of God." (21)

Colloquy.—O divine Spirit, who enforcest Thy beloved children with great vehemency to the works of virtue and sanctity, come upon my soul with a "mighty wind," enforcing her to all that which is pleasing to Thee : and to the end that she may not injure herself by indiscreet fervour, vouchsafe to conduct her in her ways, that she may arrive at last at the port of Thy perpetual glory. Amen.

5. Fifthly, this "mighty wind" caused a "*great sound*" and thunder, which was heard through the whole

(19) Dan. iii. 50.   (20) Lib. ii. in Luc.
(21) Rom. viii. 14.

city: to signify that the coming of the Holy Ghost works in the just, and by the just such works as raise an echo throughout the world, from the admirable example of their lives, sometimes from their prodigious miracles, but chiefly by the force of their word, and preaching, as was seen in the apostles, of whom it is written :—" Their sound hath gone forth into all the earth, and their words unto the ends of the world:" (22) and for this cause, Christ our Lord called two of His disciples " Boanerges," that is to say, " sons of thunder," (23) because, like to thunder, they went forth to preach throughout the world.

Colloquy.—O my beloved, let the voice of Thine inspiration sound in my ears, that by its means I may work such works as may sound, and be heard over all the world, to the edification of my neighbour, and excite them to glorify Thee, world without end. Amen.

POINT III.

" *And it filled the whole house where they were sitting.*" (24) Here we are to ponder the mysteries which lie hid in this, that this mighty wind *filled the whole house* where the disciples were sitting.

1. The first mystery was to signify that *in the law of grace, the Holy Ghost was given in great abundance and plenitude* for all kinds of works, exercises, ministries, states, and offices of the Church : Almighty God showing Himself much more liberal now, than in the law of nature, and in the written law. A certain friend of Job, who lived under the law of nature, and Elias, who lived under the written law, felt the coming of the Holy Ghost, as the sound or whistling of " a gentle wind," (25) for

<hr>

(22) Ps. xviii. 5. Rom. x. 18.
(23) Marc. iii. 17.   (24) Act. ii. 2.   (25) Job. iv. 16.

then the Holy Ghost was given greatly limited and restrained : but after the Passion of Christ our Lord, He is given like a " mighty wind," which fills the " whole house," because He is given in great abundance, with all kinds of graces, and to all kinds and sorts of persons, so that our Redeemer Himself before His death, did not give Him in so great abundance, and therefore, St. John the Evangelist said :—" As yet the Spirit was not given, because Jesus was not yet glorified :" (26) but after His Resurrection, the sluices and floodgates of heaven were opened, and there issued a flood of graces, which filled the whole earth, and renewed, and made it fertile, and therefore Isaiah said :—" The earth is filled with the knowledge of the Lord, as the covering waters of the sea." (27)

Colloquy.—I give Thee thanks, O most sweet Redeemer, for having opened the floodgates and sluices of Thy sacred body, that so Thou mightest shed forth for us all Thy blood, and in virtue thereof hast opened the floodgates and sluices of the Kingdom of heaven, to shed forth Thy abundant Spirit upon all those who seek to make profit of Thy holy Passion : O most dear Lord, shed Him forth now, anew on the house of Thy holy Church, to the end that we may all begin anew to serve Thee with fervour.   Amen.

2. This wind so filled the whole house, that it left neither chamber, nor closet, nor corner, which it did not penetrate : to signify the universality with which the Holy Ghost on His part, gives and offers Himself to all men, in what part or corner of the world soever they be, accomplishing that which the divine Wisdom said :—" For the Spirit of the Lord hath filled the whole world :" (28) and that which God promised to this people, when He said :— " I will pour out my Spirit upon all flesh, and your sons

(26) Joan. vii. 39.   (27) Isa. xi. 9   (28) Sap. i. 7.

and daughters shall prophecy, your ancients shall dream dreams, and your young men shall see visions."(29)

3. The third was to signify, that when the Holy Ghost enters with this mightiness into a soul *He fills all his house and all his family*, which are his faculties, not leaving any one empty; for He fills his memory with good thoughts, his understanding with good discourses and meditations, his will with fervent desires and resolutions; and his appetites with holy affections in such a manner, that this House is filled with truths and celestial virtues, and within it are all the acts and exercises of virtues practised with fervour, as the love of God, zeal for His glory, hope of His mercy, a reverential fear of His majesty, joy for His excellency, praise and thanksgiving for His benefits, sorrow for sins, and effectual purposes and desires of obeying God, and of suffering much for love of Him.

Colloquy.—O most Holy Spirit, vouchsafe to fill my memory and understanding with Thy illustrations, that so the thoughts which proceed from thence, may " keep holiday,"(30) joyful to Thee, and to me. O that my will, and all my appetites were filled with Thy Divinity, to the end that my desires and my propensities might henceforth be wholly divine, and conformable to Thine in all things. Fill me, O Lord, with Thine own Self, that all my " works " may be " full " (31) before Thee, so that they have nothing empty in them, which may offend or displease Thee.

4. Consider this wind filled the house where the disciples " *were sitting*:" to signify, that if I desire that the Holy Ghost should fill the house of my heart, I ought not to wander forth from it, or to " pour myself" out upon

<hr>

(29) Joel ii. 28.   Act. ii. 17.   (30) Ps. lxxv. 11.
(31) Apoc. iii. 2.

creatures, but to enter within myself, and to abide sitting and quiet within my conscience, which should be engaged in good thoughts and desires, and with some good works, and so expect the coming of this mighty Spirit, who may wholly fill it and perfect it with His abundant love. Hence it is as we have already said, (32) that when Almighty God will visit souls, He first withdraws them, and causes them to enter into themselves, and sit with repose in the chamber of their hearts, for then He presently enters with the plenitude of His gifts.

POINT IV.

"And there appeared to them parted tongues, as it were of fire, and it sat upon every one of them." (33)

First, we are to consider *why the Holy Ghost gave Himself in the form of visible fire. The reason* was, because He always takes those external forms which *represent the marvellous effects which He works in those interiorly who receive Him.*(34) In the baptism of Christ He took the form of a *dove,* to signify the innocence and fecundity of good works which He inspires and suggests. In the transfiguration of Christ He appeared *like a resplendent cloud,* to signify the dew and rain of doctrine, which He communicates, and the protection which He has over His elect. In the chamber at the last supper, He was given by Christ as *a breath,* in sign of the spiritual life which He gives us by means of the Sacraments. But on this day He appeared in the form of *fire,* to signify that as fire purifies, lightens, enkindles, carries on high, and of itself is very unitive and communicative, transforming into itself that which is joined to it : so the Holy Ghost purifies souls, consuming the rust of their sins and vices, and separating from the gold and silver of virtues, the rust and brass of sins and

<hr>

(32) Med. xx.   (33) Act. ii. 3.
(34) S. Th. 1, p. q. xliii. art. 7 ad 6.

imperfections which are mingled with them : *enlightens* the understanding with a supernatural light so excellent, that it assures us of the verities and mysteries of our faith more than if we saw them with our corporal eyes. He *enkindles* the will with the heat of charity, inflaming it in the love of God, and of our neighbours; He *elevates* hearts from earthly to heavenly things, causing them to have their conversation in heaven, and to repose there by contemplation, as in their sphere and proper place : lastly, He *unites* souls with Himself, so communicating His gifts and virtues to them, that they become one spirit with Him by the union of perfect love. This is the fire of which Christ our Lord said :—" I am come to cast fire on the earth, and what will I, but that it be kindled."(35)

Colloquy.—O most loving Redeemer, accomplish Thy desire in this earth of my soul, casting this divine fire into the midst thereof, to the end that it may consume all that is earthly, and lift me up to that which is heavenly. O divine Spirit, since Thou art " a consuming fire," (36) consume in me whatsoever displeases Thee, that so I may be made capable of receiving the light, the heat, the agility, and activity of this fire, being perfectly transformed thereinto. Amen.

2. The Holy Ghost came in form of " *tongues of fire*," rather than in the form of fiery *hearts*, because the Holy Ghost was not given to the apostles that they should love themselves only, and be converted into fire, but that with their tongues moved by this divine Spirit, they should preach to the world the law, the death, and Passion of Christ ; and exercising the office of " fire" should purify men from their errors and their sins, illuminate them with the light of true doctrine, inflame them with the

<hr>

(35) Luc. xii. 49.   (36) Deut. iv. 24.

flames of charity, and lift them up to the desire of heavenly things, uniting them with God our Lord by the union of love; Christ our Lord also fulfilling by them that which He had said:—"I came to send fire on the earth, and what will I but that it be enkindled." Moreover the Holy Ghost comes upon us spiritually in "tongues of fire," when He communicates the affections of devotion to us, which, as St. Bernard says, is the "tongue of the soul,"(37) with which she speaks with Almighty God: and when the Holy Ghost is communicated with plenitude, He is a tongue of "fire" whence inflamed affections of divine love with canticles burst forth, of which we will immediately speak.

3. There appeared *"parted tongues,"* that is to say, *divided and distributed amongst all*: in that which the apostle says, is illustrated:—"There are diversities of graces, but one Spirit,"(38) there are also many diversities and distributions of grace, of ministries, and of operations, as the gift of wisdom, of knowledge, and of faith; —the grace of healing, of working miracles, of interpreting the Scriptures, and the like, which the Holy Ghost divides and distributes amongst the members of the Church as it pleases Him, giving them tongues of fire, with which they are to make use of the graces given to them. Hence I will conceive affections of praise and thanksgiving, for the gifts of the Holy Ghost distributed amongst the members of the Church, joyful for those which He has given to my brethren, and grateful for those which He has given to me, for the one as well as the other is intended for my utility, in the same manner as in the members of the body, that which is good for the eyes is good for the hands, and that which is good for the hands is good for the eyes, because the one assists the other.

(37) Serm. xlv. in Cant.   (38) 1 Cor. xii. 4.

4. "*And it sat upon every one of them :*" which signifies that the fire of the Holy Ghost, inasmuch as rests in
Him, comes to "sit" upon us, with the desire never to
leave us, unless we ourselves drive Him from us, according
to that which Christ our Lord said : " And I will ask
the Father and He will give you another Paraclete, that
He may abide with you for ever."(39) For, if at any time
He does not forsake us, this happens through our fault, for
as the divine wisdom saith : " The Holy Spirit of discipline
will flee from the deceitful and will withdraw Himself from
the thoughts that are without understanding, and He shall
not abide when iniquity cometh in." (40)   If, therefore,
O my soul, thou wilt that the Holy Ghost sit upon thee,
and abide with thee for ever, fly all fiction and duplicity,
shake from thee all inordinate thoughts and affections, and
give not entrance to evil, for as He is a pure Spirit, He
will not enter into a depraved soul, nor dwell in a body
subject to sin, nor abide in a man who lives like a beast,
following the laws of his own flesh.

POINT V.

" *And they were all filled with the Holy Ghost.*"(41)
1. Consider, first, *the infinite bounty and liberality of
the most Holy Trinity,* as well of the Father, and of the
Son, who send, as of the Holy Ghost Himself, who is sent:
for, those who were in that chamber, being of such different dignity and merit, yet *He replenished all with His
divine gifts,* filled all with joy, and gave Himself wholly
to all, so that all remained full of the Spirit, all replenished and satisfied, desiring then no other thing but God.
He especially filled the house of their souls, all the powers
of which He completely occupied with His presence, for
He imprinted the Sacred Scriptures in their memory,

(39) Joan. xiv. 16.   (40) Sap. i. 5.   (41) Act. ii. 4.

that they might always remember them, whenever it should be needful for them. He infused into their understanding great light and knowledge of them, and of all the principal mysteries which are contained in them ; He imprinted in an instant, the whole law of love and charity, with such perfection in their wills and hearts, that though there were neither a written law nor gospel in the whole world, yet they should be a lively law, to the exact fulfilment of which the Spirit would interiorly conduct them : to conclude on a sudden, He wrought in them the full effect of His office ; for, as a pleasant wind He filled them with sweetness; as the sun with light; as fire, with celestial heat; as master, with His doctrine ; and as physician with full and perfect health ; and in a moment made them, of cowards, courageous ; of feeble, strong ; of ignorant, wise; of envious, charitable ; of ambitious, humble; and of imperfect, consummate and complete Christians in all perfection.

Colloquy.—"O change of the hand of the most high !" (42)   O infinite power of the Divine Spirit ! That change which the combat of three years, could not effect with the three strong weapons, of sermons, examples, and miracles, this day, in an instant, was effected by the Spirit of Christ, and the virtue which descended from above! Send, O good Jesus, this virtue of Thy divine Spirit upon me, that it may change me into another man, wholly made according to Thy will.   Come, O Holy Spirit, and so replenish me with Thy gifts, that I may change all my earthly habits into heavenly, and grant that I neither will, nor pretend to other things out of Thee, since I am satisfied and filled, having Thee within me.   Amen.

2. Consider, secondly, that though all were full of the

(42) Ps. lxxvi. 11.

Holy Ghost, yet *some received greater gifts than others;* as when two vessels are full of water, that which is greater contains more; so those who were more holy, and were better disposed, received greater fulness of the Holy Ghost, with more abundant grace, and consequently our Blessed Lady received more grace, and greater spiritual gladness than all the rest together, and the Apostles greater than all the other disciples, all, notwithstanding, glorifying Almighty God, for the singular benefit He has bestowed upon them. I will rejoice with and congratulate the Blessed Virgin for the gifts she received, and the great joy she felt when she saw all the disciples filled with the Holy Ghost, and the promise of her most precious Son so perfectly accomplished.

Hence I will conceive a great desire to prepare myself to receive this Holy Spirit, *with the greatest fervour I possibly can,* since He has given most abundantly to him that is prepared best; this preparation is principally to be made with these four virtues.—i. *Purity of conscience,* washing and cleansing the vessel into which the Holy Ghost is to infuse and pour His gifts.—ii. *Humility of heart,* emptying the heart of itself and of all that is contrary to this divine Spirit.—iii. *Confidence in Almighty God* enlarging the capacity of my soul, not according to the measure of my own merits, but according to the merits of Christ our Lord, and of the infinite goodness and liberality of Almighty God.—iv. *Fervent prayer,* with which these gifts are obtained, craving of Almighty God, that He would give them to me, not regarding who I am, but who He is; and the more perfectly I shall exercise these four virtues, so shall I be accordingly disposed to receive the Holy Ghost with greater or less abundance of His gifts.

Colloquy.—O most high God, who saidst to Thy

people, "Open thy mouth wide, and I will fill it," (43) behold I open my mouth with desire to draw into me Thy divine Spirit, (44) and desire to enlarge the bosom of my soul, to receive Him with great abundance : fill me, O Lord, conform me to Thy will, and enlarge me with Thy mercy, to the end that I may receive more abundant grace. Amen.

3. *All were filled with the Holy Ghost*, inasmuch as all received that which was sufficient for them to fulfil their function ; for it is the custom of God our Lord, to give to each one as much grace as is needful for the entire accomplishment of the office and function committed to him, and according to the state to which He calls him.(45) For this cause He filled the sacred Virgin, St. John His precursor, and the apostles, with as great grace as the dignity and office which He had chosen them required, and the same He now also does to those whom He calls to the ecclesiastic estate, and to the offices of His Church, as shall be seen in the sixth part.

POINT VI.

" And they began to speak with divers tongues according as the Holy Ghost gave them to speak."(46)

1. With regard to this we are to consider, first, *the especial favour which the Holy Ghost did to the Apostles*, giving them on a sudden, power "to speak in divers tongues," that they might preach the Gospel throughout the whole world; for this grace was not so much given them for their own particular profit, as for the profit of all men upon the earth : for which we are all bound to praise Almighty God, for the singular benefit which He bestowed upon them for our utility. And we should

(43) Ps. lxxx. 11.

(44) Ps. cxviii. 131.   (45) S. Th. 3. p. q. vii. art. 10.   2 Tim. iv.

(46) Act. ii. 4.

observe, that as the "confusion of tongues" was a chastisement of pride, so the gift of speaking in "divers tongues" was a reward of humility. And like as the proud, pretending to build a tower, whose top should touch heaven, were confounded with a "confusion of tongues," in such a manner that one could not understand the other, whereby they were divided, and forced to abandon their proud undertaking; even so the humble, desiring to build the tower of perfection, whose top might attain to the vision and union of Almighty God, were assisted with the " knowledge of tongues," whereby they might · unite themselves with all men, and promote and advance their spiritual building.

Colloquy.—O most sweet Jesus, give to me the true spirit of humility, and purify the tongue which Thou hast given me with the fire of love, that so I may on my part assist to raise and advance this tower of perfection, not only in my own soul, but also in my neighbours, that we may all come to the full enjoyment of Thy eternal glory. Amen.

2. The apostles *presently began to speak in these tongues,* not according to their own fancies, but moved and inspired by the divine Spirit, speaking in such a manner, and with such fervour, as He inspired them ; and so their words and whole discourses were of holy things, and after a very holy manner; and this they observed and continued during the rest of their life, as St. Paul says :—" For we are not, as many, adulterating the word of God : but with sincerity, but as from God, before God, in Christ we speak."(47)   As if He had said, in our words, we observe four conditions.—i. That they be not for any evil or vain end, but *with a pure intention* of the glory of God, of our own and of our neighbour's good.—ii. Secondly that they

<hr>

(47) 2 Cor. ii. 17.

proceed not from a violent or passionate spirit, but from a good spirit, holy and peaceable.—iii. Thirdly, that they be spoken of in the presence of Almighty God, considering that He hears us, and is witness of our words.—iv. Fourthly, that our talk be not of evil, vain, or of impertinent things, but wholly of Christ, or of things concerning Christ, and His excellencies, as we shall by and by declare.

3. The Holy Ghost, being in the soul, presently *causes her to speak with divers tongues interiorly*, that is, with divers affections of devotion, according to that which St. Paul says, " Be ye filled with the Holy Spirit, speaking to yourselves in psalms and hymns, and spiritual canticles, and making melody, singing in your hearts to the Lord ; giving thanks always for all things, in the name of our Lord Jesus Christ, to God and the Father.''(48)   These are the divers tongues of fire, with which, as has been said in the second chapter of the Introduction of this Book, we speak within ourselves with God our Lord, singing psalms and hymns with affections of praise and thanksgiving for the benefits He bestows upon us ; as also affections of love and joy for His being who He is, making great offers to serve Him, and exciting every virtue, that exercising their acts, we may make harmonious music to the glory of God our Lord.   Oh that we had heard how the Blessed Virgin spoke on that day with these " divers tongues," inspired by this divine Spirit!   What inflamed affections, what praises and thanksgivings did she utter, and how was she melted in the fire of love, speaking and discoursing with her beloved.   Oh what music of tongues so divers, yet so harmonious sounded in that chamber from the lips of those sacred singers, with the Holy Ghost as master of the choir, guiding and directing them.

(48) Ephes. v. 18.

Colloquy.—O most Holy Spirit, come into my dumb soul, and teach me how to speak with divers tongues of inflamed affections : and since Thou requirest of me that my voice should sound in Thine ears, clear it and sweeten it, to the end that its music may be sweet and pleasing to Thee, world without end. Amen.

MEDITATION XXIV.

OF THE WONDERFUL WORKS WHICH THE HOLY GHOST WROUGHT BY THE APOSTLES, ON THE DAY OF PENTECOST.

POINT I.

" And there were dwelling at Jerusalem, Jews, devout men, *of every nation under heaven.* And when this was noised abroad, the multitude came together, and were confounded in mind, because that *every man heard them speak in his own tongue the wonderful works of God.* And they were all astonished, and wondered saying one to another, What meaneth this ?" (1)

1. It is the property of the Holy Ghost to move the minds of men with the sound of His divine inspiration, and to *bring them to the place where they may hear the preachers of the Gospel,* that by means of their sermons they may acknowledge Christ and be converted. For which cause I am to render Him many thanks, and beseech Him that He cease not to bestow this benefit upon sinners; and I, on my part, will imitate these people, who, hearing this voice and the " mighty" sound, did not abide within their houses, despising and making small account of it, but presently went forth to see what it should be, and what that prodi-

(1) Act. ii. 5, et seq.

gious sound might signify; and so should I when I hear within my soul the voice of the divine inspiration, not remain idle, nor let it pass in vain, but issue forth to accomplish that to which God thereby inspires me.

·2. The apostles, who had expected the coming of the Holy Ghost in silent recollection, presently when they received Him, *issued forth from their recollection into public, and began to set forth and to preach the greatness of God in the presence of all the nations of the world.* The interior force of the Holy Ghost moved them to this; for thus He acts with those who will not that their talents be buried in the earth, or that their gifts be idle, even for a moment, but instantly come forth to the light, and are willing to be employed for the salvation of souls. With this I will confirm myself in that which has been already said,(2) that as it is a vice of pride, to issue forth to preach and to deal with souls, without having first received virtue from on high; so is it a vice of pusillanimity, not to issue forth when we have received it, and, as St. Gregory says, both extremes are very dangerous. (3)

3. Consider, *with what great spirit and efficacy the apostles declared the wonderful works of Almighty God;* for every spirit moves to speak that which is according to itself; the spirit of the world, which holy David calls " Magniloqua," speaks " proud things"(4) of the world;—the spirit of the flesh, carnal greatnesses;—our own spirit, our own greatnesses. But 'the Divine Spirit abhors these greatnesses, and will only recognise them, that He may bring them to contempt, because He holds them for things base, and only inspires and moves men to speak of the greatnesses of Almighty God, and of His virtues and excellences, of His

<hr>

(2) Med. xvii. p. 2.

(3) 3 p. p. Pastor ad Monit. xxvi.

(4) Ps. xi. 14.   S. Ber. Ser. de Spirit. de Consci. ad Monach. Cisters.

benefits and mercies, of His works and mysteries; He moves them also to think highly of God, and of all that belongs to Him ; to speak of Him when expedient, not with tepidity and coldness of mind, but with " tongues of fire," and with admirable fervour, in such a manner as to excite the hearers to great admiration and amazement, acknowledging in him that speaks the divinity of the Spirit that moves him to speak.

Colloquy.—O divine Spirit, illustrate my soul, that I may know the greatness of God, and move my tongue to speak of them with so great fervour, that Thou mayest be glorified, my neighbour edified, and myself more inflamed by Thy love.   Amen.

POINT II.

" *But others, mocking, said, These men are full of new wine.* But Peter, standing up with the eleven, lifted up his voice, and spoke to them : Ye men of Judea, and all you that dwell in Jerusalem—these are not drunk, as you suppose," but full of the Holy Ghost.(5)

1. We are to consider first that *there are never wanting wicked men to scorn the good,* and to turn to ridicule the works of God, judging rashly of them, and interpreting them in an evil sense ; as the high priest, Eli, seeing the mother of Samuel praying in the Temple, " and only her lips moved, but her voice was not heard at all,"(6) thought her to be drunk, attributing that to drunkenness which proceeded from the fervour of the spirit. And when our Lord first began to preach, His kinsmen judged His fervour to be fury ; so now these unhappy and miserable men judged them to be "full of new wine,' who were replenished with the Holy Ghost. This our Lord sometimes suffers to exercise the just in humility and patience, to let

(5) Act. ii. 13.   (6) 1 Reg. i. 13.

them see how erroneous the judgments of men are, and to teach them to make no account of them; to teach them also not to judge rashly of what they do not understand, especially of the actions of holy persons, but to reverence them with silence and admiration, or else to enquire, as some did upon this day, saying—" Quidnam vult hoc esse? —What meaneth this?"

2. The apostles, moved by the Holy Ghost, *took occasion from that derision to preach the faith of Christ*, answering the demands of some, that they might thus discover the errors of others; and so St. Peter as head of the apostles, taking the first place, said to them, that those who were with him were not full of wine, as it was " but the third hour of the day," and that such things should not be presumed of holy men, and on such a holy day, but that they were full of that Holy Spirit whom God had promised by the prophet Joel :(7) as if he had said—" These indeed, are full of wine; but not of that corporal wine which you suppose, but of another wine, much stronger, which is the Spirit of God, and His inflamed love, because He hath " brought" them " into the cellar of " His spiritual " wine," (8) and " hath inebriated them " with the abundance and sweetness of His love.

Colloquy.—O lover of souls, bring my soul into this cellar, and vouchsafe to fill her with the variety and abundance of precious wines, laid up there, filling me with charity, and with all the actions and affections which proceed from it. Thou hast drunk of this wine, and hast invited Thy friends to drink of it, saying, " drink, and be inebriated, my dearly beloved :"(9) and although I deserve not the name of a friend, yet that I may be made a friend, I beseech Thee to invite me, and give me to drink in so great

<hr>

(7) Joel ii. 28.   (8) Cant. ii. 4.   (9) Cant. v. 1.

abundance, that, as one made drunk by Thy love, I may go forth of myself, and forgetful of all other things, I may desire nothing but Thee alone. Amen.

POINT III.

1. Consider thirdly the excellent sermon which St. Peter the apostle made, giving testimony of Christ crucified, and in which he discovered the great virtues which the Holy Ghost had imparted to him, and which the preachers of the Gospel ought to have.

. The first was *great wisdom and dexterity in proposing the verities* and mysteries of Christ our Lord, proving and confirming them with most effectual testimonies from the sacred Scriptures, the Prophets, and the Psalms.

ii. The second was *great liberty of spirit*, with great fortitude and courage of heart, for Peter whom the voice of a weak maid had already forced to tremble and deny his master, now with the virtue and fortitude which the Holy Ghost had given him, confessed and preached before an innumerable assembly of men, that Christ whom they had crucified, was risen again, was their God, their Messiah, and their Saviour.   And with equal liberty he bore testimony to the same before Annas and Caiphas, and before all the princes of the priests who wondered at his constancy, and command him with threatening, that he should not " speak at all, nor preach in the name of Jesus ;"(10) these he answered very boldly, saying :—" If it be just in the sight of God, to hear you rather than God, judge ye, for we cannot but speak the things which we have seen and heard."   And the like did the rest of the apostles, who, for this cause, offered themselves to many troubles, and rejoiced " to suffer for the name of Jesus," for which cause

(10) Act. iv. 18.

it was said of them:—" and they spake the word of God with confidence."(11)

iii. The third was great *zeal and fervour in their words,* which penetrated and stung the hearts of their hearers, in such a manner that those who a little before held the apostles "for drunk," presently "had compunction in their heart, and said to Peter, and to the rest of the apostles, What shall we do, men and brethren,"(12) that we may be saved?　And they who, with execrable cruelty, cried out a little before to have Christ crucified, now with great compunction and tenderness of heart, crave to be baptized in the name of Christ.　O marvellous change wrought by the virtue of the most High !　O immense power of the Divine Spirit ! who but God Himself could give such wisdom and such fortitude, with such great fervour, to preachers so rude and cowardly ?　And who but His Spirit could change and mollify the hard and stony hearts of such an audience ?

Colloquy.—Come, O Holy Spirit, upon the preachers of Thy church, and upon the faithful who hear them, and work in the one, and in the other, this marvellous change, to the end that our Redeemer may be obeyed, and be loved by all, and Thy divine will may be known, and held in worship by all men. Amen.

2. Consider, "*they that received His word were baptized, and there were added in that day about three thousand souls ;*" (13) which number is mysterious, for the most holy Trinity chose them, *each of the three Divine Persons appropriating to Himself a thousand* of these souls as the first-fruits of the innumerable souls that were to receive His holy law; as in the same manner, in another sermon,

(11) Act. iv. 31.　　　　(12) Act. ii. 37.　　　　(13) Act. ii. 41.

five thousand were converted,(14) in recompense of the *five wounds* which Christ received on the cross. Oh what joy did Christ our Lord feel when He saw that His Father had drawn so many souls to His service, fulfilling the promise which He had formerly made, saying:—" If He shall lay down His life for sin, He shall see a long-lived seed."(15) Oh what feasts did the angels make in heaven for the conversion of so many sinners, as they rejoice so greatly for the conversion of one! (16) Oh what joy did the Virgin Mary feel, seeing so many acknowledge the Divinity of her beloved Son, in whose conversion she likewise had no little part ; for whilst the apostles preached to the people, she prayed with exceeding great fervour, negotiating with Almighty God the prosperous success of their preaching ! Oh how joyful were the apostles themselves to see so great an abundance of fish caught, with one only cast of their net, for they were engaged all that day in instructing the converted in the mysteries of their faith, in moving them to do penance for their sins, and finally in baptizing them, our Lord giving, as St. Peter offered them, the gifts of the Holy Ghost, with which they remained full of holiness and spiritual gladness. From all this I ought to draw affections of great joy and praises, rejoicing in my heart to see Christ our Lord acknowledged and worshipped by so many souls, and congratulating Him on so happy and abundant a harvest.

Colloquy.—O most sweet Jesus, how happily dost Thou begin to fulfil that which Thou saidst :—" If I be lifted up from the earth, I will draw all things to myself :" (17) now Lord, Thou art " ascended on high," and hast given " gifts to men,"(18) and in

<hr>

(14) Act. iv. 4.   (15) Isa. liii. 10.
(16) Luc. xv. 7.   '   (17) Joan. xii. 32.
(18) Ephes. iv. 8. Ps. lxvii. 19.

recompense of that which Thou hast given, hast likewise " received gifts in men," they giving themselves by Thy grace to Thee, and Thou admitting them into Thy service: give unto me likewise, O Lord, Thy gifts, and receive of me those which Thou givest me, that I may be wholly Thine, world without end.   Amen.

MEDITATION XXV.

ON THE MOST EXCELLENT MANNER OF LIFE WHICH THE HOLY GHOST INSPIRED INTO THE FIRST CHRISTIANS.

POINT I.

They who were baptised, " were *persevering in the doctrine of the apostles, and in the communication of the breaking of bread, and prayers.*" (1)

1. Here we are to consider how it is proper to the Holy Ghost to inspire into the just, whose souls He fills with Himself, three principal exercises of virtue, with which they preserve and augment sanctity.

i. The first is, to "*persevere in the doctrine of the apostles*," that is, to exercise themselves in the hearing of sermons, and in the reading of sacred and holy books, the more to confirm themselves in faith, and the more to penetrate into and to move their affections towards the doctrine of the Gospel, wholly flying all that which is contrary, or which may make us lukewarm or remiss in the faith and estimation which we ought to have of the doctrine of the apostles.

ii. The second is, to persevere " *in the communication of the breaking of bread,*" that is, in the communion of the

(1) Act. ii. 42.

most holy Sacrament of the body of Christ our Lord, which is that bread of heaven distributed to men who live on earth, to preserve and increase in them the spiritual life of grace.

iii. The third is, "*to persevere in prayers :*" he does not say in *prayer*, but in "*prayers,*" that is, in every kind of prayer such as St. Paul enumerates as "*supplications, prayers, intercessions, and thanksgivings, and psalms and hymns,* and spiritual canticles," and to pray in each of these ways, " in *every place lifting up pure hands*" to God without anger and contention."(2)

2. These three things the faithful continued to practise daily, the Holy Ghost inspiring them, for all three are necessary for the sustenance of souls, and are the most *effectual means* of all *for preserving the life of grace,* increasing the gifts of Almighty God, and obtaining the fulness of the Holy Ghost. And so in the Acts of the apostles when we read of the Holy Ghost being given, it is always when the apostles preached and laid their hands upon the faithful, or prayed : so that the faithful received the Holy Ghost by one of these three ways, *hearing sermons, receiving the sacraments,* or uniting in prayer. But their prayers were most fervent, so that as St. Luke says, " When they had prayed, the place was moved wherein they were assembled, and they were all filled with the Holy Ghost :" (3) where the place in which they were assembled, is said to have moved or trembled, to signify the fear and astonishment which their doctrine should cause in the world, and the change of hearts which they should work by their example and words, through the power of the Holy Ghost.

Colloquy.—O most Holy Spirit, my spirit is hungry,

(2) I Tim. ii. 1. ˜ Ephes. v. 19.   1 Tim. ii. 8.
(3) Act. iv. 31.

nor have I bread to sustain it; give me, I beseech Thee, these "three loaves,"(4) of doctrine, communion, and prayer, with which to relieve my wants; and although I cannot claim them as a friend, yet give them to me because of my importunity, and recompense of the labours of our most sweet friend Christ Jesus, to whom be honour and glory, world without end.　Amen.

POINT II.

"*And all they that believed were together, and had all things in common;*" (5) they sold their possessions and goods, and divided them to all, according as every man had need.

It is likewise the property of the Holy Ghost to call His elect to the Evangelical perfection which Christ our Lord preached, and He therefore inspired these primitive Christians with the desire of it, in order that they might be an example to such Religious as should succeed them.

1. First, He *called them to community life*, with great union and charity, and thus, as St. Luke expresses it, "erant pariter," "*they were together*" much more in spirit than in body; and therefore he says again afterwards, that "the multitude of believers had but one heart and one soul:" (6) for though they were many, and of different nations, dispositions, faculties, and talents, yet all were united in one love, one will, and one mind, because all had the same Holy Ghost who united them to Himself and to one another, as the soul unites together all the members of the body, although they are different.　This was what our Lord had promised by the prophet Jeremiah:—"I will give them one heart and one way."(7) And Christ our Lord obtained from His eternal Father, that which He asked of

(4) S. Luc. xi. 5.　　　　(5) Act. ii. 44.
(6) Act. iv. 32.　　　　(7) Hier. xxxii. 39.

Him on the night of His supper, that His disciples might
be one as they two were one, that the world might know
Him by this union.(8)

Colloquy.—O Eternal Father, who makes " men of
manner to dwell in a house,"(9) grant this union of
souls to all the faithful, who dwell in the house of the
Church, and to all who dwell in the house of Religion,
so that men may behold the union which exists among
those who live in Thy house, and so Thy Son may be
glorified in the world.   O Holy Spirit, to whom it
belongs to bear testimony to Christ our Saviour,
establish among all Thy disciples this sovereign union,
that by their mutual love they also may bear testimony, and so their master may be believed and
adored.

At this time those wonders *began to appear which the
prophet Isaiah foretold* when he said;—" The wolf shall
dwell with the lamb, and the leopard shall lie down with
the kid; the calf, the lion, and the sheep shall abide together, and a little child shall lead them."(10)   The calf
and the bear shall feed: their young ones shall rest together; and the lion shall eat hay like the ox.   For to
the flock of the sheep and lambs of Jesus Christ, that is
to His disciples, the Holy Ghost joined in the union of
perfect charity, those who in the day of His Passion had
persecuted Him like wolves, tigers, and lions.   Those who
had been ravenous like wolves, choleric like leopards,
proud like lions, crafty like bears, and now form but one
flock, with those who had been meek, humble, and simple,
like sheep and lambs, all living in perfect agreement, and
united together in charity: all content themselves with
the same food, and that simply drest, the lion leaving his

(8) Joan. xvii. 11.

(9) Ps. lxvii. 7.   (10) Isa. xi. 6 et 7, et lxv. 25.

accustomed fare to take that of the ox; that is, the noble adapting themselves to the fare of rude and poor labourers, and all submit themselves with great obedience to the government of a poor and humble fisherman, whom Christ had made the pastor of his flock. O " change of the right hand of the Most High!" O miracles of our Saviour's might! " Come and behold ye the works of the Lord, what wonders He hath done upon earth : making wars to cease even to the end of the earth,"(11) changing lions and leopards into sheep and gentle lambs.

Colloquy.—I give Thee thanks, O omnipotent Saviour, for these changes wrought by the efficacy of Thy divine Spirit; prosecute, O Lord, this work Thou hast begun, giving to all the faithful and to all religious this union, this equality, this obedience, and this subjection to their superiors, in order that by these miracles of Thy grace, infidels may receive the faith, and the faithful confirm themselves in it, and always increase in Thy holy love. Amen.

2. In order to preserve this union, the Holy Ghost called the faithful to have all things in common, and strictly observe Evangelical poverty.—i. For first all sold their possessions, goods, and moveables, that the price might be equally divided amongst all, according to the necessities of each, and thus they accomplished the counsel of Christ our Lord, who said:—" If thou wilt be perfect, go sell what thou hast, and give to the poor, and thou shalt have treasure in heaven." (12)—ii. Secondly, in the distribution of these goods, they did not follow their own private will and opinion, but that of the apostles, at whose feet they laid the price of what they sold, (13) to be divided by them as they chose, stripping

(11) Ps. lxxvi. 11. Ps. xlv. 10. (12) Mat. xix. 21.
(13) Act. iv. 35.

themselves by these means of all affection to flesh and blood, and to their own private will, to follow the will of the ministers of Christ our Lord.—iii. Thirdly, they renounced all property in the things which they used, so that he who possessed them did not call them his own, but that "cold word," "*thine and mine*," (14) which is the occasion of discords, and the cause of charity growing cold, was banished from their discourse; so that in heart, word, and work, they renounced all property in anything they possessed, in order to become perfect disciples of Jesus Christ.

3. Hence it followed that while all were poor, *yet none of them suffered any need*, (15) for that which one had was common to all, and that which all had was common to each, so that they held all things common for the use of all, houses were common, garments were common, meat was common, the exercises of virtues, labours, rewards, and crowns were common, so that the whole multitude were all one, and in that one many were all helping one another.

Colloquy.—O happy and blessed life, taught by Christ, adopted by inspiration of the Holy Ghost, approved by the apostles, and practised by these disciples, who were the first fruits of the Holy Ghost! (16) O most Holy Godhead, who, being One in essence, art common to the three persons ; grant to the faithful whom Thou hast called to this state of perfection, that they may be all one, and that every one together with what he has, may be common to all, that so all " having nothing," may possess " all things," and leaving all, may obtain a hundred-fold more than they left, possessing Thee the fountain of all good, world without end.   Amen. (17)

<hr>

(14) S. Chrys. in orat. de S. Phil.

(15) Act. iv. 34.   (16) S. Basil. de Const. Monast. c. 19.

(17) 2 Cor. vi. 10.   Mat. xix. 29.

4. From what has been said, I ought, if I am a religious, to draw a great desire of imitating these primitive Christians, whom the Holy Ghost has proposed as an example to religious, and many of whom, by His inspiration actually vowed this poverty, in order that it might be more secure, and more pleasing to Almighty God. Thus it was that Ananias and Saphira having sold their inheritance, and retained part of the price of it, were chastised severely by St. Peter with sudden death, who told them that they had lied to the Holy Ghost, by whose inspiration they had made that vow.(18) But if I am a secular, I will conceive desires of imitating these disciples in everything compatible with my state of life, stripping myself of all things, at least in heart, since that sentence of our Saviour applies to all: "Every one of you that doth not renounce all that he possesses, cannot be my disciple." (19)

POINT III.

"Continuing daily *with one accord in the Temple*, and breaking bread from house to house, *they took their meat with gladness* and simplicity of heart, praising God and having favour with all the people."(20)

1. It is also the property of the Holy Ghost to call the elect to several other means of preserving union and perfection.—The first is *"unanimiter,"* that is, *"with one accord,"* to repair to the Temple, and continue there, performing those exercises for which the Temple was ordained, such as hearing together the word of God, praying and assisting at the divine sacrifices, and receiving the holy sacraments, for the Temple is the school of Christ, the house of prayer, the place of propitiation for our sins, and the building dedicated to the worship of God. In such exercises these

(18) Act. v. 2. S. Aug. Serm. xxvii. de verb. Apost. et alii.
(19) Luc. xiv. 33. (20) Act. ii. 46 et 47. Luc. xxiv. 53.

disciples persevered the greatest part of the day, with very great contentment of mind, because the Holy Ghost assisted them.

2. Having performed these exercises towards Almighty God, they went, by the inspiration of the same Spirit, to one another's houses, and, lovingly and charitably inviting one another, took their bodily food with great gladness, not of a sensual kind, but spiritual, according to the words of David:—" The just feast, and rejoice before God." (21) And to their joy they united simplicity of heart, without hypocrisy, or pretence, or any murmurings against one another, but with a sincere intention of pleasing God, and maintaining brotherly charity. In them we have an example how we ought to eat, and to make that action spiritual, which in its own nature is carnal.

3. Hence it was that they were always praising and glorifying God, to the great edification of all the people, who loved them, and held them in veneration, because of the sanctity and charity which shone in them. Oh most loving Jesus, sweet spouse of just souls, with what great reason mayest Thou now say, beholding the life of this little Church Thy spouse:—" Thou hast wounded my heart, my sister, my spouse, thou hast wounded my heart with one of thy eyes," (22) that is, with the union and agreement of these just persons, who are as Thine eyes. For, as the eyes are very like one another, and open and shut together, and look both together to this, or that side, and watch and sleep together, even so these just men, as with one mind, go to the Church together, pray together, and hear Thy holy word together, and exercise the works of charity together, because all are of one heart, and one spirit, united amongst themselves, and to Thee in perfect love.

(21) Ps. lxvii. 4.   (22) Cant. iv. 9, S. Greg. ibid.

Colloquy.—O divine Spirit, since Thou art the invisible heart of the Church, infuse into all her members the spirit of life, by Thy divine inspirations, to strengthen them and unite them together in perfect concord in all things belonging to Thy service, so that they may wound Thy heart with the wounds of love, and merit that Thou shouldest love them, and increase the fire of Thy love in them. Amen.

Before I proceed further with this history, I will insert two meditations, from which the faithful of the present day may see what help they have from the Holy Ghost, towards attaining to the sanctity of the primitive Christians.

MEDITATION XXVI.

OF THE MOST EXCELLENT PERFECTION WHICH THE HOLY GHOST COMMUNICATES BY MEANS OF HIS INSPIRATIONS, AND OF THE PROPERTIES INCLUDED IN THEM.

POINT I.

Consider first, how the Holy Ghost *makes like Himself those whom He regenerates to the life of grace,* by the water of Baptism, and leads them by His inspirations to so great a height of sanctity, that like Himself they may be called *spirits,* as Christ our Lord expressly taught when He said to Nicodemus :—" That which is born of the flesh is flesh ; and that which is born of the Spirit is Spirit. The Spirit breathes where He wills, and thou hearest His voice, but thou knowest not whence He cometh, and whither He goeth ; so is every one that is born of the Spirit."(1) That is to say, as he who is born of flesh by carnal generation is in all things like him who begot him, and from whom

(1) Joan. iii. 6.

he received his nature and natural properties and inclinations; for instance, as one man begets another man like himself in that which is proper to man, although he does not actually attain to the full perfection of his nature, till he has grown to a more perfect age: so after a certain proportion, that which is born of the Holy Ghost by spiritual generation is like the same Spirit from whom he received the graces, virtues, and gifts, which are a sort of participation in the divine nature, and by virtue of these he may be called *spirit*, that is to say, a spiritual man like the Holy Ghost, who spiritually begot him. And, therefore, St. Augustine says :—" Si nascaris de spiritu hoc, eris ut ille." " If thou art born of the Holy Ghost, thou wilt be such as He is,"(2) and by His grace thou mayest live in flesh, as if thou wert a spirit, free from the influence of the flesh, full of the light of truth, rich in virtues, inflamed with fervent affections, imitating Him in His perfect method of performing His works.

Colloquy.—O most Holy Spirit, what thanks ought I not to give to Thee for this so high dignity, that Thou grantest to a man of flesh, both to be, and to be called spirit as Thou art. O most loving Father, who begettest Thy sons in such a manner as to be also within them Thyself, aiding them to grow up and to work, in order that they may come to be perfect as Thou art perfect; since Thou hast now begotten me by Baptism, instruct me what I am to do, that so my works may be like Thine, and that I may attain to be made one spirit with Thee, world without end. Amen.

Then I may discourse upon three remarkable properties of the Holy Ghost, as displayed in the work of His inspiration, which are mentioned in the words of our Lord,

(2) Tract. xii. in Joan.

quoted above, viz.—i. *absolute liberty*,—ii. *powerful efficacy*,—iii. and *great secrecy in His means and ends;* and how far we may imitate Him in these respects shall be laid down in the ensuing points.

POINT II.

1. The first property of the Holy Ghost is that—" *Ubi vult spirat,*"—" *He breatheth where He will,*" that is, He performs His work of inspiration *with great liberty*, not by force, for none can force Him ; not out of fear, for there is nothing ·that can make Him afraid; not for His own interest, because He expects no reward from His creatures; not under any obligation of justice, because none can lay Him under obligation by their merits ; He inspires only because it is His will, and because His infinite bounty inclines Him to do us this good out of pure grace. He, therefore, imparts His inspirations to such persons as He wills, at such times as He wills, and in what manner He wills, often or seldom, with great force, or with little, moving them to such things as He Himself wills, according to the disposition of His divine providence, " dividing His graces and favours,—" prout vult,"—" according as He wills."(3) At the same time He shows His infinite liberality, in giving these inspirations to all when unlooked for, and under all manner of circumstances.—i. First, He gives them to him who does not ask for them, or think of asking for them.—ii. Secondly, to him who does not deserve them, and who, on account of his sins, is unworthy of them.—iii. Thirdly, to him who will not have them, but like Saul, contradicts and resists them. (4) But after all, those to whom He gives them most frequently and efficaciously, are the just, whom He has elected as the sons of His love, of whom the apostle St. Paul says:—

----

(3) 1 Cor. xii. 11.   (4) S. Bern. Serm. xxxii. in Cant.

" Whoever are led by the Spirit of God, they are the sons of God."(5)

Colloquy.—O happy sons, who have the Spirit of God for your associate and companion! O divine Spirit since Thou breathest where Thou wilt, because Thou art essentially God, show Thy goodness to me willingly according to Thy power, frequently instructing me what to think, speak, and do, that being moved by Thee, I may be in all things like Thee. Amen.

i. *The just man, who is a perfect child of the Spirit, is guided in an excellent way by His inspiration* to do His will in all things; not evil things, nor forbidden, nor vain, nor yet trifling, because the Holy Ghost does not prompt to such things, but always to things good, holy, and profitable ;(6) and how He does these with absolute liberty of spirit; not by constraint, as a servant; not with repugnance, or weariness, like the lukewarm ; not for fear of hell, like the imperfect ; not with reward for his principal object, like a hireling ; but because he desires to please Almighty God, and love virtue ; so that, although there were no hell at all, he would not sin, because there is no hell so terrible to him as sin; and although there were no reward at all, he would not omit to perform what God commands, because he counts it his best reward to obey Him, and has within himself a living law, which inclines him to will all that God wills. It is in this conformity to the divine Spirit that his perfect liberty of spirit consists, according to those words of the apostle St. Paul :—" The Lord is a Spirit, and where the Spirit of the Lord is, there is liberty." (7) Hence it is, that as the Holy Ghost infuses His inspirations both into good and bad, because He desires in this to show His bounty ; so the just man, moved

(5) Rom. viii. 14.   (6) 1 Joan. iii. 9.   (7) 2 Cor. iii. 17.

by His inspiration, is good to all, both friends, and also enemies, and such as contradict and persecute him, showing in this that he is the son of Almighty God, and *possesses His* divine Spirit.

ii. He always does *his own will*, because he has placed his will in the will of God, and of His divine Spirit; in doing, therefore, the will of God, he does his own will, because his own will is no other than the will of God. For which reason St. Bonaventura says, that those who are conformed to the divine will, are as Gods, omnipotent, to do what they will. (8)

Colloquy.—O my soul, if thou desirest this sovereign omnipotence, only will what God wills, and thus thou wilt obtain it; resolve at length to deny thine own will, and resign it to the divine will, and thus whilst thou always fulfillest the will of God, thou wilt likewise fulfil thine own. O God of my soul, from henceforth I resolve to will what Thou willest, not by constraint, but voluntarily; not for fear of interest, but for pure love; so that my will may come to please Thee as Thine pleases me.

Hence I will gather the signs for distinguishing the inspirations of the good Spirit, from the contrary suggestions of the bad, from which proceed *repugnance, weariness, loathing*, and horror, to fulfil the will of God and His holy law. But the *fear of hell and hope of reward* may also proceed from the Holy Spirit, who does not always suggest that which is most perfect, but is wont to begin with that which is less perfect.

POINT III.

2. The *second property* of the Holy Ghost is, that when He breathes,—"*Vocem ejus audis:*" "*We hear His voice:*" where He discovers *His omnipotence* in various ways.

(8) In dicta Salutis, tit. lxxxvi. 1.

i. First, in this, that *when He is pleased to breathe into a soul no gates can be shut against Him,* nor any obstacle hinder His entrance, nor is it possible to avoid hearing His voice, that is, feeling His touch, and inspiration, and what He means and wills by it, although the man is free not to yield consent to it.(9)   And possesses the power peculiar to Himself of entering immediately, and in an instant into our understanding and will, and imprinting at once whatever knowledge or good affection He will, because He is absolute Lord of our spirit, and in it, and by it, He can speak of anything corporeal or incorporeal, at His pleasure, with or without sensible figures in the imagination.   But His omnipotence and bounty reaches yet further, for He has the power and means of breathing into us in such a manner, that we not only hear His voice, but consent to it, and obey those words which He speaks within us, yet not by force and necessity, but with unspeakable sweetness and contentment, our will being so changed, that we say with St. Paul:—" Domine, quid me vis facere ;" " Lord, what wilt Thou have me to do?"(10) Hence it comes to pass that the spiritual man, moved by the divine Spirit, has the same force and means of effecting whatever He will for the service of Almighty God, however hard and difficult, breaking down the walls of difficulties to accomplish His will, being in this point made like to the Holy Ghost, by whom he is moved.

Colloquy.—O most Holy Spirit, since Thou art absolute Lord of all my powers, knock at the gates of my soul and open them; knock so efficaciously that without delay I may open to Thee at once, that Thou

(9) S. Bern. Ser. xlv. in Cant.   Heb. iv. 12.

(10) Act. ix. 6.   S. Th. 1, p. q. cv. art. 3 et 4, et q. cxi. art. 2 ; et 2, q. clxxiii. art. 2.

mayest do in me, and with me, according to Thine own will."(11)

ii. I will consider, secondly, that as every man has his own peculiar tone of voice, by which he is recognised, and comes to be known and distinguished from others; and as Job says:—"the ear discerning words;" (12) even so the *inward inspiration of the Holy Ghost has its particular properties and signs* which the ear of the soul recognises, and thus knows that it is God who speaks, and distinguishes His voice from the voice of the evil spirit, which has very contrary signs and properties. All this is evident from the effects inwardly produced in souls; for the Holy Ghost, by His voice softens hearts that are hardened, bows down the rebellious, makes the contemptuous meek, inflames the frozen, strengthens the feeble, raises the dejected, brings back the distracted to recollection, fixes the inconstant, comforts the sad, and calms the troubled; (13) He makes the proud man humble, the angry mild, the covetous poor of spirit, such as love their own ease and convenience, temperate, and mortifiers of their flesh. And this He does with a certain kind of command and majesty, no less sweet than efficacious, terrifying the wicked with fear, that they may amend, and making the good and godly tremble, that they may reverence Him the more; but always producing in the end, justice, joy, and tranquillity. The contrary of all this the evil spirit works by his voice, although in a dissembling manner.

Colloquy.—O divine Spirit, "speak" within me, "for Thy servant heareth." (14) Thou sayest that Thou desirest to hear my voice, and I desire much more to hear Thine; "make me," therefore, "hear

(11) Apoc. iii. 20.   (12) Job xii. 11, cap. xxxiv. 3.
(13) S. Greg. 1. xxix. Mor. cap. 12.   (14) 1 Reg. iii. 10.

Thy" divine "voice,"(15) and to feel the effects of it, that I may answer Thy voice with mine, by doing such works as may resemble Thine.   Amen.

iii. Hence I will gather, that the *spiritual man, moved by the Holy Ghost, has his voices, by which he is known to be such*, because they are like those of the Holy Ghost, who moves him.   And his voices are these; modesty in his countenance, gravity in the motions of the body, purity and discretion in words, promptitude in obedience, temperance in food, joy in persecutions, constancy in labours, humility in subjecting himself to all men, diligence in the exercises of divine worship, fervour in prayer, and zeal in aiding and assisting souls.   These and other such works are the voices of him, who is a true child of the Holy Ghost, and is moved by His inspiration, and by these also he is known; for the tree is known by its fruit.

POINT IV.

3. The property of the Holy Ghost is, that although He breathes into us in such a manner that we hear His voice, yet,—" *Nescis unde veniat, aut quo vadat :*" *We know not " whence He cometh, and whither He goeth;*" for He purposely conceals His coming in, and going out, His beginnings and endings, disposing all things in a wonderful manner by His providence.

i. For, first, He hides from us the *coming* of His divine inspiration, as regards the *time, place, exercise,* and *occasion* of it.   Sometimes He comes on festival days, sometimes on working days, at one time by day, at another time by night; now in the morning, then in the evening; sometimes He comes in the church, or oratory; sometimes in the street, or in the fields; sometimes in time of prayer, mass, or sermon; at other times in the midst of our

(15) Cant. viii. 13.

business and exterior works; sometimes He enters by the sight, when we are looking at some devotional image; at other times by the ear, when we are hearing some good discourses, or by the taste, or touch, whilst we are suffering some sorrow or affliction. Lastly, it cannot be known, as He himself said to Job:—" by what way is the light of divine illuminations spread, and the heat of divine influences divided upon the earth;" (16) He would have us always rely upon His providence, and acknowledge with humility our dependance upon it, confessing that our own industry is not sufficient to obtain so great a favour, and when it is given us, that it is not for our merits, but from the liberality of the Giver.

Colloquy.—O giver of gifts, visit me often with Thy divine inspiration, and come to me by what way Thou wilt, for I desire to remain ignorant of it, in order to be humbled, believing that Thou canst favour me in any place and time.

ii. In the same manner, the Holy Ghost hides *that which He intends by His inspirations,* for, although we know it to be His will that we should obey by doing the good which He inspires us to do for His glory and our salvation, yet we know not His particular end and purpose; for many times with little beginnings, He has great ends in view, and by great impulses moves to certain things, the ends which cannot be known until the issue discovers them, as was the case with St. Paul, when he said :—" Behold, being bound in the spirit, I go to Jerusalem, not knowing the things which shall befall me there.' (17) For it is the will of the Holy Ghost, that surrendering our own judgment and will, we should obey

<hr>

(16) Job xxxviii. 24. S. Greg. xxix. Mor. cap. 12.
(17) Act. xx. 22.

His holy inspirations, depending wholly upon His loving providence as to the end which He has in view.

Colloquy.—O most loving Father, inspire me that which is agreeable and conformable to Thy holy law, for it is enough for me to know the final end which Thou hast in view, to make me obey Thee in the other means and ends which Thou ordainest.

iii. Hence I am to learn two things. (a) First, that if I am moved by the Holy Ghost, although I perform works before other which discover the virtue of my soul, yet I ought to hide from them my ends and intentions, contenting myself with their being known only to Almighty God, lest the thief of vain-glory rob me of my treasure ; nevertheless, it is necessary that my confessor and spiritual master, who governs me in the place of God, should know them all, lest Satan, transformed into an angel of light, deceive me. (b) The second is, to conceive a *great confidence* of obtaining this sanctity, since it was not without meaning that Christ our Lord said generally : " Sic est omnis, qui natus est ex spiritu :" " so is it of every one that is born of the spirit ;" to give hope to all, that every just person may come to perfection, if he live according to the grace which he received in this spiritual birth, and obey the motions of the Divine Spirit, who excites and directs him to it ; and in token and sign of this, He gives to all the just His seven gifts, as we shall immediately see.

MEDITATION XXVII.

OF THE SEVEN GIFTS WHICH THE HOLY GHOST COMMUNICATES TO THE JUST IN ORDER THAT THEY MAY SUFFER THEMSELVES TO BE GOVERNED BY HIS INSPIRATIONS, AND OBTAIN GREAT SANCTITY.

POINT I.

1. First, we must consider how the Holy Ghost, in the generation of a spiritual man, together with the three theological *virtues*, faith, hope, and charity, infuses also into him the *seven gifts which Isaiah calls the gift of "wisdom," " understanding," " counsel," " fortitude," " knowledge," " godliness," and the " fear of the Lord,"*(1) the ends and offices of which are very different from the former. It is the office of *virtues*, to incline a man to the exercise of virtuous works by his own election and free will, assisted notwithstanding, by divine grace ; and therefore can always work by their means, believing, hoping, loving, obeying, and humbling himself, as much as he will, because God's grace is never wanting to him. But it is the office of gifts to incline the just man to yield and subject himself to the impulses and motions which come to him from without, that is, from the Holy Ghost, when, with the wind of His inspiration, He moves him to do good works ; just as the use of sails is, that when the winds blow the ship may be easily moved and driven on ; and the prophet Isaiah calls them *gifts of the Spirit*, because they are the instruments by which the Holy Spirit inclines the just man to the works which he does under His inspiration. Whence is to be seen the great desire of the Holy Ghost, that we should obey His divine inspirations, since this is the end for which He imparts these gifts to us ; for which

(1) S. Th. i. 2, q. lxviii. Isa. xi. 2.

gifts I ought to praise Him " seven times a day " (2) with holy David, inviting also the apostles and saints of heaven to join me.

Colloquy.—O holy apostles, who like doves flew upon the wings of your virtues, and like clouds (3) were moved by means of the seven gifts; beseech the same divine Spirit to communicate them to me, that like a dove, I may fly in His service; and, like a cloud, I may suffer myself to be moved by the wind of His divine inspiration. Amen.

2. From what has been said, we may infer that these gifts, as St. Thomas said, are necessary to the just, in order to obtain life eternal, as well because they are always found united to grace and charity, and cannot be separated from them, as also because the instinct and inspiration of the Holy Ghost, is necessary to preserve the two parts of justice and sanctity, which are, to forsake evil and to follow good, especially in things hard and difficult, such as happen in this world.(4) And because the Holy Ghost so much desires our salvation and perfection, He hastens to bestow His favours on us, and presenting us with these gifts, in order that we may obey Him.

Colloquy.—I give Thee thanks, O most Holy Spirit, for the care which Thou takest to help my feebleness with such excellent gifts of Thy grace: suffer me not, Lord, I beseech Thee, to lose them, until by means of them I have obtained eternal life. Amen.

POINT II.

1. Next, we are to consider the manner in which the Holy Ghost, with these seven gifts, by means of His divine inspirations, *withdraws us from evil and helps us to over-*

- - -

(2) Ps. cxviii. 164.   (3) Isa. lx. 8.
(4) S. Th. supra. art. 2.

come vices and temptations, which St. Gregory expresses in the following words:—" Against *foolishness*, the Holy Ghost arms us with wisdom ;—against *dulness*, with *understanding* ;—against *rashness*, with *counsel;*—against *ignorance*, with *knowledge ;*—against *pusillanimity*, with *fortitude ;*—against *hardness*, with *godliness ;* and against *pride*, with *fear ;* (5) so that these seven gifts are weapons offensive and defensive, which the Holy Ghost gives us to attack the chief causes of temptations which beset us in the spiritual life, and to preserve it from destruction.

i. Some temptations proceed from *lukewarmness*, and from the little love which we have for the things of Almighty God, which are called *foolishness*, because the flesh does not take delight, or find any taste in the things of the Spirit, or set any value on eternal things, and therefore, as it were, loathing them, leaves them, and seeks for sensual delights, like the Israelites, who, loathing the manna, sighed after the onions of Egypt.(6) Against these temptations the Holy Ghost arms us with the gift of *wisdom*, endowing us with spiritual perception by which we are led to desire heavenly goods, discerning in them sweetness, and in earthly things loathsomeness, which He is able and accustomed to effect in a moment when He will do us this favour, and our necessity requires.

ii. Other temptations proceed from our *dulness* and obscurity in matters of faith, from which spring doubts, perplexities, clouds, distrust, and slowness, as well in believing, as in hoping, and working. Against which the Holy Ghost favours us with the gift of *understanding*, darting forth into our spirit illuminations and beams of light which dissolve those clouds, and give us peace and joy in believing.

iii. Other temptations overcome us, because from rash-

<hr>

(5) S. Greg. l. ii. Mor. cap. 26.   (6) Num. xxi. 5.

ness and precipitancy of conduct, or of so little prudence, as to be unable to find means to expel them from us as we ought; or because they assail us on a sudden, and when we are unprovided, without giving us time to think what we are to do. In such cases the Holy Ghost assists us with the gift of *counsel,* making known to us, by a special inspiration, the course that we must take to overcome them, as He inspired Joseph to leave his cloak in the hand of the woman, who solicited him to sin, and fly the occasion lest he should perish in it.(7)

iv. Against temptations which may cast us down through *ignorance,* delusion, forgetfulness, or inadvertence on our part, the Holy Ghost succours us with the gift of *knowledge,* enlightening us by His inspirations to discover the sleights of the Devil, the frauds of the world, and the deceits of the flesh, suggesting to our memory and with great sweetness inducing us to embrace those truths which are most suitable and efficacious for overcoming them.

v. To other temptations more violent, we yield through *weakness of mind,* which renders us unable to resist them, when they press us so hard, that if we do not assent to something which is mortal sin, we must lose our goods, honour, or life, or undergo some other grievous penalty; and then the Holy Ghost helps us with the gift of *fortitude,* strengthening our pusillanimous hearts by His encouragements, and animating us to suffer any temporal loss to avoid the eternal, as He succoured Susanna and the glorious martyrs in their perils.

vi. From the *hardness of our heart* proceeds our want of compassion for our neighbour, and that we do not set ourselves to do them good, or to endure the evil they do us, but break out into passions of anger and impatience, into

(7) Gen. xxxix. 12.

injurious language, and into acts of injustice, revenge, and cruelty. Against these the Holy Ghost helps us, with the gift of *piety*, softening our hearts by the touch of His tender inspiration, and moving us to mercy in those occasions which provoke us to vengeance.

vii. Finally against the temptations which spring from *pride*, presumption, ambition, and vanity, the same Holy Ghost, arms us with the gift of *the fear of God*, enlightening us by His inspirations to realise those truths which repress our pride and presumption, make us tremble at God's fearful and secret judgments, and bring down and destroy our vanity.

2. In all these occasions I will ponder the greatness of my necessity, and the efficacy of these helps, and comparing the one with the other, I will glorify the Holy Ghost, who with so loving a providence, has provided such remedies for one that stands in such need of them. And therefore, whenever I am molested by these temptations, I will instantly have recourse to Him, and crave His assistance, since it is for this end that He offers these gifts to me.

Colloquy.—O most Holy Spirit, I give Thee thanks for the fit weapons which Thou hast given me against my cruel enemies, and for Thy care in moving me to endeavour to deliver myself from them. Having such a "protector, whom shall I fear?"(8) Thou being "my light and my salvation," who shall make me tremble? "Set me beside Thee, and let any man's hand fight against me;" for although the impulses of the Devil come to overthrow me, if Thine prevent me, they will not overcome me.(9) Prevent me, Lord, amidst my perils with Thy divine inspirations, that my miseries may not overwhelm me.

<hr>

(8) Ps. xxvi. 1. 2. (9) Job xvii. 3. Ps. cxvii. 7.

POINT III.

The third point shall be to consider the manner in which the Holy Ghost helps us with these seven gifts to gain virtues *in the highest degree of perfection*, as well those which belong to the *active* as to the *contemplative* life.

1. First with the three gifts of *understanding, wisdom,* and *knowledge*, He helps us in the works of the *contemplative life*, in reading, meditation, prayer and contemplation, moving us by His inspirations, to practise them with great perfection. (10)

i. With the gift of *understanding*, He perfects us in the knowledge of the *mysteries of our faith, helping us by His illuminations, to penetrate the most inward and secret things contained in them, and that with as great certainty as if we saw them : whence descend showers of profound and subtle meditations, infused by the same Holy Ghost, with which the fire of affection is kindled in our hearts.

ii. With the gift of *wisdom* He perfects us in the knowledge of Almighty God, of His excellency and attributes, and of all things which belong to His Godhead, and impresses us with a high esteem of divine things, together with an incredible relish and sweetness in acquiring the knowledge of them ; by which relish and experience this knowledge is made more perfect, and the spirit is elevated to inflamed acts of the love of God, and of union with His goodness.

iii. With the gift of *knowledge*, He perfects us in the knowledge of things created, imprinting in us by His inspirations, the true judgment which we ought to form of them, as well with regard to what they have from God, as what they have of themselves, and the effect of this know-

(10) S. Th. 2, 2, q. viii. art. 6.

ledge is, that, like St. Paul, we count them but as dung
that we may gain Christ." (11)

2. And because prayer, that it 'may be perfect, ought to
be reduced to practice, and not consist only in knowledge
and affection, but produce the fruit of good purposes and
holy works; therefore with the gift of *counsel*, He perfects
the *knowledge of the particular things which we are to set
before us*, for the accomplishment of that which God commands us. In this manner the Holy Ghost helps us in
mental prayer; without whose favour and assistance it
would be wandering, dry, and of little profit. For as the
Wise man says, "The heart fancieth as that of a woman
in travail, except it be a vision sent forth from the Most
High;"(12)—that is to say—it suffers great distractions,
and a multitude of wandering affections and fluctuations, if
the Holy Ghost does not visit us with His inspirations, to
direct us 'and bring us to recollection. Wherefore, when I
go to prayer, I should beseech the Holy Ghost to perform
this office for me, saying to Him:—

Colloquy.—O divine Spirit, who teachest us to pray,
with "unspeakable groanings," (13) visit me with
these gifts, and assist me with Thy holy illuminations,
in order that my understanding may bud forth holy
thoughts, my will inflamed affections, and that my
other powers may be moved to perform works of great
excellence. Amen.

3. Then I will consider how the Holy Ghost, with the
three gifts of godliness, *fortitude*, and the *fear of God*,
perfects us in the virtues of the *active life*, both towards
our neighbours and towards ourselves.(14)

i. With the gift of *godliness*, He perfects us in the

(11) Phil. iii. 8.
(12) Ecclus. xxxiv. 6.   S. Bon. de vii. Itin.; Itin. ii. dist. v.
(13) Rom. viii. 26.   (14) S. Th. 1. 2, q. lxlii. art. 4.

virtues which we ought to practise towards our neighbours, imprinting in us the spirit of sons towards our superiors: the spirit of a mother towards our inferiors; and a tender and compassionate spirit towards our equals, making us ready, with the bowels of charity, to relieve the necessities of all persons, whether of body or of soul, and especially the latter, as those of most importance.

ii. With the gift of *fortitude* He perfects us in ourselves, strengthening the weakness of our flesh, and repressing its fears, and moving us to undertake great and glorious things in His holy service, laying aside all human fear.

iii. With the gift of *fear* He perfects us in our duties towards God our Lord, imprinting in our hearts the spirit of reverence and humility, by which we esteem ourselves as nothing in His presence, and give Him the glory of all those things which we do by means of these gifts, since all are His. By this *fear* He helps us to practise the counsel of the wise man, "In all thy works keep the pre-eminence;"(15) and sometimes moves us to very high and extraordinary designs in order to raise us to extraordinary sanctity.

4. Lastly, I will consider how the gift of *counsel* is a kind of sun in the midst of these seven planets of heaven, enlightening us as to what we ought to practise in the virtues, both of the active and contemplative life, that we may have greater security of choosing that which tends most to our perfection, as well as the best manner, place, and time for their exercise.(16) And because internal things are of a hidden character, and liable to many delusions, Satan transforming himself "into an angel of light," (17) the Holy Ghost assists us with the gift of counsel, that we may search for the truth, and walk in it without

(15) Ecclus. xxxiii. 23.   (16) S. Th. 2, 2, q. lii.
(17) 2 Cor. xi. 14.

being deceived. And because no man is sufficient of himself, with this same gift, He inspires us in particular with one admirable counsel, namely, never to trust to our own counsel, but to have recourse to the counsellors He has placed in His Church, according to that saying of the Wise man :—" Establish within thyself a heart of good counsel; for there is no other thing of more worth to thee than this: the soul of a holy man discovers sometimes true things, more than seven watchmen 'that sit on a high place to watch."(18) And because it is a singular gift of the Holy Ghost to have the direction of such a good counsellor, and to have a docile and tractable heart to follow His counsel, (19) I ought to ask of Him both the one and other, saying ;—

Colloquy.—O most Holy Spirit, from whom all graces proceed for the good of the universal Church, inspire my counsellors with the counsel which they are to give me, and give my heart docility and strength for embracing and following it. Amen.

THE CONCLUSION OF THE TWO FOREGOING MEDITATIONS.

From what has been declared in this and in the preceding meditation, I ought to form *three firm resolutions*, which are likewise means of soliciting and obtaining the frequent inspirations of the Holy Ghost and the use of these seven gifts in that perfection which has been mentioned.

1. The first is to trust *firmly in the bounty and liberality of the Holy Ghost*, that He will bestow this favour upon me, however feeble and ignorant, and inclined to evil I be, for to all the just, of whatever state or condition they are, He imparts these seven gifts, with the intent that they should not remain idle in them. And as the four living

(18) Ecclus. xxxvii. 17.   (19) Cass. col. xvi. c. 11. et 12.

creatures which Ezekiel saw, which had the faces of an eagle, of a lion, of a man and of an ox, although they were so different in nature, yet moved at the same rate, and that with great swiftness, following the impulses of the Spirit, each with the wings which had been given him, (20) so those men who have great talent and learning, like eagles, those who are generous and strong, like lions, those who are able to reason well, but are of weak constitution, like men, and lastly, those who are rude and laborious, like oxen, may all move at the same pace in spiritual life, and all attain to its perfection by help of the wings of the virtues and gifts which the Holy Ghost gives them, following the impulses of His fervent inspiration.

Colloquy.—O Divine Spirit, since Thou wouldst not have Thy talents lie idle, and dost chastise the slothful and wicked servant, who digs and hides them in the ground, put in exercise in me the gifts which Thou hast given me, and move me to the works which are most pleasing to Thee. Amen.

2. The second means is, *to frequent in the best manner that we can, those exercises in which the Holy Ghost is wont to communicate His inspirations,* seeing that such exercises have this force of their own nature, for which reason we may apply to them that expression in the Book of Job, the " *veins of the whisper*" (21) of Almighty God, or, with St. Gregory call them " *conduit pipes,*" through which the divine inspiration comes and enters into the soul. These exercises are reading good books, and hearing sermons, in which the Spirit is wont to enlighten us upon what we read or hear ; prayer and meditation, in which, by speaking with Almighty God, we move Him also to speak to us ;

(20) Ezech. i. 10.
(21) Job. iv. 12. S. Greg. lib. vi. cap. 19 et 20.

Holy communion and Mass, in which the same Christ is contained who merited for us these inspirations, and who, with the Holy Ghost, is the giver of them: and sometimes it will be very profitable to practise that manner of prayer by *aspirations*, of which mention is made in the introduction of this Book, joining with each aspiration, an *affection* or affectionate sigh, at one time to see Almighty God, and at another to see ourselves freed from the many miseries of this life.

3. The third means is, *to give frequent and earnest thanks for whichever of these gifts* the Holy Ghost imparts to us, esteeming ourselves unworthy of them, and to perform with exactness whatever good works, either of the active or contemplative life, He inspires us to do ;(22) rejoicing with great tranquillity in those feelings which He imparts to us by His divine light, for he who shows himself grateful for the favours and inspirations he has received, and makes due use of them as they come, will receive others much greater in future.

Colloquy.—O spouse of pure souls, who sayest :—" Arise, O north wind, and come, O south wind, blow through my garden, and let the aromatic spices thereof flow" from the trees :(23) drive from my soul the north wind of pride and ingratitude, which dries up the fountains and disperses the dews of Thy abundant mercy ; and send upon me the south wind of Thy fervent inspirations, that so all the powers of my soul may distil a great multitude of fragrant works, pleasing to Thine eyes, and profitable to my neighbours, and that I may ascend by them from virtue to virtue, until I come to see Thee in Thy holy Sion, world without end.   Amen.

(22) S. Ber. ser i. de Pent.

(23) Cant. iv. 16.   S. Ber. ser. li. in Cant.   S. Aug. in. Soliloq. cap. 18.

IV.—MEDITATIONS ON SOME OF THE FIRST PRINCI-PAL EVENTS IN THE HISTORY OF THE CHURCH.

MEDITATION XXVIII.

OF THE PLENITUDE OF THE HOLY GHOST, WHICH WAS GIVEN TO ST. STEPHEN, AND CHRIST'S APPEARANCE TO HIM IN HIS MARTYRDOM.

AMONGST the disciples of that time, one of the most eminent was St. Stephen, the first among the seven deacons, (1) whom the Apostles chose, of whom St. Luke recounts four things, which may be the subject of this meditation.—1. First, the *gifts* which the Holy Ghost gave him. 2. How well he *used* them. 3. The *favours* which God showed him for this good use of them. 4. The good end which he made, to which may be added, the reward which he enjoys in eternal glory. And the same points may be applied to the meditations of the lives of other saints.

POINT I.

1. The first shall be to consider *how liberal the Holy Ghost was with Stephen*, for it is said of him, that he was full of the Holy Ghost; from which fulness four other sorts of fulness proceeded, for he was full of *grace*, of *wisdom*, of *faith*, and of fortitude : and hence he had such great *modesty* and sweetness of manners, that his countenance seemed to resemble that of an angel's—i. The first fulness which was that of *grace* adorned his *heart* with heavenly virtues, that so he might be acceptable to

---

(1) Act. vi. 5, et vii. 57.

Almighty God. ii. The second, that of *wisdom*, adorned his *understanding* with the light of the divine truths, in order that he might penetrate them with delight, and teach them to others with profit. iii. The third, that of *faith*, enabled his *soul* to pray with confidence to Almighty God, and to work miracles for the good of men. iv. The fourth, that of *fortitude*, made him invincible against his enemies, and constant in suffering persecutions and enduring labours. The 'effect of all these four, was that he was like an angel, leading an angelic life in an earthly body.

These gifts gave the Holy Ghost freely to him, to show the riches of His grace, not only in the twelve apostles, but also in the other inferior disciples; but, without doubt this glorious man disposed himself to receive these gifts, by his great fervour, although the Holy Ghost, who bestowed them, prepared him also for their reception; and from his favour I am to animate myself to procure similar gifts, seeing the hand of this liberal giver is not straitened. I will also beseech the glorious St. Stephen to make intercession to God for me; for if by his prayer he obtained these greater gifts for Saul, who was a persecutor of Jesus Christ, he may obtain such for me; and he that could do so much with God when on earth, can now do no less in heaven.

2. Next, I will consider how diligent and fervent this holy man was in the *use and experience of the gifts which he had received* from the Holy Spirit, the same Spirit assisting him for this purpose.

i. First, through the *wisdom* which was infused into him, he preached the law of Christ our Lord, and confirmed it with such admirable and powerful reasons, that many of the learned Jews, skilful in law, going forth to dispute against him, " were not able to resist the wisdom and the Spirit that spake" (2) in him, which was the Holy Ghost, of whom he was full; and thus was fulfilled the promise made by our Redeemer to His disciples, when, speaking of occasions, He said :—" It is not you that speak, but the Spirit of your Father that speaketh in you." (3)

ii. Secondly, armed with the great and lively *faith* which he had, he did great miracles and wonders amongst the people, by which he made his doctrine credible, that all Christians might understand, that the gift of working miracles belonged not only to the apostles, but also to those who were full of grace and faith like him.

iii. Thirdly, being in the midst of a council, and compassed about with many enemies and false witnesses, who accused him of grievous faults, yet he was not troubled, nor did he lose the serenity and *modesty* of his countenance, but it shone forth so much the more by reason of the testimony of his conscience, and for the joy which he had to see himself persecuted for Jesus Christ, so that his very enemies beholding him,—" Videbant faciem ejus, quasi faciem Angeli,"—" saw his face, as if it had been the face of an angel" come down from heaven, so that that was fulfilled in him which Job said of himself;—" The light of my countenance fell not on the earth ;" (4) for neither the persecutions and false accusations of his enemies, nor the contradictions and contentions of disputation, could cause any change or alteration in him, or make him lose his grave and joyful serenity, or hang down his head for shame like Cain.

Colloquy.—Oh that I could imitate the angelic modesty of this most pure warrior, and never do anything for which I should be forced to hang down my

(2) Act. vi. 10.   (3) Mat. x. 20.
(4) Job. xxix. 24.

head in confusion and shame for having committed it! Grant me, O Lord Jesus, in the midst of my calamities such purity of soul, as may be discovered to Thy glory in the grave and joyful expression of my face.

iv. Fourthly, with great *fortitude* of mind, and without fear of his enemies, he sharply reproved the hardness of heart, and rebellion of which they had always been guilty against the Holy Ghost, their disobedience to the law, and the cruelty with which they had persecuted the prophets, and above all, the chief of them, Jesus Christ; and although his adversaries "were cut to the heart" with rage, and " gnashed with their teeth at him ;" (5) yet he was without fear, being clothed with virtue from above.

Colloquy.—I rejoice, O glorious St. Stephen, for the *fortitude* with which thou defendest the honour of thy master, honouring Him who honoured thee, and offering to die for Him who died for thee; beseech Him to vouchsafe to clothe me with the same virtue from above, that imitating thee in the combat, I may likewise attain thy crown.   Amen.

POINT II.

Stephen " being full of the Holy Ghost, looking up steadfastly to heaven, *saw the glory of God*, and Jesus standing on the right hand of God; and he said, Behold, I see the heavens opened, and the Son of Man standing on the right hand of God."(6)

In this marvellous vision, may be considered the *extraordinary favours which the Holy Ghost bestows on His elect,* and on what kind of just men,—on what occasions,—and for what causes He bestows them, that we may hence gather light to know the causes and effects of divine visions and revelations.

(5) Act. vii. 54.   (6) Act. vii. 55.

1. First, some mystery is contained in those words: " Stephen being full of the Holy Ghost, looking up steadfastly to heaven, saw the glory of God ;" and we are given to understand, that there were *two things* that made him worthy of this glorious vision.—First, that he was *full* of *the Holy Ghost*, and of His gifts and graces, as has been said.—Secondly, that *he looked up steadfastly to heaven*, not so much with the eyes of the body, as with those of the soul, longing for heavenly things, sighing after them, and praying for himself and for all others, for such favours as those God ordinarily imparts to great saints, much given to prayer and contemplation.   And although it is not safe to desire such favours, yet it is most just, that I should not make myself unworthy of them, but endeavour to obtain that fulness of grace and spirit of prayer, which disposes the soul to receive them, since our Lord promises these to all, saying, by the prophet:—" I will pour out upon the house of David, and upon the inhabitants of Jerusalem," "spiritum gratiæ et precum,"—" the spirit of grace and of prayers."(7)

2. Secondly, it is not without mystery that it is said, that he " *saw the glory of God, and Jesus standing on His right hand,*" for by this we are given to understand that the heavenly light which illuminates the interior eyes, and lifts them up to the highest contemplations, principally discovers two things:—*the mysteries of the glory of God*, belonging to His *divinity* or Trinity ; and *Jesus Christ* our Lord, with the *mysteries of His glorious humanity.*   This light discovers these mysteries after a manner so highly elevated that it is called *sight*, which, as St. Paul says,(8) ravishes the heart, and transforms it by love into the glory of that Lord whom it has seen ; for, with this sight, the soul obtains an addition to the gifts and graces which it

(7) Zach. xii. 10.   (8) 2 Cor. iii. 18.

had before, and is filled, as it were, anew with the Holy Ghost; grace, wisdom, and fortitude, are increased in it, and it remains filled with extraordinary joy and inward satiety, enjoying after a manner even in this life, that of which David said:—" I shall be satisfied when Thy glory shall appear."(9)

3. The causes for which in this vision, St. Stephen saw the glory of God, and Jesus Christ Himself were *three*, and are those for which God shows similar favours to His elect.

i. The first was, to reward, even in this life, the *services* which he had done Him in this noble confession and testimony that he gave of Christ our Lord before that council, by which he exposed himself to the perils of death; for it is the property of Almighty God to requite extraordinary services with extraordinary favours, and to give even in this life an hundredfold for that which we have done for Him.(10) And from this I will encourage myself to serve Almighty God with great fervour, since the recompenses are ordinarily proportioned to the measure of the services, for it is to the servant that David says:—" Oh, taste and see that the Lord is sweet; blessed is the man that hopeth in Him." (11)

ii. The second cause was, to strengthen him in that fight and those labours which he encountered, and to give him great encouragement against those which were yet to come; for the sight of the reward wonderfully excites a man to labour, and the presence of the captain encourages the soldier; the certainty also of Divine succour makes us undergo dangers without fear. And so St. Stephen saw Christ, his captain and helper, at the right hand of Almighty God, not *sitting*, but *standing*, to give him to understand that He was present, beholding how he fought,

<hr>

(9) Ps. xvi. 15.   (10) Marc. x. 29 et 30.   (11) Ps. xxxiii. 9.

and was ready to help him in the combat, and immediately to descend to him and crown him.

Colloquy.—O most sweet Jesus, help my little faith, in order that I may see by it, though darkly, that which St. Stephen saw with such great clearness; lift my spirit up to heaven, that I may contemplate the *reward* which Thou promisest me, the *look* with which Thou beholdest me, and the *help* which Thou offerest me, that my heart being bound with this triple cord, there may be no labour or persecution, which can separate me from Thy sweet love.   Amen.

iii. The third cause was, that by this vision *he might be an eye-witness of the truths* and mysteries which he had preached, for now, having seen them, he bore witness of them anew, exclaiming with great fervour:—" Behold I see the heavens opened, and the Son of Man standing on the right hand of God :"(12) as if he had said, Behold, how true is that which I told you, for now I see it with my eyes; I now see the heavens open, for those who believe in Christ to enter.   I see the Son of Man, whom you have crucified, now, as He Himself told you He should be, " on the right hand of the power of God ;" do you likewise behold Him, and believe in Him. (13)

4. Hence I will gather, that Almighty God *does not* bestow these favours on His greatest servants, in order that they should enjoy them for themselves, *but that they should preach and publish His glory* for the good of souls, and incite them to dispose themselves to see that which they themselves have seen, and to believe and love that which they themselves have believed and loved.   Oh, if that people had believed the glorious St. Stephen, and had lifted up their eyes to heaven, in the same spirit in which he lifted up his, doubtless they would have been

(12) Act. vii. 55.   (13) Mat. xxvi. 64.

illuminated and filled with the divine Spirit, for Christ our Lord was ready to have given Him to them with great liberality.

Colloquy.—O most loving Jesus, grant that I may believe with a lively faith whatever Thou hast revealed to us, in order that by faith I may ascend to understanding, and from this to contemplation, and in the end may come to the clear vision of Thy Godhead, world without end. Amen.

POINT III.

"And they crying out with a loud voice, stopped their ears, and with one accord, *ran violently upon him*, and casting him forth without the city, *they stoned him:* and the witnesses laid down their garments at the feet of a young man whose name was Saul." (14)

1. Here is to be considered first, the way of God's dealing with His elect, permitting the *favours which He bestows on them to be an occasion of their persecution.* By which He gives us to understand, how greatly He esteems our sufferings for His sake, since He makes the very favours, which He shows us, the cause of our having to sustain still greater troubles; although the end and issue of all is an increase of glory. Thus it happened to the patriarch Joseph, to whom Almighty God showed in a dream "the sun and the moon, and eleven stars worshipping him;" (15) his narration of which dream to his brethren, inflamed still more the envy and hatred which they bore him, and was the occasion of their casting him into the pit, and selling him to the Midianites for a slave: and in the very same way God dealt with the glorious St. Stephen. Thus I am given to understand, that if I am much favoured by Almighty God, I ought to prepare myself for great troubles,

<hr>

(14) Act. vii. 56 et 57.   (15) Gen. xxxvii. 9.

which, perhaps, may take their beginning from the present favours.

Colloquy.—O most sweet Saviour, even the troubles which are suffered for the love of Thee, are to be accounted favours; direct my life as it pleases Thee, for I will esteem nothing for a greater favour, than duly to follow Thy providence, and what Thou shalt ordain.

2. Ponder secondly, the *martyrdom* of this Saint, full of ignominy and torment. For his enemies, instead of lifting up their eyes to heaven, to behold the glory of Jesus Christ, lifted up their voice against him, as against a blasphemer, and stopped their ears, that they might not hear what he said to them, and like lions, ran violently upon him, struck him with their fists and feet, and cast him with great fury out of the city, and *there stoned him.* But the glorious martyr went like a lamb, and received those stones as if they had been diamonds of inestimable value, without either turning or hiding his face, but as the church sings, " Lapides torrentis illi dulces fuerunt— the stones of the torrent were sweet to him ;"(16) because he felt a singular sweetness in enduring and suffering for his Master; and the glory of Jesus, which he contem- plated, made sweet to him, what he suffered on earth, and transported his spirit up to heaven.

Colloquy.—O most sweet Jesus, how sweet is it to suffer contempt and sorrow to him who contemplates how much of them Thou sufferedst, and the glory Thou hast obtained by them! Oh that Thou wouldst grant me to drink of the "torrent of" the "plea- sure"(17) of heaven, that the stones of the torrents of tribulation which afflict me on earth may be sweet to me! O my beloved, since Thou drawest "honey out

(16) S. Aug. in Soliloq. cap 22.   (17) Ps. xxxv. 9. Ps. xvii. 5.

of the rock, and oil out of the hardest stone,"(18) sweeten my troubles with the *honey* of Thy comforts, and with the "*oil* of" Thy "gladness," that I may glorify Thee in them, for ever and ever.   Amen.

POINT IV.

"*And they stoned Stephen*, invoking, and saying:—Lord Jesus, receive my spirit.   And falling on his knees he cried with a loud voice, saying, Lord lay not this sin to their charge.   And when he had said this, he fell asleep in the Lord.   And Saul was consenting to his death."(19)

1. Here is to be considered the *fervour with which this glorious martyr imitated Christ our Lord* the King of martyrs, in all respects in which he could imitate Him in his martyrdom, and now in particular, prayed twice as our Lord prayed; the first time *for himself*, recommending his spirit to Almighty God; the second time *for his enemies*, craving pardon for them, and so accomplishing that command of his master:—"pray for them that persecute and calumniate you." (20) This prayer St. Stephen made with great *reverence* and *fervour*, which he expressed outwardly by bowing his knees to the ground, and crying out with a loud voice; being desirous also to give up the ghost as Christ had done, with a strong cry.

Colloquy.—O faithful soldier, true imitator of thy captain, Jesus!   O invincible charity, O love "strong as death"(21) itself! Through thee Stephen esteems it a grace and benefit to die, and prays for those that slaughter him, and when they throw stones at him to take from him his temporal life, he throws darts of prayer up to heaven, to obtain for them eternal life. Grant me, O good Jesus, grace to imitate this Thy

(18) Deut. xxxii. 13. Ps. xliv. 8.
(19) Act. vii. 58., (20) Mat. v. 44. (21) Cant. viii. 6.

soldier, as he imitated Thee, loving those who hate me, and praying for those who persecute me. Amen.

2. Consider *the cause that St. Stephen prayed for himself standing*, and for his *enemies kneeling*, and with a *great cry*, and loud voice. Perhaps he did this, because when he prayed for himself, he was assured he should be heard, since he found not in himself any impediment in the way of those things which he craved in prayer; but when he prayed for his enemies, he knew the hardness and rebellion on their parts, which put an obstacle to his prayer; inflamed, therefore, with the fire of the Holy Ghost, he prayed for them with great reverence, and with greater earnestness, and a louder voice, that his prayer might be heard; as, indeed it was. For he obtained the conversion of the most notable persecutor there present, namely, Saul, who kept the clothes of those that stoned him, and had perhaps thrown some stones with his own hands, and may be considered to have thrown them all by the hands of his associates and companions. Hence I will make resolutions of praying fervently for my enemies, persuading myself that to pray for others is a means of being heard by God in the prayers which I make for myself, as was the case with Job, who prayed for his friends, although they had behaved towards him as enemies.

3. I will meditate on the *cause that St. Stephen* prayed, *first for himself*, commending his spirit to our Lord, and *then for his enemies;* whereas Christ our Lord did the contrary, praying first for His enemies, and afterwards, when He was ready to give up the ghost, commending His spirit to the Father. The cause was, because prayer ought to begin with that which is most necessary, and of obligation, especially when it is made in a time of very great tribulation and affliction. And as Christ our Lord had no need to pray for Himself, but all we sinners, and

especially those that crucified Him, stood in extreme need of His praying for us, lest we should be drowned in the depth of hell; hence it was that out of His inward charity He prayed first for His enemies: but St. Stephen, and other just men, stand in need of praying for themselves, especially at the point of death, where the obligation is greater in proportion to the greatness of the danger, and charity began first in St. Stephen, at that which was a matter of obligation, and afterwards extended itself to that which was rather a sign of his perfection. In both these Christ our Lord would have us imitate the saint, but yet in the order here observed, for the law of charity obliges us to secure our own salvation first, and then that of others.

Colloquy.—O most sweet Jesus, receive my spirit, together with the spirits of all the faithful, both in life and death, and take it under Thy protection, so that, having served Thee on earth, I may afterwards enjoy Thee in heaven. Amen.

4. Consider, 'these two prayers ended, St. Stephen "*fell asleep*" in our Lord. To *die in our Lord* is to die in Jesus Christ, united to Him in lively faith and charity, as the holy confessors die, or to die for the confession of Christ, as the martyrs die; and both deaths are very happy; for, "precious in the sight of the Lord is the death of His saints;" and, as a voice from heaven said to St. John:—"Blessed are the dead who die in the Lord. From henceforth, now, says the Spirit, that they may rest from their labours, for their works follow them."(22) As if He had said, Those who die in our Lord, may be called blessed immediately upon their death, for now, since the death of Christ, the gates of heaven are open to them at once, unless perchance there is something

(22) Ps. cxv. 15. Apoc. xiv. 13.

in them that needs to be purged, and the Holy Ghost, with which they are filled, ordains their death to be the end of their labours, and the beginning of their everlasting rest; for the works which they did during life, and with which they prepared themselves for death, shall with great honour accompany them even to heaven. Such was the death of the glorious St. Stephen, who died in Christ, and for Christ; who, from heaven itself, from whence He had appeared to him in his combat, came now to him with thousands of angels to celebrate his victory; and he, who a little before was proclaimed by men to be a blasphemer and a sinner, is now proclaimed by angels to be a saint; and he who was stoned with stones of torment, is now crowned with precious stones, and receives the crown which his name of St. Stephen signified. He ascended accompanied by the splendour of his good works, for which he was honoured and praised by Christ our Lord, before His Father, and placed on a throne very high among the Seraphim, where he clearly beholds the divine essence by the light of glory, and drinks even to full satiety of the abundant river of delights, without any fear of ever losing them.

Colloquy.—O happy labours, whose end is everlasting rest! O sweet stones, which made so precious a crown! O precious death, that art the beginning of so eternal and glorious a life! Dear Lord, " let my soul die the death of the just," and let my life be such as may deserve such a death; and give me grace so to dispose myself for it, that " my last end be like to them,"(23) that I may ascend to enjoy Thee, accompanied by the splendour of good works, and great troubles suffered for justice' sake, to Thy greater glory. Amen.

(23) Num. xxiii. 10.

MEDITATION XXIX.

The conversion of St. Paul succeeded the martyrdom of
St. Stephen, whom he likewise succeeded in the office of
preaching Jesus Christ; for the contrivances of men cannot prevail against Almighty God, and if they take away
one preacher who makes war against their vices, the Holy
Ghost will raise another to carry it on still more vigorously,
as He did St. Paul.

POINT I.

" And Saul yet breathing out threatenings and slaughter
against the disciples of the Lord, went to the high priest,
and asked of him letters to Damascus to the synagogues;
that if he found any men and women of this way, he might
bring them bound to Jerusalem."(1)

1. For foundation of this meditation is to be considered
how great a sinner Saul was, who even from his youth conceived in his heart a detestation of Christ our Lord, and of
His holy law, supposing out of ignorance and erroneous
zeal that he pleased God by persecuting Him. And hence
it was that he was present at the death of St. Stephen,
kept the garments of those that stoned him, and consented
to his death, and was delighted to see him stoned who had
defended the faith of Christ with so great fervour. And
his hatred so increased continually, that the Evangelist St.
Luke says, that " Saul made havoc of the Church, entering
in from house to house, and dragging away men and women,
committed them to prison."(2) So that, being of the tribe
of Bejamin, he answered to that which Jacob foretold:—

(1) Act. ix. 1.   (2) Act. viii. 3.

"Benjamin a ravening wolf, in the morning shall eat the prey, and in the evening shall divide the spoil;"(3) for in the morning of his youth he persecuted Christ's sheep, like a wolf all the day, morning and evening, even to death. And thinking it little to persecute those who were in Jerusalem, he demanded authority from the chief priests to go to Damascus, and to bring bound all those who there followed Christ our Lord, with the intention of destroying them; fulfilling that which David said:—"The pride of them that hate Thee ascendeth continually."(4)

2. Then I will consider the *causes* for which *Christ our Lord permitted this*.

i. The first was, because He intended to make him a great Saint, and to erect in him a tower of great perfection, having first laid very deep the foundations of profound humility, which are drawn from the knowledge of past sins. This was fully accomplished in him; and accordingly, when he had become the apostle St. Paul, he said of himself:—"Who before was a blasphemer and a persecutor, *and contumelious*,"(5) against Christ; and again:—" I am the least of the apostles, who am not worthy to be called an apostle, because I persecuted the Church of God."(6) From his example I will learn to draw great profit from the sins I have committed, since for this cause the Holy Ghost says:—" Better is the iniquity of a man, than a woman doing a good turn;"(7) for fervent men are wont to draw strong motives from the thought of their sins to increase in virtues, especially in humility towards themselves, and in charity towards God, who forgave them: and on the contrary, the lukewarm and remiss draw vanity and presumption from their good works.

<hr>

(3) Gen. xlix. 27.

(4) Ps. lxxiii. 23.   (5) 1 Tim. i. 13.   (6) 1 Cor. xv. 9.

(7) Ecclus. xlii. 14.

ii. The second cause was in order *that Christ might show in Saul the inestimable riches of His grace*, and His infinite virtues and perfections. He showed His *charity* in loving one who so much abhorred Him ; His *goodness*, in calling one who fled away from Him ; His *omnipotence* in softening a heart so greatly hardened ; His *patience* in bearing with and waiting for one who so greatly persecuted Him ; His *mercy* in admitting him to penance, and delivering him from so many miseries; and finally, the efficacy of His *grace*, in filling with such excellent virtues one who was so full of abominable vices. Therefore, the same holy apostle writes:—" For this cause have I obtained mercy, that in me first Christ Jesus might show forth all patience for the information of them that shall believe in Him to life everlasting:"(8) and as He showed in Saul more than in other sinners, " all" His *" patience,"* that is to say, His most perfect patience ; so also He showed His *charity, goodness, mercy, liberality*, and *omnipotence*. And as, whilst He lived on earth, He showed these virtues towards Mary Magdalene, Matthew, Zaccheus, and other sinners ; so afterwards when He had ascended to heaven, He showed them .principally towards Saul ; in order that we might understand that He is always the same in love towards sinners, and in readiness to do them good, and therefore that we may always trust to obtain pardon of our sins, and deliverance from our sinful habits, since neither *charity, goodness, mercy*, nor *power* are wanting to Him to perform this for us.

iii. The third cause was in order that *Saul might be to us at once, both a warning and an example ;*—a *warning* to become more wary from his fall, and not suffer ourselves to be led by the boiling violence of our nature, or by the impulses of indiscreet zeal, or by furious anger, cloked with the title of religion; for these will easily throw us down into innumerable sins, adding new and greater sins to those already committed: and on the other hand, an example, if we fall into such sins, that we should endeavour to turn to Almighty God, after the pattern of his conversion and change of life, which was one of the most admirable that Christ wrought for our instruction, and ought to be meditated and pondered in this spirit.

POINT II.

" And as he went on his journey, it came to pass that he drew nigh to Damascus, *and suddenly a light from heaven shined round about him.* And falling on the ground, he heard a voice saying to him:—*Saul, Saul, why persecutest thou me ?*" (9)

1. Here is to be considered first, the *infinite charity* of Christ our Lord, who sitting on His heavenly throne upon the right hand of the Father, did not disdain to come down to earth, *and to appear to His very persecutor,* in the same manner that after His Resurrection He appeared to St. Peter, and St. James, and others. And thus the same St. Paul testifies :—" And last of all, He was seen also by me, as by one born out of due time;" as if he had said: After that Christ had made all His other appearances, last of all He appeared to me, as to a sort of monster, born unnaturally and out of season; for " *I am the least of the apostles.*" (10) And this appearance was a greater instance of the charity of Christ than the others were ; for the others were made to His friends, and to the disciples who sought Him and desired to see Him ; but this was made to His enemy who persecuted Him, and desired to root out His name, and the name of all His disciples. In this appearance, this good pastor accomplished

(9) Act. ix. 3.   (10) 1 Cor. xv. 8.

that which He had before spoken of Himself; for "leaving the ninety-nine sheep in the wilderness,"(11) He descended in person to seek this lost sheep, with the very same love with which He sought the others. O fire of infinite charity, which burning in the heart of Jesus Christ, canst not be hid, but daily castest forth new sparks, to inflame all with thy fervent love! It was great love, to suffer Thyself to be found by those who sought Thee not, and openly to appear to those who did not enquire after Thee: (12) but this day Thou goest very much farther, appearing to him that hated Thee, and showing Thyself to him who with unspeakable fury persecuted Thee; and instead of encompassing him with fire, to consume his body, Thou dost surround him with light to convert his soul.

Colloquy.—I give Thee thanks, O most loving Jesus, for the evident tokens which Thou givest of Thy love; illuminate, I beseech Thee, my blinded soul, with such a knowledge of them, that I may be made partaker of them.　Amen.

2. I will consider secondly, the *properties of the heavenly light* which shone round about Saul, by which are represented the properties of the inward light, which God, by the visitation of His grace, infused into sinners, that they may be converted.

i. The first is, that it came *on a sudden*, like lightning, when Saul least expected, and least deserved it; for our Lord is wont to send these visitations when we are most forgetful of them, and even when for our hardness, we are most unworthy of them.

Colloquy.—O Almighty God, who in Thy hands hidest the light, and afterwards commandest it to come again, and showest Thy "friend concerning it, that it

<hr>

(11) Luc. xv. 14.　　　　　　(12) Isa. lxv. 1, Rom. x. 20.

is his possession, and that he may come up to it:"(13)
what return shall we make Thee for the infinite charity which Thou showest in giving some part of it to
Thine enemies, making it suddenly to shine, to convert them into friends; command it, Lord, to shine
upon me, and so to enlighten the inmost parts of my
heart, that it may detach it from that which is earthly
and transfer it to that which is heavenly and eternal.
Amen.

ii. The second property was, that it *caused Saul to stop*
when he approached *Damascus*, which word is interpreted
blood, where he desired to execute his *bloody* purposes,
and prostrated him upon the ground, humbling his pride,
and stopping the current of his anger; so that although
with other sinners God our Lord, as He speaks by the
prophet Osee, hedges in their " way with thorns," (14)
drawing them to Himself with a certain violence, and
by calamities and miseries: yet He did not hedge in the
way of Saul with thorns and calamities, but with a light
which shone about him, and drew him with sweetness and
gentleness to Himself. And the same apostle relating his
own conversion, takes notice that it was " at mid-day,"
that that abundant light shone round about him; (15)
intimating by this, that when his fury had reached its full
height of malice and pride, then it was that Christ our
Lord arrested him. And, as Christ ascended the cross
in the middle of the day, to shew the fervour of the love
which He bore us: even so He was pleased to come at mid-
day to convert Saul, and to surround him in this manner
with His abundant light; declaring thus the particular
love which He bore to him, according to that which the
apostle says of himself:—" I live in the faith of the Son
of God who loved me, and delivered Himself for me." (16)

(13) Job. xxxvi. 32.

(14) Ose. ii. 6.

(15) Act. xxii. 6.

(16) Gal. ii. 20.

Where it appears that it is the property of divine grace to stop the ways of sinners, and cause them to cease from their sins, and not proceed any further in their wicked purposes, nor put them into execution: but that when those evil resolutions have deep roots, it is needful that the light be more abundant in order to convert them.

Colloquy.—O happy Saul, about whom there shone so abundant a light, well mayest thou say on this occasion that which David said :—" Unless the Lord had been my helper, my soul had almost dwelt in hell;" (17) for that journey which thou madest to Damascus would have quickly drowned thee in the bottom of hell, if our Lord had not hindered it. Beseech Him, therefore, who stopped thy course, to give me so great a light as to stop mine also, humbling my pride, bridling my anger, and prostrating me upon the ground, in order that I may be brought to myself, and be wholly converted to Almighty God. O God of my soul, although Thou hedge in my ways with thorns, yet it is needful that Thou shouldst encompass them also with Thy heavenly light, in order that I may be converted to Thee; O dear Lord, let not this second hedge be wanting to me, lest I fail perfectly. Amen.

iii. The third property was, that the light which surrounded Saul, *enlightened all parts, above him, beneath him, and on either side of him*, so that he saw nothing of any kind but by means of it; to signify that heavenly light shines about a man on every side, so that he sees nothing but with it and by it, and contemplates heavenly things without looking at all to earthly things except in order to eternal.

Colloquy.—O " true light, which enlightens every

<hr>

(17) Ps. xciii. 17.

man that comes into this world," (18) surround me with Thy light, in order that I may not behold with vain satisfaction the things that are earthly, but may look only to those which are heavenly. Amen.

3. Lastly are to be considered the *words* which Christ our Lord spake to Saul, in which His love appears in many ways.

i. For, first intending to reprove Saul, He did not do it with sharp or bitter words, but with *great love and kindness ;* for He called him twice—" Saul, Saul," in sign that He loved him and that He knew him by his proper name, and to stir him up the more, and to make him the more attentive to that which He was about to say to him. And He said to him,—" Why dost thou persecute me? " As if He had said,—What cause hast thou to persecute me? Declare it to me and I will satisfy thee ; and if thou hast none, why dost thou persecute me without a cause?

Colloquy.—O immense love of our Creator, who vouchsafes to enter into reckoning with so worthless a creature, and to reason with him, and ask him why he persecutes Him, when, if He would, He could with one word annihilate him !

ii. He likewise showed His *love* in taking the persecution of His disciples for *His own ;* and because Saul persecuted them, Christ complained of his persecuting Him. And He who on the cross did not complain of those who persecuted Him in His own person, now complains of being persecuted in those that are His, and grieves more for their afflictions than for His own.

Colloquy.—Who would not love Thee, O most loving Jesus, since Thou so lovest those who love Thee?

<hr>

(18) Joan. i. 9.

Who will dare to persecute Thy servants, since to persecute them is to persecute Thee ?

iii. Hence I will gather that it is the property of the *Holy Spirit* when He speaks to the Heart of a sinner by inspirations, and accompanies them *with heavenly light*, to *reprove* the evil of which he is guilty, and thus put him to confusion, and to say to him inwardly,—" *Man, man, why dost thou persecute me ?*"

Colloquy.—O my soul, if thou knowest who it is that speaks to thee, and who it is that is persecuted by thee, and who thou art thyself who persecutest Him, and the cause and reason, or rather unreasonableness, of thus persecuting Him with thy sins, without doubt thou wouldst be ashamed of what thou art doing, and wouldst cease to persecute Him, whom thou oughtest rather to serve and follow.

These three things Christ our Lord discovered to Saul, as we shall presently see.

POINT III.

" Saul said, Who art Thou, Lord?   And He:—I am Jesus, whom Thou persecutest ; it is hard for thee to kick against the goad."(19)

1. Here is to be considered the *manner in which* Christ our Lord illuminated Saul with His divine light, not all at once, but *by degrees*, inspiring him to ask certain questions, and returning him answers to them ; in which, as in the seed, all Christian perfection lies hid.   First, our Lord by His heavenly light infused into him a great desire to know *who it was that spake to him ;* for it is the property of those that hold intercourse with Almighty God, and have received some light from Him, immediately to desire with great fervour to know more ; for " this is eternal life,"

(19) Act. ix. 5.

to know " the only true God, and Jesus Christ, whom"
He has sent.   With this desire, therefore, Saul enquired :—
" Who art Thou, Lord?"   As if he had said :—" Discover
o me plainly who Thou art, that I may know whom I
persecute, and may desist from the evil which I am com-
mitting."   And he called Him *Lord*, out of great respect
and reverence for the majesty of Him that had spoken to
him.

2. Christ our Lord, replying to this question, answered
to more than was asked of Him, for He declared both *who
the persecuted was*, and *who the persecutor*, saying :—" I am
Jesus of Nazareth, whom thou persecutest."   As if He
had said :—" Desirest thou to know who I am ?—I am
Jesus, even the *Saviour* of him who is offending and persecuting me.   And wilt thou know who thou art?—Thou
art the *persecutor* of the same Saviour, who desires to
save and sanctify thee."   Where we see that it is the
property of Christ our Lord to teach us at the same time
by His heavenly light, both what God is, and what man
is ; what Jesus is towards a sinner, and what the sinner is
towards Jesus ; and these two pieces of knowledge go together and help one another ; for, by comparing the one
with the other, the excellency, goodness, and charity of
God our Saviour ; as also the baseness, wickedness, and ingratitude of the sinner, are made more apparent.   For
whither can any one's goodness ascend higher, than to be
the saviour of him who persecutes him ?   And whither
can any one's malice extend further, than to the persecutor of him that has saved him?

3. These two things *I ought to make my special study*
as the apostle St Paul did during his whole life ; for these
words were so deeply impressed upon him, that he always
had in his heart and on his tongue, his Saviour Jesus,
preaching the excellency of His Person, the work which

He effected of our redemption, the motive which moved Him to undertake it, the price that it cost Him, and the inestimable riches which He purchased for us. To these he joined the consideration of his own baseness and misery, together with the ingratitude and malice of offending so noble a Saviour, who of pure mercy redeemed him at the price of His own precious blood, and gained for him infinite treasures of grace and glory.

Colloquy.—O most loving Jesus, let me know Thee, and know myself: let me know myself, that I may abhor and despise myself, and may chastise in myself the sins which I have committed against Thee; let me know Thee, that I may love and praise Thee, obey and serve Thee, for the innumerable benefits which I have received from Thee. O glorious apostle, obtain for me of thy beloved some small ray of celestial light, that I may know what Jesus has been and is towards me; and what I have been, and still am towards Him, that, being enlightened with His light, I may now make a new beginning, loving what I before hated, and hating what before I loved, imitating Thee as Thou didst imitate Christ our Saviour.(20) Amen.

4. "It is hard for thee to kick against the goad:" that is to say, as he who kicks against the goad does not hurt the goad, but hurts himself, and the more violently he drives in the goad the greater is the wound that he gives himself: just so, he who resists God and the inward goad by which He urges us to serve Him, does not at all hurt God, but hurts himself, and the more he resists, the greater is the injury that he receives.

Colloquy.—O my soul, consider what thou dost when thou resistest the will of Almighty God and His holy inspiration! Although it is true that thou in-

(20) 1 Cor. xi. 1.

sultest Him very greatly, yet thou dost not really hurt His Person, but dost very seriously hurt thyself; for by this resistance thou dost make thyself all bloody, wounding thyself with sins, and bringing down upon thyself terrible pains. Enter, therefore, into thyself, and follow the sweet goading of His inspiration, doing that which He suggests to thee, and accomplishing that which He commands thee; for as it is a hard thing to resist Him, so it is a sweet thing to obey Him.

POINT IV.

' "And he, trembling and astonished said:—*Lord, what wilt Thou have me to do?* And the Lord said to him, *Arise and go into the city, and there it shall be told thee what thou must do.*" (21)

1. Here is to be considered first, this *trembling of body and this astonishment or wondering of soul*, which Saul felt, in consequence of what he had seen and heard:—*trembling* for the insults he had offered to so great a Lord,--and wondering and *astonished* as well at his own ignorance and temerity, as at the bounty and mercy with which God had not only borne with him, but had even come from heaven to call him, and to discover to him his error. All these effects, the light of heaven is wont to produce in the soul of the sinner, about whom it shines according to that expression of the prophet David:— " Thy lightnings enlightened the world; the earth shook and trembled."(22) For lightnings are divine inspirations by which the earthly sinner sees many things which he did not see before; he sees the grievousness of his sin, and the punishment he has deserved; the goodness of God, which has waited for him, and the favours He has done him. And seeing these and other things, he is afraid, and

(21) Act. ix. 6.   (22) Ps. lxxvi. 19.

trembles, and is wholly astonished, and as it were, beside himself with wonder and amazement.

Colloquy.—O eternal God, send these flashes of light into the land of unbelievers, and upon the souls of all sinners, that they may see and tremble, and depart out of their place, leaving their sins to serve Thee with loyalty.   Amen.

2. Next is to be considered, that *second question* that Saul asked, to which he was moved by an abundance of inward light, and by the perfect obedience and subjection, with which he submitted himself to Jesus Christ:—" *Lord, what wilt Thou have me to do ?*"   As if he had said:—" Behold here I am, ready to do and to suffer for Thee whatever Thou wilt, as well in punishment of my past sins, as in gratitude for present benefits : command and ordain what it pleaseth Thee, for I am ready to obey Thee.   O 'change of the right hand of the most High!' " (23)   O efficacy of the light of heaven !   Who but Almighty God could so suddenly effect such an alteration !   What other light than that of heaven, could in so short a time discover so many delusions?   He who before abhorred Christ now loves Him; he who accounted Him a breaker of the law, now accounts Him a giver of the law, whom he must obey before all; (24) he who persecuted Him now offers to follow Him and to preach Him, although he be persecuted for it Himself; and he who before obstinately followed his own judgment and will, now renounces them, and resigns his will to God's.

Colloquy.—Grant me grace, O good Jesus, always to say to Thee and to those who are in Thy place with perfect resignation :—*Lord, what wilt Thou have me to do?*"   For my desire is to do what Thou

(23) Ps. lxxvi. 11.   (24) S. Th. 2, 2, q. cxiii. art. 10.

desirest, and what Thou shalt command me by them. I do not desire Thee to say to me that which Thou saidst to a certain blind man in condescension to his frailty: "What wilt thou that I do to thee?" (25) Treat me not, I pray Thee, as one so imperfect, nor condescend to my desire; for it is not meet that I should draw Thy will to mine, but that mine should follow Thine.

3. Thirdly, I will ponder the *answer of Christ our Lord*, who would not tell him *in the way*, and as it were *in passing*, the things which he was to do, but was pleased to send him " *to the city*," there to tell him more at leisure. For God will not have things of such great importance as our salvation and His glory, listened to merely in passing. And although in every place and time, on a sudden and in a moment, He drops the light of His grace, as one that drops seed into the earth, yet that it may bring forth in due season, He chooses a suitable place and time, as we shall see below. He did with Saul.

4. Lastly, I will ponder how, as St. Luke says,—" The men who went in company with him, stood amazed, hearing indeed a voice, but seeing no man." (26) Where we are reminded of the *height and depth of the divine judments* in the calling of sinners. Saul was on his way with other wicked men, persecutors of Christ like himself, and he himself the worst amongst them all, yet notwithstanding this, God our Lord called him alone efficaciously on this occasion, and converted him to His faith and admitted him into His grace and friendship, leaving the others; in order that on the one hand we might extol His goodness in him whom He elected, and on the other hand might tremble at His justice in those whom He rejected; especially as he who was called was only this one Saul, but those who

<hr>

(25) Luc. xviii. 41.   (26) Act. ix. 7.

were rejected were many, and also his companions. But in both these particulars we ought to reverence the judgments of God, and to repress the complaints which rise up against Him in our erroneous judgment, by saying with the same apostle :—" O man, who art thou that repliest against God? Shall the thing formed, say to him that formed it, Why hast thou made me thus? Or hath not the potter power over the clay, of the same lump to make one vessel unto honour, and another unto dishonour?" (27) "Oh the depth of the riches of the wisdom, and of the knowledge of God! How incomprehensible are His judgments and how unsearchable are His ways! For who hath known the mind of our Lord? Or who has been His counsellor? Or who hath first given to Him, and recompense shall be made for him? For, of Him, and by Him, and in Him, are all things : to Him be glory for ever, Amen." (28)

5. Hence it came to pass, that these companions of Saul heard his voice, and what he said, and likewise saw some part of the outward splendour that shone about him ; but as the same apostle says :—" They saw indeed the light, *but they heard not the voice of Him that spoke;*" (29) that is, they did not hear the *words* spoken, either those words :—" Saul, Saul, why persecutest thou me?" or those others ;—" I am Jesus of Nazareth, whom thou persecutest; it is hard for thee to kick against the goad." So that although they were surprised to see Saul prostrate on the ground, and to hear him speak such things, yet they were not changed or converted at that time, although what they now witnessed may have led to their conversion afterwards, as it may well be thought that it did with some of them after the example of him, whom

(27) Rom. ix. 20.   (28) Rom. xi. 33.

(29) Act. xxii. 9.

they considered their captain when they heard him relate more distinctly what had happened to him in this journey.

MEDITATION XXX.

ON THAT WHICH HAPPENED TO SAUL IN THOSE THREE DAYS AFTER THIS APPEARANCE, AND OF THE FULNESS OF THE HOLY GHOST GIVEN TO HIM.

POINT I.

" And Saul arose from the ground, *and when his eyes were opened he saw nothing.* But they, leading him by the hands, brought him to Damascus." (1)

1. Saul, during the whole time that this vision and the colloquies with Christ lasted, *remained prostrate on the earth,* on which the light of heaven had cast him down, in order that he might be humbled, and might with more reverence see and hear what Christ our Lord said to him. At the same time that he fell to the ground his body was also weakened and enfeebled, as was the case with Daniel, (2) and is usually the case in such visions; to signify that the sight of the glorious things of Almighty God, enfeebles the strength of the flesh. And as Jacob seeing God became lame of one foot, (3) so he, who by contemplation beholds things eternal, becomes lame in the love of things temporal.

Colloquy.—O eternal God, send down the beams of Thy light upon my spirit, so as to weaken the passions of my furious flesh : prostrate me by humility even to the abyss of my own dust and nothingness, in order that I may be worthy to arise and contemplate the abyss of Thy divinity and humanity. Amen.

(1) Act. ix. 6. et xxii. 11.   (2) Dan. x. 8.   (3) Gen. xxxii. 31.

2. Saul, hearing the commandment of Christ our Lord, who said to him, "*Surge,—Arise,*" immediately *arose* like a true son of obedience, and *began to accomplish what he had purposed,* when he said :—" Lord, what wilt Thou have me to do?"   Nor did he arise from the earth with his body only, but also spiritually, arising and going forth out of the filth and error of his sins, awaking out of the sleep of death in which he lay, and rising again to a new life, leaving the earthly affections which before had fastened his heart to the earth.   And thus the apostle followed the counsel which he himself has given us in these words :— " Rise, thou that sleepest, and arise from the dead, and Christ shall enlighten thee." (4)

Colloquy.—O my soul, hear this counsel of the apostle, taken out of the book of his own experience : arise from the earth, to which thou art fallen by sin, awake from the sleep in which thou liest asleep out of slothfulness : raise thyself up to a new life, casting off the works of death; and Christ our Lord will enlighten thee with the light of His grace, in order that thou mayest hereafter see Him in the light of His glory.

3. Saul, though his eyes were open, yet *could not see,* which he himself declares to have proceeded from the brightness of the light which shone round about him ; by which is intimated that the light of heaven opens the eyes of the soul, and shuts the eyes of the body; for so great is the value that it attaches to things eternal, that it takes away the desire of seeing things temporal.   And thus those who are given to contemplation, although they have bodily eyes, yet do not see, because they do not use them out of curiosity to behold vain things, such as might disturb the sight of the soul.

<hr>

(4) Ephes. v. 14.

Colloquy.—O heavenly light, come and enlighten my inward eyes, and make them see their Creator with such clearness, that the outward eyes may be shut, and not idly cast upon creatures. O my soul, close and mortify the sight of the body, that God may clear thy spiritual sight. Amen.

POINT II.

"*And he was there three days without sight, and he did neither eat nor drink.*"(5)

1. Christ our Lord *detained Saul those three days in the city*, deferring his baptism and his being filled with the Holy Ghost, in order that in the meantime he might be catechised and well instructed in the mysteries of the faith of the most holy Trinity, and might dispose himself to receive the baptism, which is given in the name of the three divine Persons. And as Christ our Lord was *three days* in the *sepulchre* before He arose gloriously : so He would have His apostle remain *three days* in the *sepulchre* of contemplation, before he arose to baptism. The other apostles He caused to wait ten days in the city of Jerusalem for the coming of the Holy Ghost, but Saul no more than three, intending to prepare this vessel at once for Him in his office.

2. Consider the *exercises* which Saul practised during these three days, in order to imitate him as far as he is imitable.—i. In all this time he "*saw nothing*" with his bodily eyes, for beside the reason already alleged, the inward sight of his soul took away the outward sight of his body. —ii. He *neither ate nor drank*, because his spiritual joy and the suspension of his soul's powers, made him quite forget all bodily food.—iii. He *prayed continually*, as our Lord said to Ananias:—"Ecce enim orat." " For behold he prayeth."(6) With these exercises he disposed himself

<hr>

(5) Act. ix. 9.   (6) Act. ix 11.

to receive baptism and apostleship; and from his example I am to learn that these three things, restraint of the sight, rigour in fasting, and continuance in praying, dispose a man to obtain of our Lord great gifts and graces; and they are things which greatly help one another; for the restraint of the eyes and the fasting of the body tend greatly to the perfection of prayer, and again, prayer makes restraint of the eyes and fasting exceedingly sweet.

3. Consider *what great favours and graces Christ our Redeemer bestowed on Saul* in these three days, performing towards him the office of a master invisible, as He had done to the other apostles visible. For in this time He revealed and made known to him all the mysteries of our holy faith, with most abundant light from heaven, in order that he might preach them to all nations. This may be gathered from those sweet words of Ananias to him, related by the apostle:—" The God of our fathers hath pre-ordained thee, that thou shouldst know His will, and see the Just One, and shouldst hear the voice from His mouth: for thou shalt be His witness to all men of those things which thou hast seen and heard."(7)   In these three days, therefore, Almighty God revealed to him His holy will; he saw Christ and His mysteries, and from His own mouth learned His doctrine, that so he might be a witness of those things which he had both seen and heard of the same Saviour, and therefore he said to the Galatians of the Gospel which he preached:—" Neither did I receive it of man, nor did I learn it; but by the revelation of Jesus Christ."(8)

Colloquy.—O happy man, to whom God, out of His pure mercy, vouchsafed so great a grace! O God of my soul, grant me likewise grace to know Thy will, and to see with the eyes of a lively faith the just One,

(7) Act. xxii. 14.   (8) Gal. i. 12.

Jesus Christ my Lord, and hear His words, which He shall speak to my heart, that so I may become Thy witness, and may proclaim Thy mighty works in the manner that I have believed and tasted them, fulfilling in all things Thy most holy will.   Amen.

4. Some holy fathers say that in these three days happened that *vision* and stupendous *revelation* which St. Paul relates to have been given to himself, saying, that he was "*rapt even to the third heaven*," and "*caught up into Paradise*," and there heard such secret words, as it is not lawful for imperfect man to utter.   And then, also, according to the opinion of St. Augustine and St. Thomas, he clearly saw the divine essence.(9)   But however this may be, during these three days our Lord trained him in a wonderful manner, and gave him great raptures, drawing him out of himself, and lifting him up above all things created, even to the knowledge of the most sublime mysteries of the third and highest heaven, and of the most holy Trinity, communicating to him great secrets, and placing him in the paradise of divine light, where he fell into great ecstasies and excesses of love, so that when he returned again to himself, he could truly say:—"I live now, not I; but Christ liveth in me."(10)

Colloquy.—I give Thee thanks, O most sweet Jesus, for the infinite charity and liberality which Thou showedst towards so great a sinner, and Thy persecutor, on whom Thou didst bestow greater favours than on others who never offended Thee, showing in this sinner that "where sin abounded, grace did more abound,"(11) and to this son who had been so prodigal, and had so grievously offended Thee, Thou wast pleased to be still more prodigal, if it be lawful so to

(9) S. Th. in Cor. q. clxxv.   2 Cor. xii. 2.
(10) Gal. ii. 20.   (11) Rom. v. 20.

speak, in showing him mercy, for Thou not only wentest forth to meet him, but after a manner didst compel and force him to enter into Thy house; and there Thou didst adorn him with such garments, and feast him with such delicious banquets, that his elder brethren have cause to envy him with an holy envy. Since, then, Thy mercy is not diminished, force my rebellious will, I beseech Thee, to enter into Thy house; draw it out of itself, and attract it forcibly to Thee, and so transfer it into Thyself, that henceforth I may not live, but Thou mayest live in me everlastingly.   Amen.

5. Ponder, lastly, the *sweetness of Christ our Lord's manner of dealing with Saul;* for while he was at prayer, He revealed to him what was to happen to him for his cure, showing him in a vision impressed on his imagination, "a man named Ananias, coming in and putting his hands upon him, that he might receive his sight,"(12) as we shall shortly see; by which it is intimated that in *prayer* Almighty God is wont to suggest to us the means of our spiritual cure, and of our salvation and perfection.

POINT III.

"Now there was a certain disciple at Damascus, named Ananias: and the Lord said to him in a vision—Ananias! And he said, Behold, I am here, Lord.   And the Lord said to him: *Arise and go into the street that is called Strait and seek in the house of Judas, one named Saul of Tarsus.* For behold he prayeth."(13)

1. Here is to be considered first, *the various methods which Christ employs in revealing and manifesting His will to His servants.* For, to some He appears and calls them whilst they are awake, as He called Saul, taking from

<hr>

(12) Act. ix. 12.   (13) Act. ix. 10.

them their outward senses, that they may be an impediment to the inward sight.—To others He appears in their *sleep*, making use of the quietness of the senses at that time, as He called Jacob and Samuel, (14) and as it seems that He now called Ananias. Thus He intends to instruct us, that in every place and time, waking and sleeping, in church and in bed, we ought to be so recollected and composed, as to be capable of the divine inspirations, and of the favours and gifts of Almighty God, and to be able to say :—The " night shall be my light in my pleasures ;" and " I sleep, and my heart watches ;" (15) for while the body sleeps, God, who is our love, will watch within us, and make our spirit watch.

2. I will ponder the mystery contained in the *names* which are here employed to represent the marvellous works which Christ wrought in Saul.—For the street where Saul remained, was called *Rectus*, that is to say, " *straight :*" to signify that Saul now walked in *straight* and *right* ways, leading to eternal life. The house or lodging where he was belonged to a man who was called *Judas*, which means *confession and praise ;* to signify that Saul exercised himself in the humble *confession* of his sins, and in craving pardon for them, and in the *praise* of Almighty God for such manifold benefits as He had done him.—He who was commanded to seek him out, was named *Ananias*, which is interpreted, " *Cloud of our Lord*," to signify the office of such as are preachers, who, like clouds, rain down their doctrine upon the faithful, and are transported very readily wherever the wind of divine inspiration impels them : and thus, as soon as Ananias had heard the voice of Jesus Christ, he said : " Ecce, ego Domine," " Behold, I am here, Lord ;" " speak,

(14) Gen. xxxi. 11. 1 Reg. iii. 4.
(15) Ps. cxxxviii. 11. Cant. v. 2.

Lord, for Thy servant heareth;"(16) command what Thou pleasest, for I am ready to go wherever Thou shalt send me.

3. But above all, is to be pondered, the great *charity of Christ* our Lord, who did not tell Saul to seek out Ananias, but commanded *Ananias to arise and go and seek out Saul,* like the physician who goes to visit him that is sick. For as Christ came from the throne of His heavenly habitation to seek out this sinner, so He would have Ananias and His other ministers go out of their houses and forsake their own rest to seek sinners, and enter into their houses, and assist them in the business of their salvation.

Colloquy.—I give Thee thanks, O most sweet Jesus, for all the means which Thou employest for the justification of sinners; give me, Lord, I beseech Thee, the spirit of prompt obedience, which Thou gavest Ananias, and the true spirit of praise and confession, which Thou gavest Saul; take from me all slothfulness and remissness, that I may with fervour attend to the good of souls, whom Thou hast redeemed with Thy precious blood. Amen.

POINT IV.

"But Ananias answered;—Lord, I have heard by many of this man, how much evil he has done to Thy saints in Jerusalem; and here he has authority from the chief priests to bind all that invoke Thy name. And the Lord said to him, Go thy way, for this man is to me a vessel of election, to carry my name before the Gentiles, and kings, and the children of Israel. For I will show him how great things he must suffer for my name's sake." (17)

1. Here is to be considered first, how mistaken the judgments of men are, and *how easily they deceive themselves*

(16) 2 Reg. iii. 10.   (17) Act. ix. 13.

in their suspicions, especially when they are overtaken by worldly fear; for so Ananias, because of what he had heard of Saul, suspected that he was still a persecutor of Christ, as he used to be; and although Christ our Redeemer told him that he prayed, yet he could not be persuaded that he was changed. Whence I will resolve not to judge rashly of my neighbours, especially when I have my knowledge of them only upon hearsay: since he who yesterday was evil, may to-day become good, Almighty God changing his heart by His holy grace: and as I have observed the marks of guilt, to suspect evil of my neighbour, so I ought to observe with more care the signs of his change, in order to judge well of him.

Although Ananias showed himself very ready to obey Christ our Lord when He called him, yet from this human fear he proposed the difficulty that he felt in going to the house of a persecutor, and entering within the gates of one whom he took for a wolf; and he even interrupted Christ before He had finished speaking, to urge this difficulty, that he might understand how Christ would remove it. Hence I will gather, that to propose such kind of difficulties with *pusillanimity* and faintness of heart, to avoid obedience, is wrong, and ought to be far from the disciples of Christ; but to propose them with *indifference*, to know the manner how to vanquish them, and the better to accomplish our obedience, is good and conformable to the Spirit of Christ, which is sweet, mild, and very loving, as here appeared in the case of Ananias.

2. Secondly is to be considered the *answer of Christ to Ananias.* " Go," said He, " whither I send thee, for this man whom thou reckonest so evil, *is to me a vessel of election;* a vessel chosen by myself by a particular election, not for his merits, but only out of my goodness, who have changed him that was a vessel of wrath and malice, into a vessel of

mercy and grace, and filled him with the abundance of my gifts, to show in him the greatness of my charity. Moreover, I have elected him for my own vessel, and my own instrument, ' to carry my name ' throughout the whole world, and to be a teacher and preacher to all the Gentiles."

Colloquy.—I give Thee thanks, O most sweet Jesus, that Thou hast placed such wonderful treasures in a vessel so frail and worthless, in order that the excellency of them may be attributed only to Thy power, and not to his strength. (18) O glorious apostle, radiant sun, "admirable instrument, the work of the Most High,"(19) placed in the midst of the Church, to run thy course through the whole world, and give the light of faith and the heat of charity to all mortal men ; I rejoice in thy election, and the happy lots which fell to thee. Beseech our Lord, who elected thee, that He would vouchsafe to make of me also a vessel of election, full of His grace and of the love of Him, that I may also so run my course, as to obtain an everlasting crown.   Amen.

3. Christ our Lord added :—" *I will show him how great things he must suffer for my name's sake;*" as if He had said :—" I will show them to him, first by revelation, and afterwards also by experience, and will cause him to suffer much more for my name than others have suffered by his means."   And so, indeed, His divine Majesty brought to pass, for scarcely had Saul begun to carry the name of Christ through the world, before he learned by experience how burdensome it was to bear it, and began to suffer innumerable persecutions and tribulations for this cause, as he declares of himself to the Corinthians :(20) and in this our Lord aimed at three several ends.—i. That Saul should

(18) 2 Cor, iv. 7.   (19) Ecclus. xliii. 2.   (20) 2 Cor. xi. 23.

pay with these persecutions which he suffered, for those which he himself had inflicted on others ; and thus the law of justice would be fulfilled on the one hand, while on the other, our Lord was preparing for him with these tribulations a crown of glory.—ii. That we might understand that great favours and heavenly gifts are not given without great afflictions ; for, if favours be given at first, tribulations will follow after, according to the measure of the favours imparted.—iii. That the disciple might understand that he is to follow his master, and the apostle Him by whom he is sent, and the preacher of the gospel, that he must undergo those penalties which He that was author of it, first underwent.

Colloquy.—O Saviour of the world, since Thou knowest so well how to refine by tribulations the vessel which Thou hast chosen for the Kingdom of heaven, purifying it from vices, and adorning it with precious virtues ; choose me for a vessel of Thy mercy, and refine me by afflictions in this life, that I may be worthy to attain the life eternal.   Amen.

POINT V.

" And Ananias went his way, and entered into the house ; and laying his hands upon him, he said :—*Brother Saul, the Lord Jesus hath sent me,* He that appeared to thee in the way as thou camest, that thou mayest receive thy sight, and be filled with the Holy Ghost. And immediately there *fell from his eyes, as it were, scales, and he received sight, and rising up he was baptized.* And when he had taken meat he was strengthened."(21)

1. Here is to be considered the sweet *providence* of our Lord in governing those that are His, and how He uses *the help of some men, to do good to others,* and sometimes even of the less to instruct the greater : for, although He

<hr>

(21) Act. ix. 17.

could by Himself have given sight to Paul, yet He chose that Ananias should go to him for this purpose, and that he should intimate to him the obligation of baptism, and the office of witness, and apostle, which God had committed to him; and thus, however wise or holy any one may be, or however greatly favoured by Almighty God, he is given to understand, that it is needful for him to subject himself to another man, in order by this means to preserve himself in true humility. (22) In Ananias, I will consider on the one hand, the *charity* and *humility* with which he spoke to Saul, calling him "*brother*," and saying, that he did not come to him of his own authority, but was sent by Jesus Christ; and at the same time, on the other hand, how as minister of Jesus Christ, he displayed great *authority* in what he said, as the same apostle recounts in the following words:—"One Ananias, a man according to the law, having testimony of all the Jews who dwelt there, coming to me, and standing by me, said to me; Brother Saul, look up. And I the same hour looked upon him. But he said; The God of our fathers hath pre-ordained thee, that thou shouldst know His will, and see the Just One, and shouldst hear the voice from His mouth; for thou shalt be His witness to all men, of those things which thou hast seen and heard. And now why tarriest thou? Rise up, and be baptized, and wash away thy sins, invoking His name." (23) Where we see how the preachers of the Gospel ought to join *humility* to their *authority*, in such a way that the one be not an impediment to the other. (24)

2. Christ our Lord *was pleased to give sight to Saul* in a miracle *before baptism*, both in order that he might receive it with greater comfort, seeing himself to be baptized; as

(22) Cass. col. ii. cap. 5.   (23) Act. xxii. 13.
(24) 2 Cor. iii. 2.

also to declare by that miracle, the virtue of Baptism, which enlightens the soul, and removes from the eyes of her faculties the scales of vices and sins. O how joyful was Saul, when he saw Ananias and heard his message! Immediately, without any delay, he devoutly received holy Baptism, and was filled with the Holy Ghost, who imparted to him the gift of tongues, and other graces, which the rest of the apostles had received: and then replenished with this divine Spirit, he sung a thousand praises to Almighty God, thanking Him for the favours which He had done him, and offering himself from his very heart to His service. Probably also he tore to pieces and burnt the papers, which he had received from the high priest, grieving that he had been so solicitous to obtain them, and resolving to be himself a living paper and epistle of Jesus Christ, to give intelligence of Him through all the world.

Colloquy.—O angels of heaven, who rejoice at the conversion of any sinner, how much greater was your joy for the miraculous conversion of this great sinner and persecutor of Jesus Christ, when you saw him changed into a great preacher, and the friend of Christ! O glorious angels, praise Him with all your might, and rejoice with Him, that He caught this ravenous wolf, the devourer of His flock, and converted him into a meek lamb of His own field; and beseech Him to increase your joy by the conversion of many sinners, in order that His flock may be increased, heaven peopled, and God glorified, world without end. Amen.

3. *Saul "preached Jesus in the synagogues, that He is the Son of God :"*(25) in which appears the great *fervour* of this our new apostle, and the promptitude with which he

(25) Act. ix. 20.

began to discharge his office of preaching Christ; for, as he himself declares, he " condescended not to flesh and blood,"(26) and was not deterred by knowing that his own friends would persecute him, and censure him for inconstancy, in so suddenly preaching as God, Him whom until then he himself had persecuted as the enemy of God. He was not moved by these considerations to confine himself to some corner of the house where he was lodged, or to proceed by little and little, so as first cautiously to feel the minds of his nation; but, as the apostles on the day of Pentecost issued forth at once out of the chamber into the Temple, and there preached Christ crucified, even so likewise, Saul, inebriated with the wine of the same Spirit, issued forth into all the synagogues, to preach the faith of the same Christ; thus making public satisfaction for his former error, and showing himself no less fervent in preaching Christ than he had shown himself in persecuting Him, and fulfilling his own precept to us : " As you have yielded your members to serve uncleanness, and iniquity unto iniquity, so now yield your members to serve justice unto sanctification."(27) But his fervour went much further in good than it had before in evil; and he strove with the most ardent zeal after the increase of sanctity in himself and others, and even throughout the world, and that with such great constancy, that though all wondered at hearing him preach Jesus Christ, when he had come to Damascus to apprehend His disciples, he " increased much more in strength, and confounded the Jews who dwelt at Damascus, affirming that this is the Christ."(28) So far, therefore, were the sayings of men and their persecution from having any power to make him colder in his preaching, that they rather served to animate and encourage him in

(26) Gal. i. 16.   (27) Rom. vi. 19.   (28) Act. ix. 22.

it all the more; and at this same rate did he proceed the rest of his life, till he had spent it for Christ with great love, as will be seen in the ensuing meditation.

MEDITATION XXXI.

OF THE LIFE AND HEROIC VIRTUES OF THE APOSTLE ST. PAUL AFTER HIS CONVERSION, WHEREIN IS PLACED A SUM OF SUPREME EVANGELICAL PERFECTION.

The life of this glorious apostle after his conversion was a perfect pattern of Evangelical perfection, to which all apostolical men ought to labour to attain, imitating, as he said, Christ our Lord, in the same manner that he himself imitated Him ;(1) and for this end I have placed here this meditation, in which are enumerated his principal virtues, drawn out of his own epistles and the book of the Acts of the Apostles.

POINT I.

The first virtue was, his excellent *poverty of spirit*, through which he renounced all things, as the other apostles did, that he might thus be more free for the service of Jesus Christ, and for the ministry of preaching Him, and chose to experience the effects of actual poverty, especially in three particulars.

1. First, he was content, as he himself says, with "*having food, and wherewith to be covered,*"(2) that is to say, having no more than was absolutely necessary in order to live and cover his nakedness; and this contentedness was as great as if he had had the whole world, and therefore he said, We live " as needy, yet enriching many; as having nothing, yet possessing all things ;"(3) that is, we are as well contented with having nothing as if we had and pos-

(1) 1 Cor. iv, 16, et 10.   (2) 1 Tim. vi. 8.   (3) 2 Cor. vi. 10.

sessed all things. The cause of such great contentedness was, that in the midst of this outward poverty he possessed most singular spiritual riches, which gave incomparably greater comfort than all temporal riches possibly could.

2. The second and higher particular was, that he often deprived himself of that which was necessary, and *suffered the want of it with great contentedness;* and therefore amongst his labours he reckons " hunger and thirst," " cold and nakedness," and many fastings.(4)

3. He went still higher; for though he was fully occupied in preaching the Gospel, and had a right to ask relief of the faithful, and to receive it at their hands, as the other apostles did, yet *he renounced this right,* and by the labour of his hands in a mechanical art, *got his own living,* and that of his companions, in order not to charge or burden the faithful, and to give an example to all of greater perfection, according to his own declaration,—" Any man's silver, gold, or apparel I have not coveted, as you yourselves know ; for such things as were needful for me and them that are with me these hands have furnished. I have showed you all things, how that, so labouring, you ought to support the weak, and to remember the word of the Lord Jesus, how He said, It is a more blessed thing to give rather than to receive."(5)

Colloquy.—O glorious apostle, who was so sparing in receiving things temporal, and so liberal in imparting things spiritual; obtain for me of thy blessed master grace to imitate thy poverty in temporal things, that so I may obtain thy riches in spiritual. O my soul, renounce all, and thou shalt find all ; leave all things for Christ, and thou shalt possess all things in Christ ; for having Him, thou hast all things in Him,

(4) 2 Cor. xi. 27.   (5) 1 Thes. ii. 9. Act. xx. 33.

and being poor for the love of Him, thou wilt be much more contented than if thou didst abound in riches.

POINT II.

The second virtue was his most pure *chastity*, which he solemnly vowed as the other apostles did, and kept perpetually, proposing himself as an example of it, as where he says, "For I would that all men were even as myself,"(6) that is, free from the incumbrances and affairs of marriage, to pray and attend to the service of God, and to be holy both in body and spirit.   Here I will consider three things in particular:—

1. The *great account he made of this virtue*, seeing he desired that all men should be chaste, as he himself was, without regard to the consequence, that the world would thus have quickly come to an end; for he esteemed eternal pleasures more than temporal, always aiming in desire at that which was best and most perfect, although in the pursuit of it he accommodated himself to the manner of Almighty God's dealing with men, and the measure in which He imparts His gifts to them.

2. Whereas the other apostles had a custom of leading about with them some devout woman to minister to them, (7) and support them out of her means, *he would not use this liberty*, not only because he desired to live by the labour of his own hands, and not on alms, but also of the caution and delicacy which are necessary with regard to any intercourse or communication with women, from whom he who desires to keep his chastity secure should fly.

3. Although his chastity *was assaulted with great temptations, yet he manfully overcame them*, and so was doubtless the more glorious, for the glory of virtue is greater in proportion to the severity of the conflict which has been

<hr>

(6) 1 Cor. vii. 7.   (7) 1 Cor. ix. 5.

necessary for its preservation. This is the interpretation given by the saints of that which this apostle relates of himself in writing to the Corinthians: " Lest the greatness of the revelations should exalt me, there was given me a sting of my flesh, an angel of Satan to buffet me. For which thing thrice I besought the Lord that it might depart from me; and He said to me, My grace is sufficient for thee; for power is made perfect in infirmity." (8) Which was as much as to say,—in order that thou mayst be humble, it is expedient for thee to be tempted; and thy virtue, to be perfect, must be thoroughly proved; therefore the sting of thy flesh shall make it perfectly chaste, and the angel of Satan which buffets thee shall make thee patient, and pure with the purity of an angel of heaven.

Colloquy.—O Father of mercies, make the sting and annoyance of my flesh a spur to my spirit, that I may pray with fervour, and run with diligence in Thy holy service, since on Thee alone do I depend for relief.

4. Moreover, the sanctity and purity of this apostle shone forth *in other inward conflicts* which he sustained, and in which he was victorious by his great valour, with regard to which he said: " I am delighted with the law of God, according to the inward man. But I see another law in my members, fighting against the law of my mind, and captivating me in the law of sin that is in my members. Unhappy man that I am! who shall deliver me from the body of this death? The grace of God, by Jesus Christ our Lord;"(9) this is that which shall deliver me, and by virtue of which I am to overcome.

Colloquy.—O my soul, faint not, although thou see

(8) 2 Cor. xii. 7.   S. Aug. et S. Th. et alii. ibid.
(9) Rom. vii. 22.

thyself assaulted; but trust in the grace of God, that thou shalt never be vanquished. If "the flesh lusteth against the spirit,"(10) strive to make "the spirit" lust "against the flesh," so as to remain conqueror; for the sharper the combat, the more glorious will be the victory, and then thou mayest say with the same apostle:—"Thanks be to God, who hath given us the victory, through our Lord Jesus Christ."(11)

POINT III.

1. The third virtue was, very *rigorous penance* and *mortification of his flesh,* which he chastised with severity, to keep it in obedience and subjection to the spirit, as he himself declares in very strong and weighty words:—"I therefore so run, not as at an uncertainty," or as if ignorant of my reward; "I so fight, not as one beating the air," labouring in vain, and with words alone; "but I chastise my body, and bring it into subjection, lest perhaps when I have preached to others, I myself should become a castaway."(12)

Colloquy.—O my soul, if the apostle, who was assured of his reward so ran and feared, how is it that thou who art uncertain dost not hasten and run with fear? If he was not contented with beating the air, but beat his own flesh, why dost thou content thyself with words only, and neglect in the mean time good works? Chastise thy body, therefore, with penances, that it may obey the spirit, for if thou indulgest it when it rebels, it will be cause of thy perdition and reprobation.

2. Moreover, the holy apostle exercised himself in the continual mortification *of his senses and disordered appetites,* denying his own will and desires, and perfectly accomplishing that self-denial which Christ our Lord commanded us,

(10) Gal. v. 17.   (11) 1 Cor. xv. 57.   (12) 1 Cor. ix. 26.

and for this cause he said:—" Always bearing about in our body the mortification of Jesus, that the life also of Jesus may be made manifest in our bodies."(13) So that in all places, and at all times, he lived amidst mortifications, not only the inward mortifications of the spirit, but the outward mortifications of the body also; sometimes taking them on his own accord, at other times submitting to those which came to him from the hands of his enemies, and thus imitating Christ our Lord, whose life he expressed in himself, whence very frequently he was wont to say:— " I bear the marks of the Lord Jesus in my body,"(14) suffering those things which Christ suffered.

Colloquy.—O that I could obtain a mortification so continual, ample, and perfect, that his blessed life, which gave me an example of so great mortification might be manifested in it ! O sweet Jesus, who art the " way, the truth, and the life,"(15) since Thy mortification is the way to come to enjoy Thee, who art life itself, illuminate me with Thy truth, that I may embrace this perfect death, in which is manifested Thy admirable life.   Amen.

POINT IV.

The fourth virtue was, *profound and admirable humility,* joined with great sanctity, which is a rare thing, and shone in these ensuing examples.

1. Comparing himself to other men, *he always chose for himself the most humble place,* for amongst sinners he held himself the very first, and amongst saints the very last, and so he once said,—" Christ Jesus came into this world to save sinners, of whom I am the chief."(16) And another time he said,—" I am the least of the apostles, who am not worthy to be called an apostle, because I

<hr>

(13) 2 Cor. iv. 10.   (14) Gal. vi. 17.
(15) Joan. xiv. 6.   (16) 1 Tim. i. 15.

persecuted the Church of God." (17)   And passing yet further, he called himself " the least of all the saints:"(18) that is, of all the faithful.   So that he who in the eyes of Almighty God, was one of the greatest apostles, and one of the first for sanctity, was in his own eyes the very last amongst the good, and the first amongst the bad.   The cause of which was, that in this comparison, which he made of himself to other men, he much exaggerated his own sins, and forgot the sins of others: and, contrariwise, was mindful of the virtues of other men, and for the present forgot his own, only remembering his former vices. In which I am greatly to procure to imitate this humble man, and to say with him, I am the least amongst Christians, and am not worthy of the name of a Christian; I am the least amongst Religious and priests, and am not worthy to be called by this name: yea, I am the least amongst men, and do not merit the name of a man, since by my sins I have made myself a very beast."(19)

2. His humility shone in this,—that *he was not ashamed publicly to acknowledge his own sins*, and to leave them set down in writing, saying that he had been before, a " blasphemer, and a persecutor, and contumelious ;"(20) and " beyond measure had persecuted the Church of God, and wasted it,"(21) a shedder of innocent blood,(22) and who had a part in the death of St. Stephen.   And if sometimes he recounted some of his glorious works, with his account, being constrained to it by necessity, he mingled words of humility, saying,—" I am become foolish ; you have compelled me."   And elsewhere he repeated the same, and of set purpose concealed many things which he might have said, " lest any man should think of me above that which

(17) i Cor. xv. 9.
(18) Ephes. iii. 8.   (19) Ps. xxi. 7.   (20) 1 Tim. i. 13.
(21) Gal. i. 13.   (22) Act. xxii. 19.

he seeth in me ;"(23) teaching us by this example, that the truly humble inclines of his own accord to confess his sins, but not his virtues, unless constrained by necessity, having such humility, as to hold himself for vain when he recounts them.

3. His humility shone in this,—that acknowledging the great gifts which he had received of Almighty God (for the Spirit of God, as the same apostle says, is not blind to acknowledge them) *he did not attribute them to himself* or vainly boast of them, but *gave the whole glory to Almighty God, and to His grace*, and so accounted himself for *nothing* in His presence, saying :—" By the grace of God I am what I am, and His grace in me hath not been void, but I have laboured more abundantly than all they, yet not I, but the grace of God with me." And elsewhere he says :—" But for myself I will glory nothing, but in my infirmities ;" (24) for though I have planted the faith amongst you, and Apollo watered the same, yet, " neither he that planteth is anything, nor he that watereth, but God that giveth the increase." (25) And when at a certain time, the people would have adored him as God, rending his garment, rushing forth into the multitudes, and crying out he said:—" Ye men, why do ye these things? We also are mortals, men like unto you,"(26) and therefore unworthy of such an honour. This is that humility of heart, which always abideth in the saints, wherein I ought to imitate this holy apostle, if I will be made partaker of the gifts of Almighty God, remembering the words of the same Apostle, saying :—" What hast thou that thou hast not received? And if thou hast received what dost thou glory, as if thou hadst not received it?" (27)

(23) 2 Cor. xii. 11.   Ibid. v. 6
(24) 1 Cor. xv. 10.   2 Cor. xii. 5.   (25) 1 Cor. iii. 6.
(26) Act. xiv. 14.   (27) 1 Cor. iv. 7.

Colloquy.—Wherefore, O my soul, empty thyself of thyself, if thou wishest God to fill thee with Himself, for He will communicate to thee His abundant gifts, if with humility thou wilt give Him all the glory of them.

4. His humility shone in the *holy fear which he had of himself*, grounded on the knowledge of himself, for which cause he said :—" I am not conscious to myself of anything, but am I not hereby justified, but he that judgeth me is the Lord."(28)   And elsewhere he said, that he chastised his body, lest he might become a castaway ; and often he besought the faithful, that they would pray for him, which was a sign of singular humility, and of his holy fear which made him afraid, lest perhaps there were some fault in him, which might hinder the designs of Almighty God.   And above all this, humility showed itself in this, that although he knew he had received by *revelation* from Almighty God His holy Gospel, yet would he confer the same with the other apostles, " lest perhaps I should run, or had run in vain."(29)   Wherein he discovered the humble resignation of his judgment to the judgment of the Church, not willing to presume of himself, nor to neglect the more to assure himself by her judgment.

5. There shone in him *contempt of the world, and the pleasure which he took in being despised*, in glorying more by its contempts, than others in honours, and therefore he said:—" God forbid that I should glory, save in the cross of our Lord Jesus Christ, by whom the world is crucified to me, and I to the world :"(30) as if he had said, It despises me as a thing vile, and worthy of the ignominious death of the cross, and I likewise despise it. And although he was esteemed as scum, and an outcast from the world, yet he made no account of this, nor any

(28) 1 Cor. iv. 4.   (29) Gal. ii. 2.   (30) Gal. vi. 14.

reckoning of the judgments and vain verdicts of men, and was so far from taking vain contentment in them, that he said:—" Do I seek to please men? If I yet please men, I should not be the servant of Christ." (31)

Colloquy.—O faithful servant of Jesus Christ, obtain for me of thy Lord this precious gift of humility, whence arises fidelity in His service. O my soul, if thou indeed desirest to serve thy Lord, despise the vain pomps of this world, and the deceitful judgments of its children ; and glory that thou art dead and crucified to the world, and that the world is dead and crucified to thee, so that henceforth thou mayest live to God alone, for ever and ever. Amen.

POINT V.

The first virtue was *invincible and heroic patience* in his distresses, which were innumerable in all sorts of things, inward and outward, by sea and by land, at the hands of Jews and of Gentiles, as also of false brethren, as appears by a catalogue he made of them, writing to the Corinthians,(32) and how grievous some of them were, he declared by the ensuing words :—" We were pressed out of measure, above our strength, so that we were weary even of life." (33) " Our flesh had no rest, but we suffered all tribulation ; combats without, fears within ;" and he applies to himself that which is written, saying :—" For we are put to death *for thy sake* all the day long : we are accounted as sheep for the slaughter."(34)

1. His travails being such, there shone in him singular patience, in that *they appeared little to him* in comparison with the reward which he expected, and therefore, he called them, " momentary and light,"(35) and was not

(31) Gal. i. 10.

(32) 2 Cor. xi. 23 ; et vi. 5.   (33) 2 Cor. i. 8.   2 Cor. xvii. 5.
     (34) Rom. viii. 36.   Ps. xlii. 22.   (35) 2 Cor. iv. 17.

afraid of them, nor lost courage for the severity of them, but offered himself to suffer others greater; as when the prophet Agabus foretold him, that he should be bound of the Jews in Jerusalem, and that he should be delivered into the hands of the Gentiles, to which he answered,—" I am ready not only to be bound, but to die also in Jerusalem for the name of the Lord Jesus."(36) This courage proceeded from the great confidence which he had in Almighty God, and which the same Lord maintained amid similar travails, and so he says;—" We had in ourselves the answer of death, that we should not trust in ourselves, but in God, who raises up the dead, who has delivered, and who does deliver us out of so great dangers, in whom we trust that He will yet also deliver us."(37)

2. Hence he rose to so great *magnanimity*, that he said:—" I know both how to be brought low, I know how to abound; both to be full, and to be hungry; both to abound and to suffer need ; I can do all things in Him who strengthens me." (38) As if he had said, In prosperity and in adversity, in plenty and in want, I am as it were, *almighty*, not in my own strength, but in that of Almighty God, by whose power I can do all things.

Colloquy.—O Almighty God, make me, by Thy power mighty to perform whatever Thou commandest, and to suffer whatever Thou permittest, for Thine shall be the glory, since the power is likewise Thine.

3. Lastly, he had great *joy* and *consolation in his labours,* God our Lord imparting to him great delights in the midst of them, as he wrote to the Corinthians, saying:— Blessed be God, " who comforts us in all our tribulation ; that we also may be able to comfort them that are in all distress." And elsewhere he said :—" Great is my con-

(36) Act. xxi. 13.   (37) 2 Cor. i. 9.
(38) Phil. iv. 12.

fidence with you, great is my glorying for you, I am filled with comfort, I exceedingly abound with joy, in all our tribulations." And again:—"We glory also in our tribulations." And again:—"I please myself in infirmities, in reproaches, in necessities, in persecutions, in distresses for Christ." (39)

Colloquy.—O Redeemer of the world, who showedst by experience to this Thy elect vessel, how much he was to suffer for Thy name, and gavest him delight in suffering, choose me also for Thy vessel, into which Thou mayest infuse abundance of travails with abundance of comforts, in suffering them for the love of Thee. Amen.

POINT VI.

The sixth virtue was, *high prayer and contemplation*, always growing up in those things which were given to him the first three days of his conversion.

1. But in particular his prayer was *continual* which he made to God, both for himself and all the faithful, without intermission, as he himself testifies in several places, saying:—"For God is my witness, whom I serve in my spirit in the Gospel of His Son, that without ceasing I make a commemoration of you always in my prayers :"(40) himself doing that which he enjoined others to do; "I will, therefore, that men pray in every place, lifting up pure hands." (41) And this he performed in all the manners of prayer, observation, petition, and thanksgiving, as he had counselled others: and even in the prisons he prayed and glorified God our Lord, making oratories of them, to the great edification of the keepers themselves. (42)

<hr>

(39) 2 Cor. i. 4.   Ibid. vii. 4.   Rom. v. 3.   2 Cor. xii. 10.
(40) Rom. i. 9.   1 Thes. i. 2.   (41) 1 Tim. ii. 8.
(42) Act. xvi. 25.

2. He prayed *with great spirit and fervour*, not contenting himself with words alone, but much more with the affections of the heart, and therefore said:—" Orabo spiritu, orabo et mente," " I will pray with the spirit, I will pray also with the understanding,"(43) joining the inward sense of the mind with the word which proceeded out of the mouth. Hence his contemplation was so high, that being in earth, his conversation, as himself said, was above in heaven. (44)

3. He also said of himself, that he knew a man *"rapt even to the third heaven,"* and to paradise, where he saw such secrets of Almighty God, as are not lawful for a man to speak, of which point we have already spoken. In which rapture at least *our Lord must have communicated to him, the highest degree of contemplation which can be communicated in this mortal life :* and it may be supposed, that he often had other raptures, which, out of humility he concealed, as he intimated by recounting this; and when he said in another place;—" Whether we be transported in mind it is to God,"(45) that is to say, we suffer ecstasies of spirit treating with Almighty God. And it clearly appears, how sublime they were, since he says:— " Lest the greatness of the revelation should exalt me, there was given me a sting of my flesh, an angel of Satan, to buffet me." (46)

4. From this contemplation proceeded *the abundance of consolations which he received*, and the profound knowledge which he had of Christ our Lord, and of the inestimable riches of His grace, and the secrets of predestination, and His divine providence, of the excellencies and perfections of Almighty God, of the hierarchies of the angels, and of many other things which he declares in his epistles.

<hr>

(43) 1 Cor. xiv. 15.   (44) Phil. iii. 20.
    (45) 2 Cor. v. 13.   (46) 2 Cor. xii. 7.

Finally, so great was the estimation which he made of Christ our Lord, that he came to say that he esteemed all things of the world, as gold, silver, pearls, and everything else in the world, "to be but loss for the excellent knowledge of Jesus Christ my Lord, for whom I have suffered the loss of all things, and count them but as dung, that I may gain Christ."(47)

Colloquy.—O supreme science of Christ our Lord, which so much contemnest the things of the earth, and so much esteemest those of heaven ; give me, Lord, this science, that I may so know Thee, as to esteem for dung whatever is earthly in respect of gaining Thee, who art true God and true Man. Amen.

From these four considerations I may gather both a great admiration of the singular benefits which Almighty God conferred upon this holy apostle, and thankfulness for the same; as also a great desire of imitating him where he is imitable, frequenting prayer and meditation with a fervent spirit, and great alacrity, disposing myself so that I put no impediment to those favours which God desires to infuse into those who frequent this sovereign exercise.

POINT VII.

The seventh virtue was, *his most excellent charity towards Christ* with the most perfect union, that is to be found in the unitive way, which he declared when he said:—"With Christ I am nailed to the cross, and I live, now not I, but Christ liveth in me." (48) In which words he declared two wonderful manners of the loving union, which he had with Jesus Christ.

1. He was "*crucified with Christ*," being united and

(47) Phil. iii. 8.   (48) Gal. ii. 19.

nailed with Him on the cross, not with nails of iron, but of love and of imitation, glorifying in this exceedingly, and always thinking, speaking, and working conformably to this, and therefore, he said to the Corinthians:—" I judge not myself to know anything among you, but Jesus Christ, and Him crucified." (49)

2. The second manner of union with Christ was spiritual, viz., with excess of love, *leading*, as St. Dionysius says, *a life only of love*, so that, although, in truth he lived a natural life, yet he did not live a free life; for he did not rule himself according to his own will and liberty, but Jesus Christ lived in him as the beginning, rule, and final end of all his thoughts, affections, words, and works; he carried our Lord united with him by the continual exercise of love, so that he said:—" Mihi vivere Christus est;" " For to me, to live is Christ," (50) my thought is Christ, my will is Christ, my word is Christ, and my work is Christ.

Colloquy.—O happy apostle, to whom Christ vouchsafed so great a favour !   Oh that my soul were such that Christ would always live in her !   O Christ my life, live always in me, and let my life be always in Thee, world without end.   Amen.

3. *How deeply was this love rooted* in this holy apostle, who was so bold as to say :—" Who, then, shall separate us from the love of Christ? shall tribulation? or famine? or nakedness? or danger? or persecution? or the sword? I am sure that neither death, nor life, nor angels, nor principalities, nor powers, neither things present, nor things to come, nor might, nor height, nor depth, nor any other creature, shall be able to separate us from the love of God, which is in Christ Jesus our Lord."(51)

(49) 1 Cor. ii. 2.   (50) Phil. i. 21.   (51) Rom. viii. 35.

Colloquy.—O fire of love which the "waters" of many tribulations "cannot quench," but rather increase! O insatiable "fire" which "never says, ' It is enough,' " because thou art never weary to suffer labours for the object of thy love! Enkindle, O my Redeemer, this fire in my heart, that I may love Thee with so great fervour, that nothing created may content me. Amen.

POINT VIII.

The eighth virtue was, most fervent *charity and love towards his neighbours*, which sprung from the inflamed charity which he bore towards Christ our Lord.

1. This charity, as he himself said, urged him, robbing him of his heart, *to all things belonging to His service, and for the good of souls*, whose salvation he desired with all his heart, and for whom he took exceeding pains, traversing the whole world incessantly on foot, preaching throughout all kingdoms and provinces, in the streets, in private houses, and in prisons, now to many gathered together, now to some alone in particular, with great tenderness of heart. " I ceased not with tears to admonish every one of you night and day."(52) Hence he said :—" I made myself the servant of all, that I might gain the more; I became all things to all men, that I might save all." " I also in all things please all men, not seeking that which is profitable to myself, but to many, that they may be saved."(53)

Colloquy.—O most ample charity, which embracest all, and excludest none, taking the form and figure of all men, that all may take the figure of Christ, and may carry upon them the image of the celestial man.

2. Hence arose the *solicitude and zeal which he had for the good of all*, feeling and lamenting their losses as if they were his own, and so he relates this feeling amongst his

(52) Act. xx. 31.   (53) 1 Cor. ix. 19.

great labours, saying:—" Who is weak, and I am not weak? who is scandalized, and I am not on fire?"   And for this cause he said to the Romans:—" I have great sadness, and continual sorrow in my heart," (54) for the perdition of his brethren the Israelites.   And to the Galatians, who had degenerated from the purity of the Gospel, he said:—" My little children, of whom I am in labour again until Christ be formed in you."(55)   And elsewhere he calls himself by the name of a " nurse," which nurses her little ones, protesting that he desired to give his life for them, because he loved them in such sort, that he held them inclosed within his heart, loving them with the bowels of Jesus Christ, desiring to embowel them within Him, to the end they might always love Him.

3. Hence proceeded another notable excellency of his love; for much as he *desired " to be dissolved and to be with Christ," yet he restrained this desire*, finding it necessary for him to abide in the flesh for the good and help of his neighbours, and to win and save their souls, nor did he hesitate to leave the sweetness of contemplation, and to absent himself from that pleasing converse with Jesus Christ, so to save the souls of others. (56)   And this his charity extended so far, that he wished himself to be an anathema from Christ for his brethren; giving to understand, as many saints interpret, that if it were needful for the salvation of his neighbours, he would choose to be separated from the sight of Jesus Christ and of His glory, either for a long time, or until the ending of the world, for that he had no greater glory than to love Christ our Lord, to accomplish His holy will, and to gain many souls,

(54) 2 Cor. xi. 29.   Rom. ix. 2.
(55) Gal. iv. 19.   1 Thes. ii. 7.
(56) Phil. i. 23.   S. Th. 2, 2, q. clxxxii. 2,

who might love and serve Him everlastingly.(57) For
whom he might say much better than Moses:—"Either
forgive them this trespass, or if Thou do not, strike me out
of the book that Thou hast written ;"(58) for I had rather
be separated from Thee, without sin, than that so many
souls should perish through their offence.

Colloquy.—O most sublime and profound charity,
which ascended so high that thou contentest thyself
with no less than to possess Almighty God, and des-
cendest so low that thou art willing without sin to be
deprived of God, that so thou mayest please Him.
Grant me, Lord, a charity like to this, which may
place her rest in giving Thee contentment, though it
be with the loss of my own, delighting to gain many
souls who may enjoy Thee, world without end.
Amen.

4. Lastly, it is much to the praise of this charity of the
apostle, that it *extended itself even to his enemies* and persecutors, loving them as friends, and performing towards
them all the laws of love; and so he said:—"We are
reviled, and we bless; we are persecuted, and we suffer it;
we are blasphemed, and we entreat" and pray for our blas-
phemers. And again to the Corinthians he said:—"I
most gladly will spend and be spent myself for your soul:
although loving you more, I be loved less."(59) Hence,
if any, through envy, or contention, or that they thought
it afflicted him, began to preach Christ, he not only
weighed it not, nor complained of them, nor conceived
envy, nor diverted them, but rejoiced and exulted that
Christ was preached and souls profited. From all these
considerations I am to draw an inward desire of imitating
the inflamed zeal of this apostle towards my neighbours,

(57) Rom. ix. 3. S. Chrys. S. Th. et. alii.   (58) Exod. xxxii. 32.
(59) 1 Cor. iv. 12. 2 Cor. xii. 15.

good or evil, friends or enemies, beholding Jesus Christ in them, for whose sake all ought to be loved.

POINT IX.

From this charity proceed *other singular virtues*, by which the apostle discovered his perfection, some of which we will consider in particular.

1. The first was, *his great obedience* to the will of Almighty God, and to all the inspirations by which He manifested it to him; and so, being commanded to go and preach in Macedonia, or in Jerusalem, or elsewhere, he presently went, though he knew that he was there to suffer grievous persecutions and afflictions; for he made much more account of his soul than of his life, and of accomplishing the will of God than of seeking his own contentment.(60)   And having obeyed in all this, yet he did not glorify himself, nor suppose that he had done anything of moment, because he esteemed what he had done to be of necessity and of obligation; as if he had said, I am an "unprofitable" servant, I "have done that which" I "ought to do."(61)

2. The second was, great care in the *custody of his tongue,* and most exact circumspection in his words, as well in preaching as in conversing with men, as appears by what he wrote to the Corinthians:—"For we are not as many, adulterating the word of God, but with sincerity, but as from God, before God, in Christ we speak."(62) O perfect man, truly religious, who so could keep his tongue, that it did not stumble in a word, that so his religion might not be vain, nor his perfection at all diminished!(63) O that I could so bridle my tongue in speaking, as always to speak with sincere intention, following the divine inspi-

(60) Act xvi. 9 ; et xx. 22.   (61) 1 Cor. ix. 16.   Luc. xvii. 10.
      (62) 2 Cor. ii. 17.   (63) Jac. i. 26.

ration, thinking that God sees me, and always to discourse of Jesus Christ.

3. The third was, an interior *desire to profit in virtue,* and always to go forward and to advance himself in it: for after so many labours he did not imagine himself to have attained the summit, but always followed his purpose of greater perfection, and forgot those things that were past, and stretched forward to new things, even to the obtaining the reward of the high vocation.

4. The fourth was, admirable *dexterity in joining virtues together which are not united but with great difficulty,* such as humility and magnanimity, meekness and zeal, the bowels of mercy and the uprightness of justice, chastising offences when it was necessary, and resisting those who lived not conformably to the truth and sincerity of the Gospel which he preached.(64)

5. The fifth was, a great *desire to go to see Christ* our Lord, by reason of the great love which he bore Him, so that he sighed within himself, expecting the perfect " adoption of the sons of God," and further said, that Christ was his life, and that it was " gain" for him to "die" because by dying he should gain always " to be with Christ," and with this desire he said, that although he wished to be with God, yet, whether absent or present, he desired in all things to please Him.(65)   Hence proceeded that confidence and security which he had of obtaining glory, so that he might rightly say:—" I have fought a good fight, I have finished my course, I have kept the faith.   As to the rest, there is laid up for me a crown of justice, which the Lord the just judge will render to me in that day; and not only to me, but to them also that love His coming."(66)   Hence likewise proceeded that great prompti-

<hr>

(64) 1 Cor. v. 5.   Gal. ii. 11.
(65) Rom. viii. 23.   Phil. i. 21, et 23.   (66) 2 Tim. iv. 7.

tude and generosity of mind with which he offered himself to die for Christ, for the good of souls, which he declared by the works of his whole life ; for his life was nothing else but a continued death for Jesus Christ and his neighbours, and therefore he said:—" For Thy sake we are put to death all the day long," and are handled and " accounted as sheep of slaughter." And elsewhere he says:—" We who live are always delivered unto death for Jesus' sake." And again:—I protest "I die daily by your glory, brethren, which I have in Christ Jesus our Lord."(67)

6. Finally, when occasion offered, *he laid down his life for Christ our Lord ;* and though the manner of his death appeared easy, for probably he was not crucified, as St. Peter was, yet the cause of this was, that his whole life after his conversion had been, as we have said, " with Christ nailed to the cross,"(68) bearing the marks and signs of His Passion; fulfilling in his body that which was wanting to the sufferings of Christ, applying their virtue and efficacy to His body, which is the Church, at the expense of his own labours; and with this fervour he was prepared to undergo the death of the cross, if it had been granted to him: he even desired to die a thousand different deaths, to manifest by them the great love he bore to his Lord and master.

Colloquy.—O celestial master, who, after Thou ascendedst into heaven, madest election of this new disciple, and didst so elaborate and polish him with Thine own hand, as to despoil him of all earthly affections, and clothe him with heavenly. I humbly beseech Thee by his merits that Thou vouchsafe to accept me for Thy disciple, so assisting me with Thy copious grace, that I may imitate Thee, as he imitated

(67) Rom. viii. 36. 2 Cor. iv. 11. 1 Cor. xv. 31.
(68) Gal. ii. 19; et vi. 17.

Thee, that I may come to enjoy Thee in his company for ever and ever. Amen.

MEDITATION XXXII.

OF THE VOCATION OF CORNELIUS THE CENTURION: AND THE REVELATION WHICH ST. PETER HAD CONCERNING THE CONVERSION OF THE GENTILES.

POINT I.

" There was a certain man in Cæsarea, named Cornelius, a centurion of that which is called the Italian band, *a religious man and fearing God with all his house, giving much alms* to the people, *and always praying to God.*"(1)

1. Here consider *the excellent virtues with which this man disposed himself to receive the favours* which God conferred on him, illuminating his understanding to receive the faith of Christ, and imparting to him the plenitude of the Holy Ghost, together with the gift of tongues, as to the other apostles.

i. He was "*very religious,*" i. e., much given to things belonging to the worship of God, and to the works of His holy service.—ii. He feared God, flying from all which was sin: he accomplished the two parts of justice, which are to decline from evil, and to follow good. And the example which he gave was so effectual, that all his family imitated him, for such as the master is, such are the servants, and such as the father of the family, such are those likewise of his household.—iii. He was a great alms-giver, giving liberally to the poor who asked of him, not making any difference or exception.—iv. He was *much addicted to prayer*, for it is said of him, that "he prayed always;" that is to say, with great frequency and continuation in

(1) Act. x. 1.

the hours assigned to it. Thus it appears that he observed the custom of praying at the ninth hour, as he himself affirms, saying, " I was praying in my house at the ninth hour," (2) and though he was a Gentile by nation, yet he exercised himself in such works, for both Almighty God mercifully prevented him with His assistance, and he carefully profited by the example which he observed in the godly, with whom he conversed in that city; this man, Christ our Lord, doth set before us for our confusion, who having the faith of Christ, and enjoying the benefit of the holy sacraments, yet with all this, perform not that which a heathen and a soldier did.

2. Then will I consider *the manner in which Almighty God called him*, to impart to him the light and perfection which was wanting in him. For he " saw in a vision, manifestly, about the ninth hour of the day, an angel of God, coming in to him, and saying to him, Cornelius. And he beholding him, being seized with fear, said: What is it Lord? And he said to him: Thy prayers and thy alms are ascended for a memorial in the sight of God. And now send men to Joppa, and call hither one Simon, who is surnamed Peter, he will tell thee what thou must do." (3) In which appears the sweet providence of our Lord in thus attending to the salvation and perfection of His elect: for when He sees any one do on his part what he is able, and according to his knowledge and forces by divine assistance, He speedily approaches to instruct him in what he knows not, and to give him new assistance to perform what else he could not, using to this effect, when necessary, extraordinary and miraculous means, as He did in this occasion: whence I will conceive great confidence in this fatherly providence of Almighty God, and will

(2) Act. x. 30   (3) Act. x. 3.

render Him continually praises for so singular favours imparted to us by its means.

Colloquy.—O my beloved, how shall not I have great care of Thee, seeing Thou hast so great care of me? My salvation shall be most sure if Thou take it into Thy charge, beholding with especial providence what is wanting in me, that Thou mayest presently supply the same. Grant me, dear Lord, to perform all I know and can, and discover to me by Thy divine light what I do not understand, assisting me with Thy grace to fulfil the same. Amen.

3. The *angels*, especially our guardians, *are instruments and ministers of the divine providence, in the work of our salvation*, and to them it appertains, to assist invisibly those that pray, and to present to God their works and prayers: (4) and so this angel who guarded Cornelius appeared to him in the time of prayer, and said to him two things:—

i. First, that his *prayers and alms had ascended into the remembrance and sight of God*, so that they did not remain below on earth, but flew and ascended up to heaven : nor was God forgetful of them, but had them present in His remembrance and in His sight, where they solicited and negotiated the salvation and perfection of Cornelius, and both of them ascended together, because prayer helps alms, and again alms assist prayer.

Colloquy.—O my soul, if thou desire to negotiate thy salvation with Almighty God, send to Him beforehand these two solicitors, against whom there are no gates shut in the Kingdom of heaven, "for the prayer of him that humbleth himself shall pierce the clouds, ...and he will not depart till the Most High behold;" and if thou "shut up alms in the heart of the poor, it shall obtain help for thee against all evil."(5)

(4) Heb. i. 14. Tob. xii. 12.
(5) Ecclus. xxxv. 21. Ibid. xxix. 15.

ii. The angel told Cornelius *to send for St. Peter*, and he would tell him what he should do. By which we see that the divine providence, although it governs us by angels in those things which men cannot do, yet in those things which they can do, He will govern by them: and so the angel would not tell Cornelius what he was to do, although he could, but remitted him to St. Peter, to the end that he might receive them from his mouth, and inspired St. Peter to come to instruct him. Whence I will learn to subject myself to such sort of government as God has appointed, as well to honour His ministers, as to keep us in humility, for the mutual necessity we stand in one of another, as we have observed in the meditation on Saul and Ananias.

POINT II.

Cornelius " called two of his household servants, and a soldier who feared the Lord, of them that were under him. To whom, when he had told all, he sent them to Joppa.. And drawing nigh to the city, Peter went up to the higher parts of the house, *to pray about the sixth hour.* And being hungry, he was desirous to taste somewhat. And as they were preparing, there *came upon him an ecstasy of mind.*" (6)

1. Here I will consider the laudable custom of the apostles, in the practice of prayer, *choosing and assigning for prayer, place, time, and hours convenient.* For St. Peter, in order that he might pray, went up to the highest and most retired place in the house, whither the noise of the people that were below could not ascend. By which is represented the work of perfect prayer, which is the ascending of the soul to Almighty God, withdrawing ourselves from the noise of importunate imaginations, which boil in the inferior parts of the soul.(7)

(6) Act. x. 7.   (7) S. Damas. S. Th. 2, 2, q. lxxxii. art. 17.

Colloquy.—O eternal God, who commandest that to pray I enter into my closet, and "shut the door," to the end that with more quietness and silence I may offer up my prayer "in secret;"(8) vouchsafe to assist me with Thy grace, that I may enter into the most high closet of my spirit, there to pray and to worship Thee in spirit and verity. Amen.

2. He *chose also the sixth hour for prayer*, as Cornelius had done the ninth, following in this the custom of the just of Israel, who prayed three times a day, viz. : at the third hour, which is about nine in the morning: and at the sixth, which is about noon: and at the ninth, which is three in the afternoon: which custom of David and Daniel, all the apostles observed with greater exactness and reason.(9) For at the third hour the Holy Ghost came down upon them: at the sixth Christ ascended on the cross: and at the ninth He gave up the ghost, and descended to take the spoil of Limbo. Hence will I conceive a very firm and stable purpose of assigning hours for prayer, and when the hour shall be come, of leaving all things to comply with my prayer, as St. Peter did on this occasion, who, though he was hungry and desired to eat, yet for this omitted not his prayer, but set himself to it before meat, giving food first to his soul, and then to his body.

3. Christ our Lord, to impart extraordinary favours to His elect, is wont to choose place and time fit for the purpose, *and that ordinarily a retired place, and the time of prayer*, for when a man on his own part approaches to God, and ascends by spirit into His presence, then God imparts to him those especial favours which He can and will: for even so in this occasion He suspended the senses of St. Peter, and elevated him in spirit, to the end that he

(8) Mat. vi. 6.
(9) Ps. liv, 18. Dan. vi. 10. Act. iii. 1. Cass. l. 2, cap. 9.

might see the secrets of God, and this suspension is called:
—" Excessus mentis,"—" ecstasy of mind :" for the soul
issues out of itself, and is elevated above itself, and far
above its own forces: and when the same is done with interior violence, it is called—Raptus, a rapture, (10) for
God violently draws the spirit, and causes it to ascend, as
to St. John, to see His divine mysteries.(11)   Whence I
will gather, that notwithstanding it be not secure, to wish
and procure such ecstasies, yet I ought to seek and desire
that ecstasy of love, which may pluck me out of myself,
and may transport me into Jesus Christ, to the end that I
may say with the apostle St. Paul:—" I live, now not I
but Christ liveth in me,"(12) because forsaking all temporal things, and myself with them, I cease to be my own
and begin wholly to be Jesus Christ's, delighting to think
on Him, to speak of Him, and in all things to please Him.

Colloquy.—O God of love, cast upon me this excess
of love. O omnipotent love, ravish my heart, and
transport it thither where Thou art, that I may always
be with Thee united by love, and Thou mayest always
live in me, governing me by Thy love.   Amen.

POINT III.

In this ecstasy of mind, St. Peter " *saw the heaven
opened,* and a certain vessel descending, as it were a great
linen sheet, let down by the four corners from heaven to
the earth ; wherein were all manner of four-footed beasts,
and creeping things of the earth, and fowls of the air.
And there came a voice to him : Arise, Peter : kill and
eat. But Peter said, Far be it from me, Lord : for I
never did *eat anything that is common and unclean.* And
the voice spoke to him again the second time : That which

____

(10) Act. x. 10. 2 Cor. v. 13 ; et xii. 2.   (11) Apoc. iv. 2.
(12) Gal. ii. 20. S. Dionys. cap. 4, de Divi. Nom.   S. Th. 2, 2, q.
clxxv. art. 2.

God hath cleansed, do not thou call common. And *this was done thrice*, and presently the vessel was taken up into heaven."(13)

1. As Christ our Lord, when He preached in this mortal life, used parables and similitudes to discover the mysteries of the Kingdom of heaven; even so, also spiritually is He wont *similarly to imprint in our imagination figures by which the mystery He discovers is represented*, as He did here with St. Peter, and with St. John, in the revelations of the Apocalypse, and even to this hour also is accustomed to communicate Himself after this manner to whom He will. But it is my business, only to form in my imagination if I conveniently can, the images and figures of those things which He has revealed to me in His faith; for example, Christ made a little infant, laid in a manger, bound to the pillar, or nailed on the cross, to move me by the means of these figures to a greater love of our Lord, who is represented in them; all other things I will leave to His divine providence, that He perform that which shall be most expedient. But in this *present* figure shines forth the infinite charity of God our Lord, in vouchsafing to admit into His Church, and into heaven also, as far as He is concerned, all the sinners of the world, the covetous, the carnal, and the proud, figured by those three kinds of living creatures, beasts, serpents, and birds, gathering them, not only out of that little corner of Judea, but from the four corners of the world; for to this end He descended from heaven to earth, and clothed Himself with the most pure sheet of His humanity; for this He exhibited to Himself His Church, white and pure, without stain or blot; for this He directed the preaching of the four Evangelists, whose doctrine is from heaven, for the salvation and life of the world.

(13) Act. x. 11.

Colloquy.—I give Thee thanks, O most sweet and most merciful Jesus, for the infinite charity with which Thou callest all sinners, and desirest to lay all upon Thine own shoulders, to carry them to the kingdom of heaven. O my beloved, how admittest Thou such savage beasts and serpents into a sheet so white and pure? Their abode ought to be in the deserts, and in the holes and caves of the earth; why dost Thou, then, draw them thence, and put them in this precious sheet to bring them to heaven, and to place them in those eternal tabernacles? Henceforth I will no more doubt of Thy infinite mercy, since it shows itself so ample in redressing our misery.

2. I will consider, secondly, *what that voice signified* which spoke to St. Peter, and in him to all the ministers of Jesus Christ. "*Occide et manduca :*" "*kill and eat.*" As if He had said, Since thou art hungry, and desirest to eat, kill these savage beasts, these serpents, and these devouring birds, and eat of them; to signify that it is proper to priests, confessors, and the ministers of Christ, to kill sinners, as touching their sins, taking from them their carnal and beastly life which they led, by means of the sacraments of Baptism and Penance, and forthwith to eat them, and to incorporate them with the Church as members, and to unite them with Jesus Christ by charity, and similitude of life; for Christ our Lord detests and rejects living sinners,—to wit, such as live and continue in sin; but admits within Him such sinners as are dead to sin, because this death brings to them a new being, and life of grace.

Colloquy.—O eternal God, since Thou commandest Thy ministers that they kill and eat, Thou, O Lord, vouchsafest to kill and eat by their means, assisting them efficaciously to accomplish that which Thou commandest with so great mercy.

3. Then will I consider *the answer of St. Peter*, who at that time was not assured of the will of Almighty God concerning the admission of the Gentiles into the Church of Jesus Christ: and this he signified *in refusing to eat those creatures, which were held unclean* according to the ancient law. But a voice from heaven said to him:— "That which God hath cleansed, do not thou call common: that is to say, Refuse not to admit to my faith and religion, those whom I have chosen in my eternal ordination to be holy, although they appear to thee to be profane. Whence appears how contrary it is to the spirit of Christ, that preachers and confessors should abhor sinners who fall at their feet, how sinful and abominable soever they be, since God draws them thither to convert them, and to make them just.

Colloquy.—O immense charity of Jesus Christ, how many ways dost Thou take to manifest the love which Thou bearest to sinners? Who shall abhor to receive them, since Thou abhorrest not to call them? Who shall refuse to eat this meat, which Thou declarest to be holy? Give me, dear Lord, this hunger of saving sinners, that I may eat them with great contentment, and may incorporate them with Thee by grace, whom Thou attractest by true penance. Amen.

4. Consider, lastly, how *this voice sounded three several times, to the end that it might penetrate and be imprinted the deeper in the heart of St. Peter ;* even as he was thrice examined concerning his love towards Jesus Christ, and was commanded by Him three several times to feed His sheep. And immediately that sheet was received into heaven, to show that God held heaven open for all such heathens as should be converted to Him, although they were most grievous sinners.

Colloquy.—Rejoice, O my soul, beholding that sheet taken and assumed up to heaven, full of beasts, serpents, and devouring birds, i. e., of grievous sinners, not living, but dead; dead indeed to sin, but alive to grace. Study to kill in thyself the life of the old man, and to rise again with Jesus Christ to the life of the new man, that entering with Him into heaven, thou mayest sit on a seat in the throne of His glory, world without end. Amen.

POINT IV.

"Now whilst Peter doubted within himself what the vision that he had seen should mean; behold the men who were sent from Cornelius, enquiring for Simon's house, stood at the gate. Arise, therefore, and get thee down, and go with them, doubting nothing; for I have sent them......And the day following he arose and went with them......And the morrow after he entered into Cæsarea. And Cornelius waited for them, having called together his kinsmen and special friends." And Peter, understanding from Cornelius what had happened to them, began to preach Jesus to them, and as " Peter was yet speaking these words, *the Holy Ghost fell on them* that heard the word, and "*they spoke with tongues*, magnifying God."(14)

1. Our Lord Christ sometimes does not *express the meaning of the visions He discovers to His servants*, which He does out of His providence, partly to ground them in humility; partly that by means of prayer they may obtain this understanding of Almighty God; as also to give to them at the most convenient time and opportunity, as it happened to St. Peter on this occasion; who, obeying the voice of the Holy Ghost, went to the place where Cornelius and his people expected him, and preached to them

(14) Act. x. 17, et seq.

Jesus Christ crucified with so great fervour, that all believed, and received the Holy Ghost, together with the gift of speaking in divers tongues.

2. In this place is to be considered the infinite liberality of Almighty God, in *imparting so great gifts to Gentiles*, according to that which St. Peter said in this place:—" In very deed I perceive that God is not an acceptor of persons, since He bestows so liberally a gift so precious as the Holy Ghost on men who had been beasts and serpents, and who had adored these base creatures for gods, and on those who had had, so to speak, tongues of serpents, to blaspheme God, and to poison their neighbours, he bestowed tongues of fire, with which to glorify God, and to publish His singular greatness. And although God illuminated them by little and little, and softened them by the sermon of St. Peter, yet on a sudden, and in an instant, He changed, justified, and filled them with His gifts and graces, giving them great cause for joy, all receiving baptism by the order of St. Peter, and together with baptism new increase of grace, and of joy; the apostle likewise greatly rejoicing in these first fruits of the Gentiles, which this day he offered up to his master, to whom be all honour and glory, for ever and ever. Amen.

(V.) MEDITATIONS ON THE LIFE AND ASSUMPTION OF OUR LADY—HER BLESSEDNESS AND VIRTUES—DEVOTION TO HER AND ON THE HAPPINESS OF THE BLESSED IN HEAVEN.

MEDITATION XXXIII.

OF THE ADMIRABLE EXERCISES OF VIRTUE, IN WHICH THE BLESSED VIRGIN OUR LADY EXERCISED HERSELF AFTER THE COMING OF THE HOLY GHOST.

To make an end of the glorious mysteries of Christ our Lord, whose glory was in a certain manner complete, when He had His mother glorified with Him, I will here insert meditations of the *life, death, and Assumption of the glorious Virgin our Lady*, who after the coming of the Holy Ghost, as the Church gives us to understand in the Gospel, which is sung on the day of her Assumption, chose the better part of Mary, yet not absolutely leaving the part of Martha, but performing its highest duties, exercised herself, not only in serving God by contemplation, but also in attending to the spiritual good of her neighbours, for the glory of her Son, and for the comfort and increase of the primitive Church, which was the principal cause why Christ our Lord took her not immediately with Him up to Heaven, but left her for almost fifteen years here on earth, that in His absence she might perform those offices which He Himself was wont to perform, towards His disciples, as we shall presently see.

POINT I.

The Blessed Virgin our Lady, illuminated by the Holy Ghost, retired not into the deserts, as Mary Magdalen did, but chose to lead, after the example of her Son, *a common life* amongst the other disciples in order to assist them with her example, keeping with great perfection the *Evangelical counsels*, of whom the disciples themselves learned to keep them.

1. First she embraced Evangelical *poverty*, taking a vow to that effect, unless she had made it before, which seems more probable; but then she kept the same with greater strictness, living on the alms which the apostles distributed amongst the faithful and other widows, (1) contenting herself much better than did St. Paul, (2) having wherewith to sustain and to clothe herself, for she held as yet very fresh in memory, the gall, the vinegar, and the nakedness of her Son upon the cross, in comparison of whom all which she suffered seemed little. And, therefore, as truly poor in spirit, she always desired to feel in herself greater effects of poverty, and with it conjoined her sister humility, which the saints call by the same name, on which we will, therefore, make a special meditation.

2. She practised most excellent *obedience*, not only to all things which Christ our Lord left established in the Evangelical law, but also those which St. Peter and the other apostles ordained to be observed in the universal Church, she being the first in obeying and subjecting herself to all such ordinances, recollecting that saying of her Son:— " Whosoever shall do the will of my Father that is in heaven, he is my brother, and sister, and mother;"(3) and therefore she would in nothing more demonstrate herself to be the mother of Christ than in obedience to Christ, and to those whom He had constituted in His place.

Colloquy.—O Sovereign Virgin, I rejoice that thou art the Mother of Christ my Lord by a double title,

(1) Act iv. 35.   (2) 1 Tim. vi. 8.   (3) Mat. xii. 50.

both because thou engenderedst Him in thy womb, and because also thou conceivedst Him in thy spirit by perfect imitation; it only remains, O Lady, that thou be His mother by a third title, engendering Him likewise spiritually in the hearts of the faithful; engender Him, I beseech thee, within my soul, obtaining that He may always live there, world without end.   Amen.

3. She excelled all others in *chastity*, of which, as has been said in the second part, Med. 4, she made a vow, and kept it perpetually with a purity more than angelical, for which cause holy Church calls her not only Virgin of virgins, but also *virginity* itself, saying:—"Holy and immaculate virginity," "I know not with what praises I may extol thee."   I only now add, that as the Ark of the Testament was made of the wood sethim, a wood incorruptible, was gilded with most pure gold, "intus et foris," ",within and without:"(4) even so this Virgin adorned her incorruptible chastity with most pure virtues, as well with those which perfected the body in exterior works, as those which perfected the spirit in interior, that so she might be, as the apostle says, "holy," by pre-eminence, "both in body and in spirit."(5)   Amongst others we will consider some which St. Ambrose recounts for the custody of chastity.(6)

i. The first was rare *modesty* in all the exterior motions of the body, with a certain celestial composure in her countenance, in her gait, and in her manner of speaking, insomuch that the exterior comportment of her body was a model of the inward sanctity of her soul; and by her outward carriage might well be known the beauty of the interior building, in which, as it were, rays of the divinity shone most marvellously.

(4) Exod. xxv. 11.   (5) 1 Co:. vii. 34.

(6) Lib. 2, de Virginib.

ii. The second was admirable *silence*, full of wisdom and discretion, speaking only when it was needful, and that in very few words, and with a very humble voice, as it appears by what is related of her in the Gospel. And on this account her lips are compared to "a scarlet lace, and" her "speech sweet,"(7) giving to understand that she was very sparing in her words, but yet with tokens and signs of singular charity, as was said in its proper place.

iii. The third was singular *temperance* and abstinence, observing in her refection a certain celestial rule, which St. Ambrose relates, saying, (8) " Cibus plerumque obvius, qui mortem arceret, non delicias ministraret." Her ordinary kind of meat was such as was to be found everywhere, which she took in such quantity as might suffice to keep her from dying of hunger; nor did she eat it for the pleasure's sake. Moreover, after the Ascension of her Son, she accomplished that which He said :—" Can the children of the bridegroom mourn, as long as the bridegroom is with them? But the days will come when the bridegroom shall be taken away from them, and then they shall fast." (9) She therefore fasted very rigorously, but especially when she petitioned anything of Almighty God for the good of the universal Church, joining fasting and penance with prayer, as she related afterwards to St. Elizabeth.(10)

iv. The fourth was very admirable *watching*, for as the same saint says, she only slept so much as was necessary to sustain nature, and when she could no longer resist it; neither then was she altogether idle, for, her body sleeping, her soul watched, either repeating what she had read, or continuing what she had interrupted, or executing something which she had proposed, or proposing something anew, with divers affections of spirit, according to that

(7) Cant. iv. 3.   (8) p. 2, Med. vii. et. p. 3, Med. ix.
(9) Mat. ix. 15.   (10) S. Bon. in vita Christi.

of the Canticles, saying:—" I sleep, and my heart watched." (11)

v. The fifth was great diligence in all exterior works, which belonged to the worship of God, to the service of her Son, to the management of her poor habitation, and to the good of her neighbours, performing the works of religion, of piety and mercy with great punctuality. This virtue St. Ambrose notices, annexing it with the former in these words:—" How shall I recount the small refection of the Virgin Mary, and her great labour and occupation?" Her exercise was such as surpassed her forces; her food was so little that nature almost fainted; her occupation was so continual that she admitted no interruption; she ate so seldom, that sometimes she passed whole days without food.

vi. The sixth virtue was most vigilant *custody of her heart*, whence, as the Wise man says, " life issueth out :"(12) so that when she went abroad, although it were in company, yet " nullo meliore sui custode, quam se ipsa utebatur"—" she had not a more secure keeper of herself than she herself," who always watched in the custody of her senses, composed her bodily motions, and kept her heart purely intent upon her God, whom alone she studied to please without making any account of the vain judgments and sayings of men:— " Arbitrium mentis solita non homines, sed Deum quærere." " She sought as judge and witness of her conscience, not men, but Almighty God," whose glory, as she always regarded it, so she always wished it, and, as far as in her lay, procured it.

Colloquy.—O sovereign Virgin, more pure than the very angels of heaven, I rejoice that thou art the mirror of virgins, the pattern of Religious, and the mistress of Evangelical perfection. Implore thy Son

(11) Cant. v. 2.   (12) Prov. iv. 23.

to adorn me with thy holy virtues, that I may perfectly fulfil all His counsels.   Amen.

POINT II.

Notwithstanding our Blessed Lady *always* practised most sublime prayer and contemplation, as has been said in the second part,(13) yet as she increased in years, so she *likewise increased in the gifts of God, particularly in this:* —here are to be considered certain things in which we may imitate her, according to our ability.

1. The first is, that she entirely, by a special privilege, *was exempt from the four impediments of prayer* and contemplation which the glorious St. Bernard calls, "guilt gnawing," "care pricking," "sense coveting," and "troops of vain thoughts troubling the imagination;"(14) for the Blessed Virgin was not like to the Sulamitess, which is a soul captive and taken prisoner by her own passions, who troubles herself for those chariots of Aminadab, averting herself from the sight of our Lord in holy prayer, until He call her effectually four times, saying:—"Return, return, O Sulamitess; return, return, that we may behold thee:"(15) for this most sacred Virgin always beheld Almighty God, nothing being able to divert, nor to withdraw her sight a moment from Him.

2. To this it greatly availed that *she had in her very perfectly all the virtues which dispose to prayer* and contemplation, which she made use of to ascend to heaven; especially a most lively faith in the divine mysteries, great confidence in God our Lord, profound humility, and above all, inflamed charity, with supereminent wisdom, and the other gifts of the Holy Ghost.   And as these virtues were now at their full growth in her, so likewise her contem-

(13) Medit. iv.

(14) Serm. xxiii. in Cant.   (15) Cant. vi. 12.

plation was the more perfect, for which cause the angels said of her with great admiration :—" Who is she that goeth up by the desert as a pillar of smoke, of aromatic spices, of myrrh and frankincense, and of all the powders of the perfumer?"(16)   As if they had said :—" Who is this that is full of the myrrh of mortification, and of the incense of prayer, and of the odoriferous powder of all virtues, which, being cast upon the coals of charity, ascend up as a most sweet smoke of contemplation, which always mounts and ascends so high, that we lose sight of it?"

Colloquy.—O most holy Virgin, I rejoice that living in earth, thou always hast thy conversation in heaven, soaring so high that thou causest great admiration to the angels themselves, who behold thee.   Draw me, O pious Virgin, after thee in the odour of thine examples, and enkindle in my soul so great a fire of charity as may consume in her all that is earthly, and may lift her up to contemplate that which is heavenly. Amen.

3. This lady *frequented very often the places in which her Son had wrought the mysteries of our redemption;* she visited the Garden of Gethsemane, the mount of Calvary, the holy sepulchre, and the mount of Olivet, whence He ascended up to heaven, and the sacred chamber in which the Holy Ghost descended, and first ordained the most holy Sacrament of the altar.   All these visits she made with great reverence and devotion, and with very high contemplation of the mysteries which were wrought in them, receiving new illustrations concerning them.

Colloquy.—O sovereign Virgin, how happy were he that might follow these thy steps and paces in this journey, ascending with these to the mountain of myrrh,

<hr>

(16) Cant. iii. 6.

and to the little hill of incense, beholding as thou beheldest that which Christ suffered on this mountain, and the manner in which He prayed on this hill. Lead me, O Lady, in thy company, and so direct me that I may ascend with security, and so illustrate me that I may contemplate the same with profit of spirit. Amen.

4. This excellent lady *prayed most instantly in every place and in every time*, and that with the greatest continuation that ever pure creature prayed, accomplishing in this the counsel of her Son, who says:—"That we ought always to pray, and not to faint:"(17) for she prayed and contemplated both day and night, and yet wrought with her hands; and although she slept, as has been said, yet she frequently thought on Almighty God, who visited her with visions no less delightful than those of Jacob, when sleeping he saw the Kingdom of God, in figure of that ladder, which standing upon the earth, touched heaven.(18) And generally in her contemplation, she received extraordinary favours, far greater than all the Saints of the New and Old Testament ever received. Almighty God appeared often to her as He did to Moses, speaking with her, not by figures, nor in dreams, but mouth to mouth, and face to face, with the greatest clearness that is compatible with this mortal life. She was rapt, like St. Paul, even to the third heaven, and entered into paradise itself, where she heard the secrets of God, which it is not lawful to utter to men. She was elevated in spirit like St. John the Evangelist, to see the things that were to come, and that with greater light than he. She saw several times the heavens open, as did St. Stephen, and her Son sitting upon the right hand of the Father. Finally, such and so great were her delights, that the angels admiring her,

(17) Luc. xviii. 1.   (18) Gen. xxviii. 12.

said :—" Who is this that cometh up from the desert, flowing with delights, leaning upon her beloved?" (19)   As if they had said,—" Who is this who ascends up by contemplation as high as heaven, and in this ascending receives abundance of delights, with so great favours, that she always leans upon her beloved, united with Him by perfect love, and leaning upon Him by very firm and assured faith.''

Colloquy.—O most holy Virgin, I rejoice to see thee so full and abounding in delights, and so united by love unto thy beloved ; well hast thou deserved them for the manifold labours which thou hast suffered for His sake ; well mayest thou say with David :—" According to the multitude of my sorrows in my heart, Thy comforts have given joy to my soul."(20) Impart, O my lady, some little drop of this celestial liquor to me thy servant, that I may take delight to run in the way of the divine commandments, with enlargement of heart, like thine.

5. This devout Lady, *communicated every day with extraordinary faith* reverence, and devotion, receiving her Son in the Blessed Sacrament to unite herself with Him daily anew, and delighting herself to see Him and enjoy Him in this Sacrament, till she might come to see Him in His glory.   In every communion she received such augmentation of grace, by reason of her most excellent disposition, as it is impossible to declare in words.   Oftentimes also, Christ our Lord shewed Himself to her in the same form, which then He had, and as He has done since to many others of His servants.

Colloquy.—O most holy Virgin, I rejoice to see thee every day renew that first joy which thou feltest in the Incarnation, receiving sacramentally into thy

(19) Cant. viii. 5.   (20) Ps. xciii. 19.

breast Him whom thou then receivedst into thy bowels. For His sake, I humbly beseech thee, obtain for me such disposition to receive Him, that here He so fill me with His grace, that hereafter I may enjoy Him with thee in His glory. Amen.

POINT III.

As the Virgin our Lady entered every day into the wine cellars of her Son, so she *burned in desire to exercise accordingly all the acts and works of charity :* whence arose in her a most inflamed zeal of the glory of God, and salvation of souls, but perfectly ordered; wherein we may all imitate her.

1. First; she vehemently *desired the salvation of all men,* which she solicited by prayers, and by all means she possibly could, now praying for the preachers of the Gospel, that God would give them efficacy in their words, and for sinners themselves, that God would vouchsafe to touch their hearts. And it may be believed, that by her prayers, at the first and second sermon of St. Peter, so many thousands of men were converted. As also St. Paul, for whom she prayed no less than St. Stephen did. She likewise prayed for the martyrs, that God would give them constancy and victory. And holding her hands lifted up to Almighty God, much better than Moses did, when the people of Israel overcame, how should not they overcome for whom she prayed?

Colloquy.—O sovereign Virgin, pray for this thy servant, when he fights against his enemies, for, thou praying for me, I shall overcome by thee, and thine shall be the glory of my victory.

2. *She likewise assisted souls with the rare example of her life,* which was indeed a dumb preacher, but most effectual to provoke and move to all virtue, for there shone in her

a certain divinity so great, that, as St. Dionysius said of her, unless faith corrected the understanding, all would take her for God, as her Blessed Son was.(21)

3. She assisted *with her words,* instructing the apostles in the mysteries of faith, which she knew with more particularity, and with greater light of heaven than they, comforting and encouraging the faithful who had recourse to her, not only from Jerusalem, but from the furthest parts of all the world. For, as St. Ignatius, martyr, said, all desired to see her as a miracle of celestial sanctity.(22)

4. But her charity went yet further, for, as by the inspiration of Almighty God, she went from Nazareth into the mountains of Judea to visit Elizabeth, and by her means justified John the Baptist—even so by the same inspiration *she undertook now also certain journeys.* For she was at Ephesus, as the Fathers of the council of Ephesus affirm : and she went to Antioch, as she herself promised St. Ignatius; and in like manner she went to other parts, to help and comfort the faithful who desired to see her, and to strengthen them in the faith, as also to spread it among the Gentiles.(23) For, although she was a great lover of quiet and recollection, yet charity forced her to issue forth (as is said in the book of Canticles) to visit the vineyards of the Church, and to see if they flourished, and whether the flowers of the new Christians produced the fruit of good works.(24)

5. Finally, at this time, and on this account, as the same St. Ignatius relates, *she endured great murmurings and persecutions from the Scribes and Pharisees,* and from all those who abhorred and persecuted her Blessed Son :

(21) Dionys. Carthus. cap. 3, de Divi. Mon.
(22) Epist. i. 2.
' (23) Tom. ii.   Act. Cons. Ephes. cap. xxvii.   Epist. iv. inter Epist. S. Ignat.
(24) Cant. vii. 12.

in which persecutions she showed herself very patient and joyful, rejoicing to suffer some contempt for the name and honour of her Son, and with this her marvellous example of patience, she greatly encouraged those who were persecuted, that they should endure them with the like patience. But her soul was greatly afflicted at the fall of certain feeble souls; for with more reason than St. Paul she might say:—" Who is weak, and I am not weak? Who is scandalized, and I am not on fire?" and that of the psalm,—" The zeal of thy house hath eaten me up,"(25) and all my inward parts, as it did those of her Son, when He beheld the sins of those that profaned it. But all this moved her to pray with greater fervour, and to procure with greater solicitude the salvation of souls, to His glory who created and redeemed them.

Colloquy.—O sovereign Virgin, if thou sufferedst no pains in bringing forth thy natural Son, Jesus Christ, thou dost now suffer them in the bringing forth of thine adopted sons, the whole human race. Thou art "clothed with the sun," and holdest the " moon under" thy "feet," and on thy head there is a "crown of twelve stars,"(26) and notwithstanding all this thou criest out through grief, to bring forth this son, and form Christ within his heart. Cry out, O Lady, I beseech thee, for me, and cease not to cry until thou hast engendered Jesus Christ within me, so that He may live in me, and I in Him, world without end. Amen.

POINT IV.

The last circumstance from which we may know the height of sanctity to which the Blessed Virgin attained is the *manner in which she performed her actions,* for she

_____

(25) 2 Cor. xi. 29. Ps. lxviii. 10.   (26) Apoc. xii. 1.

was not only "in all her works exquisite,"(27) but as the Wise man admonishes, most excellent, increasing every day by innumerable degrees of excellence; for in every work she employed the utmost of her spiritual strength, working with the greatest possible affection of heart. And forasmuch as Christ our Lord pays those who are fervent in ready money, rewarding them immediately, and giving them all the increase of grace and charity, which they have merited by the work they have wrought; for this reason the Blessed Virgin, in all her works, redoubled her spiritual strength, and doubly augmented the charity with which she loved ; and thus when she returned a second time to exercise her acts of love, she loved with a more redoubled intention than before, and after this manner went adding and augmenting day by day with incomprehensible increase; for charity, as St. Thomas says, has not in this life any bound or limit in increase, and the fire of the Blessed Virgin's love never said, "it is enough."(28)

1. Hence it is that she most eminently *fulfilled that precept* which says:—"*Thou shalt love the Lord thy God, with thy whole heart, and with thy whole soul, and with thy whole strength ;*" for she employed them all in loving Him with all the faculties she had, and with all the perseverance that was possible for her in this mortal life, to which she was excited by all the motives that she had to love her Son, as has been considered in the fourth part.

2. After the same manner most excellently did she *accomplish that petition of the "Our Father :"*—"*Thy will be done in earth as it is in heaven,*" for she fulfilled it in all things, both great and small, with as great love, with as great purity of intention, and with as great diligence and

(27) Ecclus. xxxiii. 12.
(28) S. Th. 2, 2, q. xxiv. art. 7.   Prov. xxx. 16.

fervour, as the angels fulfil it in heaven, and even with much greater, those only excepted which are peculiar to the state of the blessed.(29)

3. She also seriously endeavoured day by day to extend and *enlarge her heart,* so as to receive greater gifts of Almighty God, arising from that great confidence which she had in the abyss of His bounty.(30) Whence it happened that as Isaias said, she every day renewed her fortitude, giving it new increase, recovering new feathers, and like an eagle, flew and soared to the height of perfection, ran without labour, and walked without weariness, rejoicing as a giant to run her course with great celerity, even to its summit.(31)

Colloquy.—O glorious Virgin, daughter of the supreme Prince, how beautiful are the steps and paces of thy feet, studded with such divine virtues! Oh how prosperously dost thou proceed every day, like the " morning rising," fair as the moon, bright as the sun, terrible as an army set in array." (32) Thou beginnest thy works like to the morning, increasing in light "even to perfect day;"(33) thou dost prosecute them like to the full moon, filling them with the fulness of conformity to the will of God ; thou dost perfect them like the sun with singular excellence, illuminating with them the whole world, and inflaming them with the love of their Creator ; and finally all thy works are as an army of virtues set in goodly array, terrible to the devils, and pleasing to the elect, whose protection thou art. Take me, I beseech thee, under thy protection, that through thy favour I may increase daily, from virtue to virtue, until I come to see the God of gods in His hill of Sion, world without end. Amen.

<hr>

(29) Medit. i. p. viii.   (30) Isa. xl. 31.   (31) Ps. xviii. 7.

     (32) Cant. vi. 2.   (33) Prov. iv. 18.

MEDITATION XXXIV.

ON THE GLORIOUS DEATH OF THE BLESSED VIRGIN.

POINT I.

1. In the first place let us consider the *lively and inflamed desires of the Blessed Virgin*, especially in the latter years of her life, to go and see Almighty God, and to be united to her Son, which arose, not from the irksomeness she had of this present life, nor from any aversion to the toil she sustained, but only from pure love, which, when very vehement, greatly desires the presence its beloved, and nowhere finds rest until it sees Him.

i. And because she was well skilled in the knowledge of the Holy Scriptures, *she drew thence the words of her affection;* sometimes speaking to herself she said with David:—" Woe is me, that my sojourning is prolonged; I have dwelt," for a long time, " with the inhabitants of Cedar, my soul hath been long a sojourner :"(1) at other times speaking with Almighty God she said:—" As the hart panteth after the fountains of water, so my soul panteth after Thee, O God. My soul hath thirsted after the strong living God, when shall I come and appear before the face of God ?"(2) " Bring my soul out of prison, that it may praise Thy name; the just wait for me,"(3) until Thou give me the crown of justice, which Thou hast promised me. Other times speaking with the angels that visited her, she repeated to them that of the Canticles :— " I adjure you, O daughters of Jerusalem, if you find my beloved, that you tell Him that I languish with love ;" (4)

(1) Ps. cxx. 5.   (2) Ps. xli. 2.   (3) Ps. cxli. 8.
(4) Cant. v. 8.

tell Him that my spirit fails, and my flesh faints for the desire I have to see and enjoy Him.

ii. Moreover it is to be believed that sometimes there was within the heart of the Blessed Virgin that holy contest between the love of God and her neighbour, which St. Paul also felt when he said:—"I am straitened between two; having a desire to be dissolved and to be with Christ, a thing by far better: but to abide still in the flesh is needful for you;" (5) for the love of God urged the Blessed Virgin to be dissolved, and to be with Christ; but the love of her neighbour, whose necessity she saw, told her that it was necessary to remain as yet in the flesh, to do good for them; and forasmuch as she was perfectly resigned to the divine will, in a state of the most excellent obedience, she said what St. Martin afterwards said:— "Lord, if I be necessary to Thy people, I refuse not the labour, Thy will be done."

Colloquy.—O ineffable Virgin, who wert neither overcome by labour, nor to be overcome by death, who neither fearest to die nor refusedst to live, only seeking the will of Almighty God. Oh that I might live in such a manner, as to imitate thy fervent desires, with thy holy resignation, desiring death with joy, and enduring the present life with patience.

iii. At length, when the Blessed Virgin felt that but a few days of her mortal life now remained, she began with new fervour to prepare herself for her departure, exercising most high and noble acts of virtue, saying that of the Canticles:—"*Stay me up with flowers, compass me about with apples, because I languish with love:* (6) as if she had said, whilst speaking to her own faculties, The force of love consumes my life, let it, therefore, produce new flowers,

<hr>

(5) Phil. i. 23.　　　(6) Cant. ii. 5.

and celestial fruits, let it bud forth meditations, affections, and most odoriferous works, which may assuage my sickness, and dispose me to my end.

2. In these three things I ought to imitate the Blessed Virgin, and prepare myself for death, *with inflamed desires of seeing God*, with perfect resignation to the divine will, and with more perfect works, and increasing fervour, when I foresee that I am approaching my last hour ; for it is not a small fault to be lukewarm in the desire of seeing God, and of attaining eternal happiness; thus we read, that there is a certain kind of purgatory in the other life, which is called the purgatory of desire, in which is purged the lukewarmness of those which had not a fervent desire of seeing God. (7)

POINT II.

In the second place we are to consider *what preceded the death of the Blessed Virgin.*

1. Although God our Lord preserved the Blessed Virgin from original sin, yet *He would not preserve her from the death of the body,* which is its punishment, but wished her to suffer it like all other men, by which we may see how irrevocable the sentence of death is. This likewise He permitted, that in this the Virgin might imitate her Son, who died to redeem us by His death ; and that her merit might be the greater by overcoming this natural repugnance of the flesh to die; for St. Paul says:—" We would not be unclothed, but clothed upon" with the garment of glory, " that that which is mortal may be swallowed up by life:" (8) and that she might also by her death give to all a rare example of virtue, and might have compassion on those that die, having herself sustained that combat and repugnance of the flesh, because she was to be our

(7) Blos, in Moniti. Spirit. c. xiii.   (8) 2 Cor. v. 4.

advocate at the hour of death. Hence I am encouraged to beseech the holy Virgin to succour me in that hour, and obtain for me one favour out of the multitude she received at that time, saying unto her very devoutly those last words of the Ave Maria:—"Pray for us sinners, now and at the hour of our death, Amen:" and that other hymn which says,

> " Mother of grace, O Mary blest,
> To thee, sweet fount of love, we fly,
> Shield us through life, and take us hence,
> To thy dear bosom when we die."*

2. The appointed time being come for the glorious departure of the Virgin, her Blessed Son *sent to her the Archangel Gabriel, to declare to her the joyful tidings.* He came, therefore, beaming and resplendent, as when he came to bring her the message of the Incarnation of the divine Word. And it is very probable that he now entered with the same salutation as then, saying:—" Hail full of grace, our Lord is with thee, blessed art thou amongst women," by reason of the blessed fruit of thy womb Jesus, from whom I have been sent to announce to thee, that now the hour is come when He will take thee to Himself, and reward the services thou hast done, and gladden the court of heaven, who are anxiously waiting to enjoy thee in their company.(9) Oh what deep feelings may we think the Blessed Virgin had when she heard these tidings ; on the one hand, full of jubilees of joy, she said with David:—" I rejoiced at these things that were said to me, We shall go into the house of the Lord:" (10) and on the other, with great resignation she repeated that answer which once before she had given to the same angel, saying:—" Behold the handmaid of the Lord, be it

* *Caswall's Breviary Hymns.*

(9) Nicep. 1. 2. cap. xxi.   (10) Ps. cxxi. 1.

done to me according to thy word." These two affections of the Blessed Virgin I ought to ponder and retain in my heart, for the hour when the news of my approaching death shall be announced to me, for God desires me to receive it with joy and resignation.

3. The apostles, *together with many other disciples* miraculously came to assist *at the death* of the Blessed Virgin, rather for their own advancement, than for her comfort, although she greatly rejoiced to see them present.(11) All lamented her departure, and recommended themselves to her prayers; she again comforted them all, giving them wholesome advice and according to the example of her Son, prayed for them, and gave them her blessing with great affection, offering herself to be their faithful advocate in the Kingdom of heaven.

Colloquy.—O most sweet Mother, we remain orphans on earth, if thou ascend and mount to heaven, yet if we be assured of thine assistance from heaven, we shall live secure here in earth. Ascend, therefore, in good time, since by thy benediction thou dost leave us a pledge that we shall follow thee, and enjoy with thee thy Son in eternal glory. Amen.

POINT III.

1. The hour being now come, *Christ our Lord descended from heaven to take up His Mother*, fulfilling in her the promise He had made to His apostles, when He said to them :—" If I shall go and prepare a place for you, I will come again and will take you to myself." (12) And it is certain that He brought with Him an innumerable multitude of holy angels to be present at her death, driving thence all the devils, so that none of them durst appear

(11) S. Dionys. cap. iii. de Divin. Nom. S. Damas. S. Juven. Lipoman. Ser. de Assump. B. Virg.

(12) Joan. xiv. 3.

there, not yet approach her holy dwelling. Oh what cheerful words did the Son use to His Blessed Mother! Our understanding truly cannot conceive them, unless by that which is written in the Canticles ; He said, therefore, to her with great love :—" Arise, make haste, my love, my dove, my beautiful one, and come, for winter is now past," and the end of thy labours is arrived.—" Come from Libanus, O my spouse," (13) and from the high mountains of most fertile virtues, on which thou hast hitherto dwelt: leave this miserable world, which is a den of lions and a mountain of tigers, come and thou shalt be crowned with the crown of justice, which thou hast so well deserved.

2. The Blessed Virgin seeing her Son, and hearing the words which He spoke to her heart, out of the great charity which was in her, besought Him to comfort His apostles and disciples, by pouring upon them His fruitful benediction.   And immediately remembering how her Son gave up the ghost upon the cross, she *repeated the same words which He pronounced, saying :*—O my Father, inasmuch as God, and my Son, inasmuch as man, "*Into Thy hands I commend my spirit,*"(14) and saying this, she gave up the ghost. Oh how precious was the death of this sacred Lady in the eyes of Almighty God, in whose sight the death of His saints are so precious.

i. Her death was precious, because she died not so much from any bodily sickness, as from the *vehemence and excess of love* which consumed her corporal strength; and therefore she might say that of the spouse :—" I languish with love,"(15) "and I am wounded with charity ;" which wound penetrating to her soul, drew it forth from her body, that she might behold Him who had wounded her with the wound of His inflamed charity.

(13) Cant. ii. 10.   Ibid. iv. 8.

(14) Ps. xxx. 6.   (15) Cant. ii. 5.

ii. *She died without pain,* her Son contenting Himself with the pain she endured when she saw Him die upon the cross. And moreover the jubilee of her soul which she felt in the presence of her beloved was so very great, that she felt not her departure from her body, that being accomplished in her which the divine Wisdom says, that "the torment of death shall not touch" the just, because their souls "are in the hands of God."(16)

iii. *All her works,* which were many and most noble, *then linked themselves together,* and Almighty God manifested them, that they might accompany her, and fill her with confidence and joy. For, if "blessed are the dead who die in the Lord,"(17) how much more blessed is she who died in Christ, and from the pure love of Christ, with such great abundance of excellent works which accompanied her? If the servant be blessed, whom the Lord "shall find watching" when He comes to His house, how much more blessed shall this Virgin be, who never slept a deadly sleep as the foolish virgins did, nor any light sleep, as the wise did, but always watched? If "the just," as the Wise man says, "hath hope in his death,"(18) what far greater hope had the Queen of the just in the last hour of her death? Oh that my soul might die the death of this glorious lady, who by excellence deserves the name of just, and that my last end might be like to hers!

Colloquy.—O most holy Virgin, that my death may in some sort resemble thine, obtain for me that I may live wounded with love, and be so full of good works that the torment of death may not touch me. It is but just that the corporal torment of death should touch me, since it is a penalty which I have merited by my sins, but let no spiritual torment touch and

(16) Sap. iii. 1.   (17) Apoc. xiv. 13.   (11) Prov. xiv. 32.

afflict me with disordinate fear, diffidence, and dejection of heart.   Amen.

POINT IV.

1. After the Virgin gave up the ghost, *her body was interred with great pomp*, both of heaven and earth, so that we may say of her what Isaias said of Christ Himself:—and her "sepulchre shall be glorious:"(19) for thither hastened the most glorious creatures both of heaven and earth, viz., *the Apostles, and many disciples, who went singing hymns and praises to Almighty God and His mother*, as the Holy Ghost inspired their hearts and mouths: the choirs of angels also came, followed the sacred corpse, and remained three days at the sepulchre, making celestial music, and honouring their Queen there entombed.(20)

2. Her sepulchre was likewise glorious, *for the great miracles which Almighty God* wrought at the presence of her venerable body. For, although while she lived she wrought no miracles, partly through humility, and partly to leave this glory to the apostles and preachers of the Gospel, partly also because her whole life was nothing but a continual miracle, and much more glorious than the life of St. John the Baptist, yet, in dying, her Son would honour her with conspicuous miracles, as He honours other saints.

3. It was glorious, because though the apostles and other disciples were afflicted at the death of the Blessed Virgin, yet it is to be believed, that *by and by Christ our Lord manifested to them the glory of His mother*, and filled their hearts with spiritual joy, they certainly persuading themselves that they had in heaven a true mother and advocate, who would there be careful of them.

(19) Isa. xi. 10.
(20) S. Dionys., S. Dams, S. Juven., Lipoman. ut supra.

Colloquy.—O sovereign Virgin, I desire, as far as I may, to accompany thy body with my spirit, to enter amongst the choirs of apostles and angels, and to sing with them thy due praises. It was most meet that as thy body was the glorious sepulchre wherein the eternal Word was, as it were, buried for nine months, He should now give to thy body a glorious sepulchre, in which to repose for three days. And since during thy whole life it was employed in praising and glorifying thy Creator, and after three days is to return to perform the same exercise perpetually, it was with great reason that during these three days the angels should in its stead serve as a tongue to glorify Him, whom hitherto it had ever glorified. I give Thee thanks, O eternal Word, for the honour Thou didst confer on Thy worthy Mother ; and for her sake I humbly beseech Thee to grant me such a death, that I may merit to enjoy Thee in her company in glory, world without end. Amen.

MEDITATION XXXV.

OF THE ASSUMPTION OF THE BLESSED VIRGIN, AS REGARDS HER SOUL,
ABOVE ALL THE CHOIRS OF ANGELS, AND OF HER ESSENTIAL
GLORY AND CORONATION.

POINT I.

The first shall be to consider *the glorious ascent and entrance of the Virgin into the empyreal heaven :* for immediately she gave up the ghost, her holy soul being now loosed from the body, in an instant *flew to heaven,. and there was glorified.*

1. Meditating this after our manner, we may suppose that this took place not in a moment, but by little and little.

i. Therefore I will ponder the *sweet and mutual embraces of the mother and the Son,* in that first meeting, with ineffable joy. For there was accomplished that which was written:—" His left hand is under my head, and His right hand shall embrace me :"(1) for while she lived in the body, He sustained her by the contemplation of the mysteries and works of His humanity, signified by the left hand; but when she died, He immediately embraced and environed her soul with the clear sight of His divinity, figured by the right hand. O how joyful was that blessed soul in that first instant, and with what affection of mind did she repeat that of the spouse, saying:—"I found Him whom my soul loveth; I held Him, and I will not let Him go," (2) until He bring me and carry me with Him to the house of my mother, that celestial Jerusalem.

Colloquy.—O sovereign Virgin, obtain for me such purity of life and such fervour of charity, that my soul, departing from my body, may immediately fall into the arms of her beloved, and may ascend with Him to the house of my mother, where thou, my true mother, dost dwell, rejoicing with thy Son, world without end. Amen.

ii. I will ponder the *noble troop of the three angelical hierarchies which accompanied the Blessed Virgin,* and celebrated her Assumption, saluting her, as St. Athanasius says,(3) with salutations of singular glory, and rejoicing to conduct her to their exalted city; they congratulated with her for the great wonders which Almighty God had · wrought in her, and all with one voice resounded the salutation of the angel Gabriel, in which was contained an epilogue of her excellencies. And I, entering in spirit amidst these hierarchies, will likewise praise this glorious Lady,

(1) Cant. ii. 6.   (2) Cant. iii. 4.
(3) Ser. de Assumpt. Virg.

celebrating her triumph, as the Hebrews did the triumph of Judith, saying :—

Colloquy.—O glorious Virgin, "thou art the glory as well of the militant as of the triumphant Jerusalem;" "thou art the joy of Israel," as well of such as see God by contemplation in this life, as of such as behold Him clearly in the other.   "Thou art the honour of our people," (4) because thou hast always wrought manfully, having loved chastity without ever knowing man : for this thou shalt be ever blessed, and for thy sake all those shall be blessed who shall be under thy protection.

iii. I will ponder, thirdly, how this sacred Virgin ascended, not *carried by the hands of angels*, as Lazarus the beggar was into Abraham's bosom, but *by the hands of her own Son*, and between His own arms, for He here repaid the services and fostering care she showed Him in His infancy, when she sweetly bore Him in her arms. Hence proceeded the great admiration of the celestial hierarchies, when they said :—"Who is this that cometh up from the desert, flowing with delights, leaning upon her beloved?"(5)   As if they had said, Who is this ascending from the desert of the dry and barren world, where there is nothing but labour and sorrow, and notwithstanding this, she ascends so rich, prosperous, and bountiful, full of celestial delights, leaning, not upon herself, nor upon the angels, but upon her own beloved?

2. In like manner did the sacred Virgin enter into the empyreal heaven, to the unspeakable joy and content of all the celestial citizens, and of the most Holy Trinity.   For the eternal Father rejoiced to have with Him His beloved daughter ; the Son, to have with Him His most sweet mother; and the Holy Ghost, to enjoy in His company

(4) Judith xv. 10.   (5) Cant. viii. 5.

His beloved spouse. O what joyful receiving! O what sweet kisses of peace! O what amorous embraces! O what tender discourses passed between such a daughter and such a Father, between such a mother and such a Son, between such a spouse with His espoused, and between the three divine Persons, to honour so great a princess! All this I am to reverence with great silence and admiration, because it is infinitely more than I am able to conceive.

3. From what has been said, I am to form an inward desire to *follow in spirit the glorious Virgin in this journey*, and begin to dispose myself to it. i. *In heart I should forsake the world*, imagining that to me it is a desert, and deprive myself of all its sensual delights, so to become capable of spiritual. ii. *I should strive to ascend daily and profit in virtue*, not relying on my own strength, nor putting my trust in the arm of flesh, but relying upon the arm of Almighty God, placing in Him my whole confidence. iii. *I must always rejoice in Almighty God*, and delight in what belongs to His service, to the end I may abound in His gifts and graces, and be, as the apostle Paul says, " rich" in Christ Jesus, " so that nothing be wanting" to me " in any grace, waiting for the manifestation of our Lord Jesus Christ."(6)

POINT II.

1. We are next to consider *the essential glory of the soul of this Virgin our Blessed Lady*.

i. If to all the just, as Christ our Lord says, there shall be given " good measure, and pressed down, and shaken together, and running over," (7) what measure did He grant to His Mother? If with the same measure with which we mete, it shall be measured to us again, *what*

(6) 1 Cor. i, 5 et 7.(7) Luc. vi. 38.

measure, as it were, without measure, shall she receive of God, who never has any limited measure in loving and serving Him.   The measure of the Virgin in the service of her Son was always good, with every kind of goodness, without the mixture of any fault; full of all graces and virtues, with the plenitude of all good works, without failing in any respect; pressed with labours and mortifications; shaken together and running over with the keeping of the Evangelical counsels, performing much more than she was bound to, and always desiring to do much more, without putting any limit or measure to her desire. If, therefore, Almighty God reward the just, with a measure of glory, which a thousand times excels their services, how did He reward the excellent measure of His mother?   Only God Himself who gave it, and the Virgin who received it, know the immensity of this measure; to us it suffices to know that the sacred Virgin remained full and satisfied, proving the truth of that which says,—" I shall be satisfied when Thy glory shall appear."(8)

ii. We may also imagine that *our Lord said to her what* Holofernes said to Judith:—*" Drink now and sit thee down, for thou hast found favour before me."*   And the Virgin might answer as Judith did: " I will drink my lord, because my life is magnified this day above all my days." (9)   For, the most sacred Virgin drank and was filled, because her understanding was filled with the clear vision of Almighty God, Three and One, drinking of that immense sea of His infinite wisdom, with such abundance that the Cherubim, who are called the fulness of knowledge, in comparison with her seemed empty.   Her will was filled with the beatific love of God, she entered the " cellar of " His " wine," and drank of the delicious wine of charity, until she was inebriated, and that with such

(8) Ps. xvi. 15.   (9) Judith xii. 17 et 18.

excess of love, that the Seraphim, who are said to be inflamed with love, in comparison with her, were frozen. Her spirit was wholly filled with the peaceable possession of that infinite good which it had desired; and she was engulfed so deep in the bottomless sea of the joys of her Lord, and drank of the running river of His delights with such great fulness, (10) that in comparison of her, the angels themselves seemed to be exceedingly thirsty.

iii. Lastly, then did Almighty God employ (if I may so say) the rest of His bounty and omnipotence, *in filling the desires of His Mother with as great fulness as was convenient for a pure creature*, rendering to her the reward for the many times she had given Him to drink, not a cup of cold water, but the milk of her own breasts, until He had drunk His own fill. Then did He put His Mother to the breasts of His divinity, that she might be filled with the infinite sweetness of His milk; then did He likewise recompense her for the draught of that bitter chalice, which, for His sake she drank in His Passion, giving her to drink of the most delicious charity of His glory, with which draught she quite forgot all her past pains and bitterness, because the sweetness of the one was incomparably greater than the bitterness of the other. He entirely wiped " away all tears from" her " eyes," (11) chasing away for ever all mourning and lamentation, and all the miseries of the old man, and renewing her with the glorious dowries of the new.

Colloquy.—O most glorious Virgin, I rejoice at this thy glory, and at the joy and fulness which thou receivedst at this celestial table, where thou art seated with thy blessed Son, and close by His side eatest and drinkest what He Himself eats and drinks; much better hast thou deserved this seat and this society than the apostles have, since thou remainedst with Him in His temptations, much more faithful than they. And since the measure that is given thee is so abundant, remember us who are hungry and thirsty, who live on earth, and distribute amongst us at least some little crumbs.   Amen.

2. Hence I will conceive a firm purpose of imitating the Blessed Virgin in that measure with which she served Almighty God, with the four conditions before mentioned, animating myself with the hope of the glory which God will give me, a thousand times greater than my works merit of their own nature, for which reason St. Paul said: —" that the sufferings of this time are not worthy to be compared to the glory to come, that shall be revealed in us."(12)

POINT III.

The third shall be to consider *the Coronation of the holy Virgin* our Lady, with the other circumstances of her glory.

*1. For, first, the sacred Virgin *was lifted up far above the nine choirs of angels*, to a glory incomparably greater than all theirs, for her Son placed her at His right hand in a throne of great majesty, with greater demonstrations of love than Solomon placed in another throne his mother Bethsabee. Then was accomplished that of David:—" The queen stood on thy right hand in gilded clothing, surrounded with variety."(13) For, as Christ our Lord is said to sit at the right hand of His Father, because He enjoys the best goods, both of grace and glory, that there are in heaven ; even so this holy Virgin sits at the right hand of her Son, because, after Him she holds the highest degree of glory above all the choirs of angels, and above the

(12) Rom. viii. 18.   (13) 3 Reg. ii. 19. Ps. xliv. 10.

other blessed spirits, for by how much the name of mother is more glorious than that of servant, by so much is the Virgin's throne higher than that of all the other saints.

Colloquy.—I rejoice, O queen of angels, for the exalted height of thy throne, and may this thy sitting upon the right hand of thy Son be productive of much good. Oh how fitly does this garment of the gold of charity become thee, bordered round about with such a variety of virtues! If the first angel, who afterwards fell by reason of his pride, was adorned in paradise with nine kinds of precious stones, that is to say, with all the perfections of the nine angelic choirs; how much more shalt thou be adorned, with all the perfections of the living and precious stones of the celestial Jerusalem!(14) O mother of mercy, behold my nakedness, and obtain for me the wedding garment of charity, with the other precious pearls of virtues, that I may be worthy to appear in the presence of my God, and to enjoy Him in thy company. Amen.

2. The sacred Virgin *was crowned by the most holy Trinity*, with most precious crowns.—The Father crowned her with a crown of *power*, giving her after Christ absolute power over all creatures, both of heaven, earth, and hell, accomplishing that of the divine Psalmist:—"Thou hast crowned" her " with glory and honour," " and hast set" her " over the works of thy hands." (15) The Son crowned her with a crown of *wisdom*, giving her a most clear knowledge, not only of the divine essence, but also of all other things created, and of all those things which appertain to her dignity of our mother and our advocate.—The Holy Ghost crowned her with a crown of *charity*, infusing into her, not only the love of Almighty God, but also the

(14) Ezech. xxviii. 12.   S. Greg. lib. xxxii. mor. cap. 18.
(15) Ps. viii. 6.

inflamed love of her neighbours, with a most ardent zeal for their good and salvation. Oh, in what a state of admiration and astonishment were the three hierarchies of angels, when they saw the Virgin adorned with such crowns! The Seraphim stood amazed at the fervour of her charity; the Cherubim admired the plenitude of her knowledge; the thrones the abundance of her peace; the dominations the greatness of her power; the virtues the excellence of her gifts; and the other angels the sovereignty and perfection of her sanctity.

Colloquy.—Rejoice, O my soul, at this crown of the glorious Virgin; be glad that thou hast a mother in heaven of such power and greatness, who can by her intercession help and remedy all thy miseries; and of such great wisdom that she knows perfectly well all thy necessities, and understands thy desires and petitions; and of such great charity and zeal, that she desires their accomplishment much more than thyself. O most sweet Mother, crowned by thy Son " with mercy and" with abundance of "compassion," beseech Him that He would vouchsafe to crown me with them in this life, that I may obtain the crown of the next, Amen.

3. Moreover, the most holy Trinity crowned the sacred Virgin with three *crowns of accidental glory*, which divines call garlands, or crowns of laurel, which never lose their verdure, namely, the laurel of a virgin, of a martyr, and of a teacher. For this Lady was the Virgin of virgins; she was a Martyr in the Passion of her Son, in the manner already shown, and the teacher of our religion, the mysteries of which she taught even to our teachers.

Colloquy.—O sovereign Queen, how well hast thou deserved these crowns in heaven, for the abundant

(16) Medit. xlvii. 4 p.

fruits which thou hast produced here in earth! For thou didst produce the fruit of thirty as Virgin; of sixty as Teacher; and of a hundred as Martyr. It is therefore meet that such precious crowns should answer to such labours; and that I also may be worthy of them, obtain for me that I may produce abundant fruit of holy works. Amen.

4. Lastly, this sacred Virgin was crowned *with the crown of which mention is made in the Apocalypse,* for as there concurred in her the excellencies and virtues of all the orders of saints that are in heaven, so was she crowned with their rewards figured by the twelve stars. For there shone in her eminently, and with great advantage, the faith and hope of the patriarchs,—the light and contemplation of the prophets,—the charity and zeal of the apostles,—the fortitude and magnanimity of the martyrs, —the patience and penance of the confessors,—the wisdom and discretion of the doctors,—the sanctity and purity of the priests,—the solitude and prayer of the hermits,—the poverty and obedience of the monks,— the charity and purity of virgins,—the humility and endurance of widows, with the fidelity and concord of the holy married, and by consequence she received the rewards and crowns of them all with incomparable advantage, for to her agreed with strange peculiarity that which the Wise man says:—" Many daughters have gathered together riches; thou hast surpassed them all:" (17) which means, many souls have gathered together great treasures of merits and virtues, but thou hast gathered together more than all. Arise, therefore, my soul, in spirit, and behold with the eyes of' faith, this mother of the true Solomon, with the crown of glory with which her Son crowned her on the day of her

---

(17) Prov. xxx. 29.

entrance into heaven, and on the day of the gladness of her heart.   Contemplate the ineffable joy of this sovereign Queen, and the affection with which she renewed her ancient Canticle, saying :—"My soul doth magnify the Lord, and my spirit hath rejoiced in God my Saviour. Because He hath regarded the humility of His handmaid; for behold, from henceforth all generations shall call me blessed.   Because He that is mighty hath done great things to me, and holy is His name." (18)

Colloquy.—O glorious Virgin, may all the generations, both of heaven and earth, with one voice call thee blessed, since thou now hast in thy possession what before thou didst hold only in hope.   He who is mighty always did great things in thee, but this day He sealed them all with the crown of glory which He gave thee in reward of thy great humility.   Thou art crowned with stars, because the saints who imitated thee are thy glory and thy crown, and by thy intercession and assistance they have obtained their victories.   Therefore with great humility do they " cast their crowns" before thy feet, confessing that by thy means they have obtained them.   O pious advocate, and most potent mediatrix, succour me by thy intercession, that I also may be thy joy and thy crown, fighting with such valour in this life, that by thy means I may obtain the victory, and win the crown of eternal glory.   Amen.

(18) Luc. i. 46.

MEDITATION XXXVI.

POINT I.

The first shall be to consider the *incorruption of the most sacred body of the Blessed Virgin* the three days it remained in the sepulchre, Almighty God preserving it with the same integrity which it had during life.

i. For although this sacred Virgin was conceived after the natural order of other men, yet was her soul preserved by especial privilege from the stain and guilt of original sin, as has been said in its place ;(1) so also, though she died a natural death, as the other daughters of Adam, yet by special privilege her body was preserved from the corruption which was the pain of guilt, so that she fell not into that malediction which God gave to man when He said :— "Dust thou art; and unto dust thou shalt return."(2)

2. The *causes* of this privilege were three.

The first was, in *reward of her virginal purity*, which was miraculous and unheard of, for it was bound by a strong vow, and kept with great constancy throughout her whole life; and therefore was to be rewarded with a miraculous and extraordinary reward, but most proportionable to her, namely, the preservation of the integrity of so pure a body without corruption for all eternity.

ii. The second cause was in reward *of the extraordinary and miraculous purity and sanctity of her soul*, into which never entered the gnawing worm of guilt, nor the contaminating dust of sin, nor any savour of earthly Adam; for which cause it was most just that the worms should not

(1) 2 p. Medit. iii.　　　　　　(2) Gen. iii. 19.

touch her sacred body, and that it should not be converted into earth or dust, but be preserved most entire, like to the body of the heavenly Adam, in regard of whose sanctity David said:—"Nor wilt give Thy holy one to see corruption." (3)

iii. Hence arises the third cause, for it was *becoming to the honour of Christ our Lord, whose flesh was, as it were, one and the same,* with the unspotted flesh of His most pure mother, from which His was taken.   And as the flesh of Christ never felt corruption, so, as St. Augustine says, it was reasonable that the flesh of His mother should not be touched or tainted, for in it was, in a certain manner, that of her Son. (4)

Colloquy.—O blessed Mother of our Saviour Jesus, Ark of the New Testament, built of the incorruptible wood of setim, gilded all over "with purest gold,"(5) to be made the worthy habitation of Him who was the propitiation of the whole world ; I rejoice at the incorruptibility of thy body, and of the most pure gold of thy virtues, with which thou didst adorn thy spirit. Obtain for me, sovereign Virgin, that " incorruptibility of a quiet and a meek spirit, which is rich in the sight of God,"(6) that freeing my soul from all corruption of sin, my body may likewise be freed from the corruption which it has deserved by it.

POINT II.

1. *The body of the sacred Virgin rose again the third day,* issuing forth from the sepulchre alive and glorious, through the virtue and omnipotence of her Son, to whom it seemed but a small favour to preserve the body of His blessed mother uncorrupt until the day of the general resurrection,

<table>
<tr><td>(3) Ps. xv. 10.</td><td>(4) Serm. de Assumpt.</td></tr>
<tr><td>(5) Exod. xxv.</td><td>(6) 1 Pet. iii. 4.</td></tr>
</table>

and therefore He would anticipate that time by raising it up the third day.

. i. The first cause of this favour was, because *the Son of God, loving His Mother so vehemently, would accomplish and fulfil*, not only the desires which her blessed soul had to see God, but also *the natural desire it had to be reunited with the body*: which desire the souls of the other blessed have, of whom it is said in the Apocalypse that they cry with the voice of a great desire for the resurrection of their bodies.(7)   And because both the body and soul of the Blessed Virgin were always greatly united and conform in accomplishing the will of God, it was great reason that God should immediately join them together, that with the same conformity they might praise Him everlastingly.(8)

ii. The second was to *give us hope of our own resurrection* by believing that not only Christ, true God and Man, rose again, but also His Mother, a pure creature ; and thus to excite in us great desires to see her, pretending and "minding the things that are above, not the things that are upon the earth,"(9) where Jesus Christ is, with His Mother sitting at His right hand.

iii. The third cause was, that with all propriety, even from that time to the day of judgment, and for everlastingly, *there might be preserved in the Virgin the name of the Mother of God*, because this name does not properly agree to her soul alone, but to the union of body and soul.   In order also that she might perform in heaven, in our behalf, the office of a mother and advocate by appeasing the anger of her Son, and showing Him her maternal breasts, as the Son appeases the anger of the Father, by showing Him His precious wounds ; and that thus we might have in heaven

(7) Apoc. vi. 10.   (8) S. Greg. lib. ii. mor. cap. vi.
. (9) Colos. iii. 2.

"a help like unto himself,"(10) in the glory of soul and body, as Adam had in the earthly paradise.

2. For these and other causes mentioned in the preceding point, God decreed to raise the Virgin, and unite her soul to her body. Oh how great was the joy and gladness of this lady for this new benefit, and how sincerely did she renew this third day her accustomed canticle, saying:— "My soul doth magnify the Lord, and my spirit hath rejoiced in God my Saviour; because He that is mighty hath done great things to me," having thus glorified my soul and body. Oh what content did that glorious body experience on seeing itself united to that blessed soul, and receiving from it those four dowries of bliss and glory! For it was made a thousand times more resplendent than the sun, and far more beautiful, without comparison, than the full moon; for it now remained impassible, agile, and wholly spiritual, without any fear of hunger, cold, weariness, or any other kind of misery; for all this ceased on her being raised again to a new life, never more to die again.

Colloquy.—I give Thee thanks, O eternal Word, for this new and singular favour which Thou hast shown to Thy Mother, careful of Thine own honour and for hers; for it is the glory of children to have glorious parents. I rejoice, O glorious Virgin, for this new privilege granted thee this day by thy blessed Son, in fulfilling the desire of thy soul, and glorifying thy body like His own; pray for me in His presence, show Him the breasts which thou gavest Him when He was a tender babe, that He may likewise fulfil the desires of my soul by favouring me in such a manner that I may faithfully serve Him in this life, and that He may hereafter glorify me in the life to come. Amen.

(10) Gen. ii. 18.

POINT III.

ʹ The third shall be to consider *the Assumption of the glo-rified body of the Virgin to heaven.* And although we know not perfectly the manner in which this came to pass, yet we may meditate upon it as upon the Ascension of Christ our Lord, imagining that the resurrection of the Virgin took place here on earth, by her soul coming from heaven to unite itself to her body, as will come to pass at the general resurrection and day of judgment.

1. There were *millions of angels guarding the sepulchre, making celestial music,* as has been said, and thence crying forth to Christ our Lord, repeated, perchance, that of the psalm:—"Arise, O Lord, into Thy resting place, Thou and the ark which Thou hast sanctified;"(11) for it shall be Thy rest to bring with Thee the same ark, in which reposed the infinite treasure of all sanctity.

2. By degrees this sovereign ark *began to ascend between the arms of Cherubim and Seraphim,* piercing the clouds with jubilee and ineffable joys of mirth and gladness until she came to the empyreal heaven. There her beloved Son with incredible delight received her, introducing her, as did Solomon, into the Holy of Holies, namely, into the most high and sublime place of that celestial temple. He crowned her like the ark, with a crown of most pure gold, encompassing her whole body with ineffable brightness and beauty, which surpassed the beauty of the empyreal heaven in which she now was. Oh how brilliant did that heaven shine when renewed with the light of such a sun and such a moon as was Christ our Lord and His blessed mother! Oh how joyful were the angels at the glory of such a queen, by whose intercession they now hoped that the seats of that Kingdom would be repaired! Oh how

---

(11) Ps. cxxxi. 8.

contented was this humble mother to see herself lifted up
from the lowest of the earth, even to the top of the highest
heaven !

Colloquy.—I rejoice, O most holy Mother, for the
two stars of glory which are given thee; one to thy
soul, as it is to the other blessed; and another by
special privilege, straightway given to thy body.   Oh
how well hath thy Son performed His promise in
giving thee a crown of glory for one of ashes, oil of
gladness instead of mourning, and the garment of
praise for the spirit of sadness; and wishing thee
immediately to possess in this thy land double rewards,
with unceasing pleasure. Lift up, O most holy Mother,
my spirit to heaven, where thou art seated at the
right hand of thy Son, for it is meet that where the
Mother is, there the Son should be, and where the
body is, there "the eagles also be gathered together."
(12)   Oh that there were given to me wings of an
eagle, that flying on high I might contemplate the
glory of the glorified body of this Blessed Virgin !
Lift thyself up, my soul, with great joy, ascend far
above thyself, and above all things created; forget the
things of the earth, and sigh after those of heaven,
where thy celestial Father is, and thy glorious Mother.
Imitate the humility she had in this life, that thou
mayest be exalted with her in the other.   Amen.

MEDITATION XXXVII.

ON THE HEROIC HUMILITY OF THE BLESSED VIRGIN, FOR WHICH
SHE WAS EXALTED ABOVE ALL THE CHOIRS OF ANGELS.

Although the most holy Virgin our Lady excelled much
in all sorts of virtues, yet with singular excellency *did*

(12) Mat. xxiv. 28.

she excel in humility, to which we may attribute her exaltation, following the rule which St. Paul sets down of Christ our Lord, saying:—" Now that He ascended, what is it, but because He also descended first into the lower parts of the earth? He that descended, is the same also that ascended above all the heavens, that He might fill all things;"(1) the same may we say of His Blessed Mother, who ascended above all creatures, because she humbled herself more than all: and the glorious crown of twelve stars which she has in heaven has been given her for [twelve heroic acts of humility, which she exercised here on earth: which I will insert in this meditation, gathered from all that has been said in the meditations of her life, especially in the second part. And because there is a humility towards God, and a certain humility towards men, and the Blessed Virgin was most eminent in both, we will speak of them all in the three ensuing points.

POINT I.

First is to be considered, the heroic humility which the holy Virgin had *concerning the gifts she received of our Lord;* this virtue manifestly shone in these her actions.

1. The first act is, *her concealing these gifts with singular silence,* without discovering them either by words, motions, or exterior signs, from no human respect, nor from any apparent title to glorify God, or to profit her neighbour, unless in cases of necessity, in which our Lord willed and ordained that they should be discovered. For excepting in these cases, he that manifests the gifts which he has received in secret, puts himself in peril, as St. Gregory says, of being robbed of them by the thieves of vain glory, pride and presumption. (2) And for this cause true humility with great asseveration says that of

(1) Ephes. iv. 9.   (2) Hom. xi. in Evang.

Isaiah ;—"My secret to myself, my secret to myself." (3) And he repeats it twice, to signify how seriously he keeps this secret, and enjoys it with himself alone. This act did the Blessed Virgin exercise by concealing the revelation of the angel, and the mystery of her conception, without discovering it even to her own spouse, St. Joseph, whom yet she loved so tenderly. For this cause, worthily does her beloved call her, "a garden enclosed, a fountain sealed up :"(4) for she hid and enclosed with silence, the graces she had received of Almighty God, in nowise discovering them, till God Himself manifested them.

2. From this act follows the second, which is her having *in horror her own praises*, and hearing them much against her will, and with a holy displeasure and affliction; because, as St. Gregory says, when an humble person is praised by others, either he does not acknowledge in himself the good he hears, or if he acknowledge it, fears to lose it, through the vain complaisance of him that praises: or else perchance God rewards him with this temporal meed, to exclude him from the eternal.(5) This act, did the Virgin exercise in a most elevated manner, when the angel saluted her with words of such great honour, calling her "full of grace," and "blessed among women:" for as she was humble, she was troubled, and appalled, as it seemed to her that such great excellence could not be in so vile a person, so base an estimation had she of herself.

3. Hence arises the third act of humility, which is, that when God Himself wishes His gift to be discovered in any one, or discovers it by some certain means, the person should presently give the whole glory to God, and praise and bless Him, saying that of the prophet David :—"Not to us, O Lord, not to us, but to Thy name give the glory :"

(3) Isa. xxiv. 16.

(4) Cant. iv. 12.   (5) S. Greg. lib. xxii. mor. cap. v.

(6) and with the same affection desires that every one else should also give glory to God for the same cause, saying with the same David:—"O magnify the Lord with me, and let us extol His name together."(7) This did the Blessed Virgin, when she saw that our Lord had revealed to St. Elizabeth the secret mystery that she was the Mother of God, and when she heard the excellent things she related of her, for at the same instant she gave the glory to God only, saying:—"My soul doth magnify the Lord, and my spirit hath rejoiced in God my Saviour; because He hath regarded the humility of His hand-maid, for behold from henceforth all generations shall call me blessed:"—By which she excited St. Elizabeth, to attri-bute the whole work to God alone, thus openly confessing her own littleness.

Colloquy.—O glorious Virgin, who, like another Job, didst never behold "the sun when it shone," nor "the moon going in brightness,"(8) because thou didst never take pleasure in the glory and praise which proceeded from men, but didst always give to God alone the glory of His gifts. With great reason art thou clothed in heaven with the true sun of jus-tice, and holdest under thy feet the moon of this world, crowned with stars, shining "for all eternity."(9) O blessed Mother, obtain for me such a degree of humility, that I may be worthy of such a crown. Amen.

POINT II.

Consider the heroic humility this Virgin showed in *her subjection to God our Lord, and to men for the love of Him,* and to ponder the acts in which this humility appears most.

(6) Ps. cxiii. 9.

(7) Ps. xxxiii. 4.

(8) Job xxxi. 26.

(9) Apoc. xii. 1. Dan. xii. 3.

4. The fourth act is *to choose*, as David said, *" to be an abject in the house of my God,"*(10) and as much as a person can, to set himself in the lowest place, although God have given him the first; for so this holy Virgin did, when she saw that God would set her in the highest place of all His house, after His Son, and make her His Mother; for with true humility she chose the lowest place, such as is wont to be that of servants, and called herself the "handmaid" of our Lord. And for this cause St. Luke according to her desire, reckons her in the last place, after the apostles, and the other women;(11) of whom she who had before been a public sinner was one; and for this cause likewise when she came to Bethlehem, she was pleased with true humility to choose for her dwelling the vilest place in all the inn, which was the stable.

5. The fifth act of humility is *her subjecting herself to, and obeying all the laws and ordinances of God, and of His ministers,* though in things contrary to her honour and reputation, without admitting privileges or exemptions, though she had sufficient occasion for it; and although she was not obliged by precept, yet she delighted to obey as others did, and to humble herself more than others, even then when she might have been excused the humiliation, as Christ our Lord humbled Himself to the law of circumcision, and made Himself " obedient even to the death of the cross." This did the Virgin perform most punctually, observing the law of purification, though not obliged to do so, and although it were a blot and detriment to her honour, because that law was given for women who were unclean, and who had conceived by the work of man, which had no place in her, yet would she conform in this respect

(10) Ps. lxxxiii. 11.
(11) Act. i. 14. _ S. Ber. in ibid. signum magnum apparuit.

to other women who brought forth sons, as if she had been one of them.

6. The sixth act of humility is, *to subject and humble oneself, not only to our betters and equals, but also to our inferiors*, giving the first place to all, and anticipating them with compliments and courtesies of honour, winning their love in all this, according to the counsel of the apostle, saying:—" In humility let each esteem others better than themselves," " with honour preventing one another."(12) This did the Blessed Virgin perform when she went to visit her cousin Elizabeth, and saluted her first; though the greater in dignity, as St. Ambrose says, and humbled herself to her that was much inferior to her, employing her person in her service.(13) And the same she observed towards all, as true mistress of humility, subjecting herself " to every human creature for God's sake.'(14)

7. The seventh act of humility is, *to serve others in base and humble offices, and to perform them with delight*, as if we were born, not to be served, but to serve in the manner that Christ our Lord said,—" The Son of Man is not come to be ministered unto, but to minister, and to give His life a redemption for many,"(15) which He performed most exactly, by exercising Himself in the office of a carpenter, and obtaining His livelihood by the labour He performed in the service of other men; and afterwards by serving His disciples, even to the washing of their feet; giving us an example to accomplish that to which St. Paul exhorted us, saying:—" By charity of the spirit serve one another."(16) This the Blessed Virgin exercised most exactly, for, as the poor wife of a poor artificer, she employed herself in all the humble offices of her house, help-

(12) Phil. ii. 3.   Rom. xii. 10.

(13) Luc. i. 40, in Luc. et ibid. Beda.   (14) 1 Pet. ii. 13.

(15) Mat. xx. 28.   (16) Gal. v. 13.

ing to gain her food by the labour of her hands, looking upon herself in this also as a handmaid, whose office it is to serve the rest of the house ; for even so, with more humility than Abigail she said :—" Behold let thy servant be a handmaid, to wash the feet of the servants of my Lord."(17)

8. With this degree of humility another likewise is joined as companion, which is *to refuse,* as far as lies in one's power, all *offices and places of honour,* and those commissions which are much esteemed amongst men ; looking upon oneself as unfit to perform them, or unworthy of them ; also to fly the honour which they draw with them, and to accommodate oneself to one's humble estate, living quiet and content with it.　This the Blessed Virgin performed, who, as St. Thomas says,(18) wrought no miracle in her life, nor would ever preach in public; and if she instructed the apostles and other disciples in the mysteries of the faith, it was in secret and privately, leaving the honour of public preaching to the apostles, and embracing that rule which afterwards St. Paul delivered, saying :— " I suffer not a woman to teach;"(19) yea, it is rather to be believed that in the Temple and in other congregations and sermons she was present, and heard them as other women, and with great humility worshipped the priests of Jesus Christ, at whose hands she received the Holy Communion, not only holding herself unworthy to have such power, but not so much as desiring that her Son, by special disposition, should communicate it to her.

Colloquy.—O most glorious Virgin, with great reason was bestowed on thee that throne of glory which thou hast in heaven, since thou didst humble thyself so much here on earth.　It is most just that thou

(17) 1 Reg. xxv. 41.

(18) 3 p. q. xxvii. art. 5, ann. 3.　　　　(19) 1 Tim. ii. 12.

shouldst there have the first place after thy Son, because here thou didst always choose the last. With reason, too, are all the angelical hierarchies subject to thee, since thou didst subject thyself as a handmaid even to men. And seeing thou didst so observe the counsels of humility, help me, that by thy example I may observe them, and humble myself here on earth, that God may exalt me in heaven above. Amen.

POINT III.

The third shall be, to consider the heroic humility which this holy Virgin showed *in the humiliations of poverty, and of injuries which came from the hands of men,* which are true touchstones by which to discover the perfection and excellence of humility towards God, and towards men.

9. Beginning, therefore, at the easiest, the ninth act of humility is, *to delight to be poor, and to exercise all that appertains to poverty,* and to the humiliations which thence proceed. For, supposing that voluntary poverty is no disgrace amongst Christians, yet, when it is not evident that the exercise of poverty is voluntary and not of necessity, it causes contempt among men; and so it is a rare humility for a person to bear himself in all things as truly poor, and to suffer himself to be treated by others in the manner that poor are treated, and this not by force, but by free election. This humility did the Blessed Virgin practise with great pleasure and content, in all occasions that occurred. In Bethlehem she was repulsed by all when she craved a lodging of them, and, therefore, she repaired to the refuge of the poor in winter time, which was a stable. In her purification she would not offer up a lamb, but a pair of turtles, or two young pigeons, as one that was poor. In Egypt, and after her return to Nazareth, she always embraced the contempt of poverty, delighting that

all should treat her as they were wont to treat other poor women such as herself.

10. The tenth heroic act of humility is, to *support with patience and silence the ignominy that is incurred against one's honour and reputation*, neither excusing nor defending one's self, or complaining of the injury done, but quietly holding one's peace, and accepting the ignominy and humiliation with great content for the love of God; and in this there are divers degrees:—i. to suffer with patience the injuries and contempts which happen by our own fault;—ii. and greater is it to suffer injuries without being at all in fault, holding our peace though false witnesses be produced against us;—iii. much greater is it to suffer them when they happen on occasion of any good work, for which we rather deserve praise and glory; —iv. still greater is it to *suffer all this*, not only from enemies, or strangers, but from our own brethren, friends, and kindred. Such was the humility which Christ our Lord had in the injuries and contempts He suffered in this life: and the same His most holy Mother exercised, when her spouse, St. Joseph, perceiving her to be with child, suspected that she was an adulteress, and determined to dismiss her, which she, notwithstanding, suffered, holding her peace, and not defending herself, as we have pondered in its place.(20)   And it is to be believed, that not at this time only did the Virgin suffer such injuries, but many times was made partaker of the false testimonies which were uttered against her Son.   And when Christ's kindred persecuted Him, and bound Him as one that was " become" (21) mad, they perhaps turned also against His mother, because they saw she stood in her Son's defence; but she held her peace, and endured all, rejoicing more than the apostles, " to suffer reproach for the name of Jesus." (22)

(20) 2 p. Medit. xiv.   (21) Marc. iii. 21.   (22) Act. v. 41.

11. The eleventh act of humility, which is linked jointly with the former, is, *to bear with serenity and peace of mind reprehensions and rejections, dry and distasteful answers,* as well internal, which we feel in treating with Almighty God, when He discomforts us, or denies, or defers what we ask Him, as external, which our superiors give us, or our neighbours, though without any fault of ours, and though some degree of contempt towards us ensue. For, to suffer on such occasions without excuse, complaint, or disdain, is an act of heroic humility, in a wonderful degree pleasing to our Lord ; and for this, as St. Bernard says, (23) the spouse was greatly pleasing to him, whom, therefore, he called beautiful, because, being sharply reprehended, and threatened, she held her peace, when he said unto her :—" If thou knowest not thyself, go forth and depart out of my house." This humility did the Blessed Virgin many times, and on divers occasions, as when her Son being only twelve years old, answered her and St. Joseph sharply, saying :—" How is it that you sought me? did you not know that I must be about my Father's business?"(24) And at the marriage, another time He said to her, with a certain severity, and as though He would refuse what she asked,—" Woman, what is it to me, and to thee? my hour is not yet come." (25) And others telling Him at another time, that His mother and His brethren stood without, seeking to speak with Him, He answered as it were with great rejection, saying :—" Who is my mother, and who are my brethren?.. whosoever shall do the will of my Father that is in heaven, he is my brother, and sister, and mother.'' (26) In all these occasions which have a certain appearance of reprehension and repulse, the holy Virgin ever preserved great humility and silence, as we

<hr>

(23) Ser. xlv. in Cant.   (24) Luc. ii. 49.   (25) Joan. ii. 4
(26) Mat. xii. 48 et 50.

have considered in its place ;(27) and in this manner she behaved herself in many like occasions, and with many other persons, supporting them with great tranquillity and peace of heart.

12. The twelfth act of humility is, *not to withdraw ourselves when any of our own kindred and friends are contemned or calumniated, but patiently to take part with them*, and to share with them in their confusion, as Job, who, as himself said, was not afraid, nor terrified at the contempt of his own kinsmen,(28) to wit, to see himself contemned by them, or to see them contemned by others. But much more valiantly did the Blessed Virgin exercise the same, who would assist and be present at the contempt and ignominies of her Son, placing herself close by the cross, nothing disdaining that all should suppose her to be the mother of that man, so ignominiously condemned to die, and to be crucified between two thieves ; and for this respect she suffered many injuries, and ardently desired to suffer many more, as we have noticed elsewhere. (29)

These are the twelve acts of humility which shone in the Blessed Virgin, fulfilling that which the Holy Ghost says :—" The greater thou art, the more humble thyself in all things, and thou shalt find grace before God ;"(30) and so, indeed, the holy Virgin found it in this life, and was afterwards crowned with a crown of twelve shining stars, in reward of her twelve kinds of humiliations, and elevated to a most high throne of glory, where, together with her Son, in more exalted dignity than the apostles, she judges " the twelve tribes of Israel."

Colloquy.—O most holy Virgin, I rejoice to see thee crowned with so many crowns of justice by thy

(27) 2 part, Medit. xxx.   3 part, Medit. ix.
28) Job. xxxi. 34.   (29) Part 4, Medit. lx.   (30) Ecclus. iii 20.

blessed Son. It is fitting that she who was encompassed with such heroic acts of humility should be adorned with rays of such great splendour; and that she who, to humble herself, became subject to all men, should be now seated on a throne of majesty to judge them all. And since thou now art on a throne of glory, not to be a judge, but a gracious advocate; beseech thy Son to crown me with mercies in this life, that I may obtain the crown of justice in the next. Amen.

MEDITATION XXXVIII.

ON THE DEVOTION TOWARDS THE BLESSED VIRGIN AND OF THE GOOD WHICH COMES TO US BY IT, AND IN WHAT IT IS TO BE MANIFESTED.

POINT I.

First, let us consider the *manifold reasons we have to love and serve the Blessed Virgin* with all our strength, placing her in the second place after her Son, meditating in each reason and motive what I can and ought to do for her sake.

1. The first reason is, *because the most Holy Trinity loves this Virgin more than all the angels and saints together*, on account of the excellent sanctity which she possesses above all creatures, conforming my love to that of God, and loving her more, who, on account of her great sanctity, deserves to be more beloved. From whence I will conceive several affections of spiritual joy and contentment in the favours granted to the Blessed Virgin, rejoicing that she is so greatly beloved by God, and that she has found grace before Him; rejoicing likewise for her sanctity, and for all the other virtues which she possesses, giving thanks to God for having bestowed them upon her, and beseeching

the same Virgin to procure me a share in them, to the end that I likewise may be beloved by God, and may find grace before Him.

2. The second reason is, *because she is the Mother of this same God, and the Mother of our Saviour and our Lord,* who, for the great love He bears her, desires that all should love and serve her, as the greatness of her dignity deserves, reputing all our service to her, as rendered to Himself.   For, if He said of the poor :—" So long as you did it to one of these my least brethren, you did it to me," (1) how much rather will He say, That which you did in the service of my Mother, you did to me?   If, therefore, I sincerely love Jesus Christ for the great debt of gratitude I owe to Him; I ought also to love, not only His eternal Father, with whom He is one and the same God, but also His Mother, with whom He is one and the same Spirit, for the singular love He bears her.

3. The third reason. is, *because she is also our Mother, and loves us most tenderly ;* and this alone is surely sufficient to make us love her, and render and pay love for love, since it is the property for sons to love their mothers, and more especially such mothers who so fondly love them. Wherefore, like that disciple whom Jesus loved, who presently hearing those words which He spoke upon the cross, " Behold thy Mother," forthwith took her for his own, and loved her with an especial love ; even so I also ought to take her for mine, and to love and serve her with singular diligence, esteeming it as a signal favour to be allowed to have her for my Mother.

4. The fourth reason is, *for the good offices which she does continually in my behalf in heaven,* which justly oblige and bind me to love her, as my supreme benefactress after God.—i. For first she *prays continually for us,* much better

<hr>

(1) Mat. xxv. 40.

than Jeremias did for his people, and for all the holy city, because she is our advocate and mediatrix with her Son. —ii. She is *greatly solicitous for our good*, so that she not only hears the petitions of her clients, but even before they ask her, she represents their necessities to God, as she did at the marriage in Cana of Galilee, when out of mere compassion she said to her Son :—" They have no wine," as we have contemplated in its proper place ; and as St. Augustine says :—" Sicut omnibus Sanctis est potior, ita pro nobis omnibus Sanctis est solicitior ;" " as she is more powerful than all the saints, so is she more mindful of us than them all."(2)—iii. " She is *very powerful in obtaining remedies for our evils* with great speed and readiness, on which account St. Anselm says, that sometimes we are sooner heard invoking the name of the Blessed Virgin, than invoking the name of her Son; not that her Son is not incomparably more powerful and merciful than His Mother, but because He being also our Judge, sometimes His justice defers His mercy, and He delays to hear us because of our sins, but the Blessed Virgin not being a judge, but an advocate, is wont only to show mercy, and by her prayers appeases the divine justice, and causes Him to succour us with speed. (3)   Hence is to be gathered that which the same saint says, that fervent devotion to the Blessed Virgin is a sign of predestination, because this advocate carefully solicits for her clients, as we meditated in the second part,(4) all the means of their predestination until they attain their end, and she brings them with her into glory. She also affords a remedy in all our perils and necessities, so frequently, and with such assurance, that St. Bernard made bold to say, " O Blessed Virgin, let him alone cease to praise thy mercy, who having faithfully

---

(2) Serm. de Nativit.

(3) De lib. de excellent. Virg. cap. vi.   (4) Medit. iv.

called upon thee, ever found himself forsaken in his necessity;"(5) as if he had said, All ought worthily to praise thy mercies, because, whosoever has recourse to thee, finds a remedy for his necessity. All these reasons being well weighed, I ought to kindle in my soul the fire of devotion towards our Blessed Lady, humbly beseeching her Son to give me this love towards His Mother, and the same Mother that she would vouchsafe to obtain it for me.

Colloquy.—O most loving Mother, whose special "dwelling" is not in the house of Esau, who is hated, but in the house of Jacob, who is beloved, "taking root" in God's "elect"(6) for heaven; I desire to love thee with all my heart, to serve thee as a mother, and to imitate thy virtues as a son. Admit me into this house of Jacob, wherein thou inhabitest, and cast roots in my heart, whereby I may compass my desire, exercising myself with great solicitude in thy holy service.

POINT II.

Secondly, let us contemplate *the devotion which the Holy Ghost has inspired into the universal Church towards our Blessed Lady*, noting some excellent things, in which the same is expressed and declared; these I am to consider, performing on my part what I may, thus to correspond with the inspiration and desire of the Holy Spirit.

1. First she shows it *in ~~adoring and worshipping~~ her*, an adoration less than that of God, but greater than that of all the saints, and is called by excellency—" Hyperdulia:" and through respect she attributes to her certain titles proper to God, and this for the singular excellency with which such qualities are found in her, as when she is called, " Mother of mercy, our life, our sweetness, and our hope." She likewise calls her the " gate of heaven," and

(5) Ser. de Assump.   (6) Ecclns. xxiv. 13.

asks of her that which otherwise is proper to God Himself to grant, as to "~~unloose the bands of the guilty~~," to "give ~~light to the blind~~," to "~~take from us all our evils~~," and " to show unto us Jesus, the fruit of her blessed womb."(7) All which the Blessed Virgin performs, obtaining the same of our Lord by her holy prayers; with this affection, therefore, ought I to honour this Blessed Lady, and to repeat the words of holy Church, with the same spirit and affection with which she repeats them.

2. Secondly, she shows it, because, by divine inspiration she *dedicates many churches*, and those exceedingly sumptuous, in honour of the Blessed Virgin, adorns them with very devout pictures, and exhorts the faithful to visit them, God our Lord confirming all with innumerable miracles, which He works for our sake. And for this end also, congregations and religious orders are instituted, devoted to the service of the Blessed Virgin, which she receives under her protection, gaining extraordinary favours, as well in general as in particular, for those who dedicate themselves in an especial manner to her service ; and this without exception of persons, for whosoever serves her, finds grace and favour in her eyes, and I shall likewise find the same if I offer myself sincerely to her service.

3. This devotion is shown in the *frequent commemoration and recourse which the Church has to her* in all seasons: ordaining for this purpose many yearly feasts, one almost every month, and in some also two or three : and every week dedicates the Saturday to her honour, with a particular office and Mass : and for every day has appointed a particular office for our Blessed Lady, with indulgences to those that recite it ; and before the greater office is begun, the Church always salutes her with the Hail Mary, and ends with some antiphon to the same Virgin ; and with

(7) Hym. Eccles. Salve Regina, Ave Maris Stella.

the ringing of the bell, invites us every day to salute her
with the Hail Mary; and, in some parts, the same is done
thrice a day; in the morning, at midday, and in the evening.   Finally, she approves of, and exhorts us to use the
Rosary in her honour, making a psalter of a hundred and
fifty Hail Marys, which answer to the psalter of David,
containing a hundred and fifty psalms, with fifteen Our
Fathers, inserting to every one ten Hail Marys, as if to
make a pause or stay in the fifteen steps of this divine
temple, and answers to the fifteen gradual psalms, that we
might glorify *her* with this celestial music, who always
ascended by all the degrees of virtue.   And for those who
cannot every day recite so many, is allowed the chaplet of
sixty-three Hail Marys, in memory of the number of
years she lived in this world; and to excite us to the
exercise of them, the Church grants great indulgences to
all those who recite these rosaries.   Our Lord Himself
also confirms this devotion, with many great and marvellous
miracles, out of the love He bears to His Mother, and that
which He desires all men to bear her.

Colloquy.—O most sweet Jesus, since Thou so much
desirest us to honour Thy most holy mother, efficaciously inspire into me this devotion, aid me to exercise those works with great fervour, which Thy spouse
the Church ordains and exercises for this end.

THE MANNER OF RECITING THE ROSARY OF OUR LADY WITH SPIRIT AND DEVOTION, JOINING WITH IT MENTAL PRAYER.

Amongst the devotions used towards our Blessed Lady,
the most notable is that of *the rosary*, which we have assigned.
And because vocal prayer is greatly perfected when it is
joined with mental, the clients of our Blessed Lady have
invented several means of joining them together when
they recite their beads.   I will here put down *three of*

those that are most profitable, to the end that every one may choose that which most helps his own devotion, or he may use now one, now another, to take away tediousness by this holy variety.

1. Before one begins the rosary, he should perform what we spoke of in the Introduction of this Book, chapter v., framing his intention after the following manner. I must raise up my heart to God, who is there present, and making Him a profound reverence, I will then humbly *beseech Him to assist me* with His grace, so to recite this rosary, that it may be pleasing to Him: next I will *offer to Him all the thoughts, words, affections,* and desires which I shall have, directing all to His glory, and to the glory of the Blessed Virgin, our Lady, in thanksgiving for His benefits bestowed upon me, and in satisfaction for the sins and negligences which I have committed in His service, begging of Him to grant me the virtues which I require, and whatsoever else I need to serve Him with perfection. And if the rosary is to be offered for other necessities of the Church, or for any particular person living or dead, here this offering is to be made; yet we must note, that though there are four ends to which I may direct my prayer, viz., the glory and praise of Almighty God, for His great majesty, thanksgiving for His benefits, satisfaction for my sins, and obtaining of virtues: yet if I offer up the rosary for another person, although I transfer to him the satisfaction which otherwise would have fallen to myself, I may still offer up the rosary for myself, without prejudicing him in the other three intentions.

2. This offering being made, I will recite *one Our Father, and ten Hail Marys,* with deliberation and attention, not contenting myself with attending to the bare words only, lest I should omit any of them; but also to the sense of them, or to the person to whom they are

directed which is God our Lord, or our Blessed Lady: who, although she be in heaven, sees, hears, and understands my prayer; and I may so speak to her, as if she were by me here on earth. Having recited the ten "Hail Marys," I will make a brief meditation according to one of the following methods.

THE FIRST MANNER OF RECITING THE ROSARY, BY MEDITATING THE WORDS OF THE "HAIL MARY."

THE first manner of reciting the rosary, or chaplet, is according to that method of praying by words, which we have declared in chapter ix. of the Introduction of this Book, *dividing the prayer of the Hail Mary into six or seven principal words;* and every ten Hail Marys, to take one of them for matter of meditation, as was pondered in the second Part.

1. In the *first ten* I will meditate these words, " *Hail Mary,*"(8) considering the excellencies which are contained in this most sweet name of Mary. In the second ten I will meditate the second words, "*full of grace,*"(9) contemplating the immensity of graces and virtues with which our Lady was replenished. In the third ten I will meditate the third words, " *the Lord is with thee.*"(10)—In the fourth ten, the fourth words, " *blessed art thou amongst women.*"—And in the fifth, those other words, " *blessed is the fruit of thy womb, Jesus,*" considering the excellencies of the most sweet name of JESUS, and the most celestial benedictions, which come to us by His means.—In the sixth ten I will meditate the sixth words, " *Holy Mary, mother of God,*"(11) reflecting on the exalted gifts which are contained in the election of the sacred Virgin for this high dignity, and the privileges which, on this account, are granted to her.—And finally I will meditate on what

(8) Medit. iv.   (9) Medit. vi.   (10) Medit. xxi.
(11) Medit. iii.

is contained in the last words, *"pray for us sinners, now, and at the hour of our death, Amen :"*(12) considering the efficacy of the prayer of the Blessed Virgin, the great need I have of her intercession, especially in the hour of death, imagining with what affection I would pronounce these words when I shall find myself in that final transit, and endeavouring to say them now with the same fervour.

2. With this brief meditation, I am to *join various affections :* some concerning God our Lord, and others concerning the Blessed Virgin; admiring their excellencies and virtues, rejoicing that she is adorned with them, glorifying and praising Almighty God for having given them to her, and exciting desires in myself to imitate her in them, always saluting her in each with this word, " Hail," which is to be repeated with every one of the other words with great affection, saying, Hail, most holy Mary.— Hail, full of grace, full of charity, full of humility.—Hail, thou who hast God with thee, who art His Mother, and who possessest Him for thy Son, &c.

3. Lastly, I will conclude *by begging the virtues which I have considered in the most holy Virgin*, or other things, which I find to be wanting in me, directing my prayers sometimes to Christ our Lord, through the merits of His most holy Mother; at other times to the same Mother, that she would obtain them for me from her Son; and lastly, to the other Persons of the most Holy Trinity, with the titles and colloquies of which mention was made in section 1 of the Introduction of this Book.

After this manner the Our Father may sometimes be taken for matter of meditation, meditating at every ten Hail Marys one of the seven petitions, as is to be found in part 3, meditation xiv. And sometimes also I may meditate on the ten verses of the canticle, " Magnificat,"

(12) Part 3, Medit. ix.

taking one or two verses at every ten, and thus endeavour to excite various feelings and affections, such as are set down in part 2, meditation xii.

THE SECOND MANNER OF RECITING THE ROSARY, BY MEDITATING WITH IT THE FIFTEEN MYSTERIES.

1. The second, and more usual manner of reciting the rosary, is to take, for matter of meditation, *the fifteen principal mysteries of Christ our Lord, and of His Mother,* meditating at every ten Hail Marys, on one of the mysteries, which are distributed into three divisions.

i. The first are the *joyful mysteries,* which were sources of great joy to the Blessed Virgin, and are:—The Annunciation of the angel.—The visitation of St. Elizabeth.—The birth of Christ our Lord.—His Presentation in the Temple.—And the finding in the Temple amongst the doctors. Of all which, meditations have been made in the second part of this book. And inasmuch as every mystery comprehends several points, lest it might be tedious always to meditate on the same thing, I may one day meditate one point, and another day another, in the manner they are there assigned.

ii. The second set of mysteries are called *sorrowful,* because they were very painful both to Christ our Lord, and to His Mother, whether she were present at them, or when she heard, and considered them. They are, the prayer in the garden, with the heaviness of Christ, and His sweating blood,—the scourging at the pillar,—the crowning with thorns,—the carrying of the cross, and the crucifixion: on these many meditations have been made in the fourth part.

iii. The third are the *glorious* mysteries, in which the glory of Christ our Lord, and of His Mother, are comprehended, and shine forth. They are, the Resurrection of

Christ, His Ascension into heaven, and His sitting on the right hand of His Father, the coming of the Holy Ghost, the Assumption of the Blessed Virgin, and her glorious crowning in the Kingdom of heaven; and on these we have already meditated in this fifth Part.

2. These things presupposed, at every ten Hail Marys *three things are to be performed.*

i. To *call to mind the mystery,* or some part of it, *meditating and considering briefly the greatness and perfection* of Christ our Lord, and of His Mother: the things which they there do, or suffer: the joy, sorrow, or glory which they receive: the heroic virtues which they exercise: and the great good which results from thence to all men, and in particular to myself; considering the particular causes which I have to rejoice, to grieve, or to glory in what is represented in these mysteries.

ii. And in this kind of meditation I may detail myself more or less, according to the devotion which I feel, or according to the time that is offered me: always procuring to pass to the *second part,* which is the more essential, that is to say, *to move the will to the exercise of those affections of joy, or of sorrow,* which the mystery excites in me, making affectionate colloquies with Christ our Lord, or with His Mother, or with the most Holy Trinity.

(a) If the mystery be *joyful,* as is that of the Incarnation, I may exercise these acts by *pausing and saying with inward feeling :*—" I give Thee thanks, O eternal Father, for having vouchsafed that Thy blessed Son should be made Man for the love of us. I rejoice in the infinite bounty, charity and mercy which Thou didst manifest in this work. O that all the world would praise and glorify Thee for the same! O divine Word, I give Thee thanks for having chosen the holy Virgin for Thy mother, and vouchsafing to make Thyself a little infant in her womb. O most holy Virgin, I rejoice that thou wast chosen for the Mother of God, and at the great joy thou didst experience at the glorious tidings which the angel gave thee of it. I rejoice likewise in the prudence, chastity, humility, and perfect resignation which thou didst discover in this embassage. O that I might obtain some part in these thy joys, and also imitate these thy virtues! Obtain for me, O bountiful Mother, what I desire, that having obtained it, I may serve thee devoutly with the same. Amen."

(b) If the mystery be *sorrowful*, I am to exercise affections of *sorrow*, proportionable to those things which we have said before. Considering, for example sake, the mystery of the garden, I may say: I give Thee thanks, O eternal Father, for having permitted Thine Only-begotten Son to suffer such agonies for the remedy of my offences. O my Saviour, I am truly sorry to see Thee so sad and so afflicted for my sins, sweating blood to wash me from them. O my sins, which so afflict Him who is my God! O would to God I had never sinned, nor given the occasion of so great torments, O my God, by offending Thee! Would that my sorrow were like Thine, and that I could shed abundance of tears for my offences, since Thou didst shed for them such abundance of blood! O most holy Virgin, how great was thy sorrow, when thou didst understand what thy Son suffered in this garden! O what feeling hadst thou for our sins, considering the pains thy Son suffered for them! Beseech Him, therefore, to make me partaker of these sorrows, since it is just that, the fault being mine, I myself should endure the pain.

(c) After this manner colloquies and affections may be framed *in the other mysteries*.

iii. This done, I should add the *third* thing, which is, *to propose to Christ our Lord, and to His holy Mother, the necessities and miseries which I suffer*, craving and beseeching a remedy for them; alleging as a claim to obtain it, the joy or sorrow which they received in the mystery, making very effectual purposes to imitate some virtues of the sacred Virgin, of which we will speak immediately.

3. But if any one, for want of time, or for other causes, cannot stay to meditate upon the mystery, it suffices, after having said the ten Hail Marys, *to call to mind at least the mystery*, and to make a brief colloquy and petition to our blessed Lady, saying:

Colloquy.—I rejoice, O sovereign Virgin, at the joy which thou receivedst in this mystery, by which I beseech thee to obtain for me pardon of my sins, and grace to imitate thy holy virtues.   Amen.

And in the *sorrowful and glorious* mysteries the same is to be done proportionably, saying: I am sorry, O sovereign Virgin, for the sorrow which thou didst suffer on this occasion.   Or: I rejoice in the glory and joy which thou didst receive in this mystery, by which I humbly beseech thee, &c.

4. This brief mental prayer being ended, as has been said, concerning one mystery, I am *to resume the vocal*, reciting ten other Hail Marys.   And if, by the former motion and feeling, my heart be still fixed on the same mystery, I may permit it; for such affections are not contrary to the intention which is required in vocal prayer, but rather perfect it in an excellent manner.

5. Having recited the whole rosary, I *will briefly examine the manner in which I have recited it*, being sorry for the distractions, drynesses, and other defects, which I have committed in it; and giving thanks to Almighty God for any good feeling which He has given me, resolving to recite it the next time with greater fervour and devotion.

6. Lastly, I may state, that notwithstanding we reduce the mysteries of the rosary to the number of fifteen, yet we may sometimes, instead of those which are named, take some other similar ones, which have some affinity with the former.   For with the joyful mysteries we may sometimes join the Conception of the Blessed Virgin, her Nativity and Presentation in the Temple, the Circumcision of the Child Jesus, with the imposition of His name, the Adoration of the Magi, the flying into Egypt, and returning from thence.   With the sorrowful mysteries may be joined, the taking of Jesus Christ, the blow which He received in the house of Annas, the cruelties which He sustained in the night of His Passion in the house of Caiphas, the ignominious treatment of Herod, and His being esteemed worse than Barabbas.   And sometimes the seven words which Christ our Lord spoke upon the cross may be taken for matter of meditation, meditating one at the recital of every ten Hail Maries, contemplating the feeling of the Blessed Virgin when she heard them spoken, as may be found in the fourth part Meditation xlv.

THE THIRD MANNER OF SAYING THE ROSARY, BY MEDITATING THE VIRTUES OF OUR BLESSED LADY.

The principal thing in which we are to manifest our devotion towards the Blessed Virgin our Lady is, the *imitation of her heroic virtues*, and in this we shall be greatly assisted if we meditate upon them in the recital of the rosary, taking one virtue with every ten Hail Marys; in one ten, her humility, in another her purity, in another her obedience, or patience, or charity, and so of the rest, fixing the eyes and intention upon three things.

i. Upon the heroic acts which the Blessed Virgin exercised in that virtue, after the manner which we have mentioned in the thirty-seventh Meditation, when speaking of her humility, admiring her sanctity, rejoicing in it, glorifying God, who gave it to her, and exulting for the reward which He has given for such virtue.

ii. To fix my eyes upon *the want which I have of that virtue,* and upon the contrary faults and defects into which I fall, grieving for them with great confusion and humiliation, and beseeching this sovereign Virgin to obtain pardon for me for what is past, with grace to amend for the time to come.

iii. To make some *steadfast purposes,* with the greatest determination that I can to imitate the Blessed Virgin in these acts of virtue, choosing for this purpose some particular virtue, and trusting in the favour of this pious Mother, that she will assist me to execute my good purposes.

It will much help in this method of meditation to know the especial virtues of our Lady, which have been treated of in the preceding meditations, as in those of her Presentation and Purification, where we have laid down six, like to the six white leaves of the lily, with the six golden springs of inward affections which shone in her, which we may meditate whilst reciting her chaplet.

MEDITATION XXXIX.

OF THE LIVES OF THE SAINTS, AND OF THEIR BLESSED DEATH AND REWARD.

Since in the treating of this fifth part, as also of the third, many meditations have been inserted, which may serve for the feasts of the Apostles, Martyrs, Doctors, Virgins, and other Saints, therefore I will here only put down one, for all in general, which may easily be applied to each in particular, meditating the same of one which we shall say of all.

POINT I.

1. The first shall be to consider the immense *liberality of Almighty God* towards His elect, *in communicating to them the innumerable gifts of His grace*, to make them holy, of which St. Paul makes a brief enumeration of these words: —" Whom He foreknew, He also predestinated to be made conformable to the image of His Son,...and whom He predestinated,...them He also justified; and whom He justified, them He also glorified."(1)

i. First, God our Lord, of His own bounty and by the merits of Jesus Christ His Son, predestinated and " *chose*" *them*, " *in Him before the foundation of the world*, that" they " should be holy and unspotted in His sight,"(2) marking them, that they might be " vessels of mercy,"(3) wherein He would put and manifest the riches of His grace.

ii. To execute this sovereign election, *He created them in their time,* leaving innumerable others in the abyss of their nothingness. Then He called them efficaciously to His faith and Christian religion, making them members of His Church by the means of baptism, permitting many others to perish in the flood of infidelity. And if at any time after they chance to sin, He returns to call them effectually to do penance, suffering others to die in their sins.

iii. He *preserved them from grievous sins,* drew them forth from great dangers, assisted them in most grievous temptations, preventing them with many inspirations and sweet benedictions, that they might exercise heroic acts of virtue; and He exalted them with many gifts and graces, that they might be great before Him.

iv. Moreover, He displayed an especial providence over

<hr>

(1) Rom. viii. 29 et 30.   (2) Ephes. i. 4.   (3) Rom. ix. 23.

them, by *calling them to that office and state of life which was most convenient for them* to make them holy, either to the priesthood, to Religion, or to the prelacy, giving to every one sufficient helps, by means of which he might satisfy his obligations.

v. Lastly, He ordained them *what kind of death they should die*, that their passage .to glory might be more secure: for, as the Psalmist says:—"Precious in the sight of the Lord is the death of His saints:"(4) by which is concluded the whole course of their blessed election, to be conformable with Christ our Lord in glory, as they were conformable in life.

2. All these considerations ought to be *motives to excite within me various affections :* some towards Christ our Lord, praising Him for the favours which He has conferred upon His saints themselves, rejoicing for the gifts which Almighty God has bestowed upon them; others, with regard to myself, acknowledging the favours which in this behalf He has bestowed on me, and giving Him thanks for the desire which He has to make me holy and clean in His sight, beseeching Him to help me, because of myself I can do nothing.

Colloquy.—O Holy of holies, who saidst unto Thy people :—" Be holy because I am holy ;"(5) give me what Thou commandest, that I may obtain what Thou desirest to give me. And since holiness itself is Thine, prevent me with Thy abundant grace, that I may ascend to the highest degrees thereof. Amen.

Of these five benefits, which have here been recounted, I shall speak more at length in the sixth part, which now ensues.

POINT II.

The second shall be to consider *how well the saints*

<hr>

(4) Ps. cxv. 15. ;   (5) Levit. xi. 44. 1 Pet. i. 16.

answered to their vocation, and how well they profited by the favours which they received during their life, meditating the most remarkable virtues which they exercised whereby to aspire to such great sanctity.

1. These may briefly be reduced to three sorts, which are drawn from what Christ our Lord said :—" *If any man will come after me, let him deny himself and take up his cross and follow me.*"(6)

i. First, they excelled in the *abnegation and mortification of themselves*, conceiving a holy hatred of themselves, of their own flesh, and of self love. Those who were great sinners performed great penances, deplored their sins with great contrition, and confessed them so humbly, that some of them left them written in papers and books, for their own perpetual humiliation, and those who fell not into grievous sins, to preserve themselves from them, afflicted their flesh with great austerities, to keep it subject to the spirit, chastised severely every little fault, as if it were great, showed themselves herein to be of the band of Jesus Christ, in crucifying " their flesh, with the vices and concupiscences," and mortifying " the deeds of the flesh" with the fervour of the " spirit."(7) And as Christ our Lord when crucified received four wounds in His hands and feet, of which He died, and a fifth in His side, the more to confirm His death, even so the saints crucified the disordered delights of their senses, the unbridled concupiscences of their appetites, the depraved wishes of their self will, and the wandering thoughts of their imagination and judgment, and with these four mortifications did die to sin. But not content with all this, desiring to make their happy death the more assured, they mortified their natural love in many things of themselves lawful, to be farther

(6) Mat. xvi. 24.   (7) Gal. v. 24. Rom. viii. 13.

removed from falling into those which were unlawful.(8) For they renounced their fathers, friends, goods, honours, and their pleasures, which they might lawfully possess; they abstained from many things which they might do without offence, thus to die to the world and to self love, to live more perfectly to Jesus Christ: and with this generous violence which they offered to themselves, they bore away the kingdom of heaven.(9)

Colloquy.—O valiant Saints, who, by your continual mortification, despoiled yourselves " of the old man, with all his deeds,"(10) to clothe yourselves with the new man, with his works; beseech your Captain, Jesus Christ, to assist me with His grace, that I may overcome my own nature, endeavouring and striving to enter by the strait gate of the mortification of my flesh, that so I may obtain the perfect renovation of my spirit. Amen.

ii. The saints excelled in *daily bearing the cross of Christ our Lord* with great fortitude, patience, and perseverance. (11) They showed their fortitude in the battles which they had, both interior and exterior, with the Devil and his ministers, with their enemies and with their friends, under the pretext of piety; the end and intent of which were to despoil them of their faith, chastity, humility, Evangelical poverty, or their vocation to Religion; and in these they fought most valiantly, and suffered much to issue forth victorious. They showed their invincible patience in the labours and calamities which occurred, in sickness, sorrow, poverty, infamy, false witnesses, and many other like afflictions, which, though they felt as men, yet assisted with the grace of God; they rejoiced in them, glorying to bear the cross of Jesus Christ, and His precious mortification

(8) S. Greg. lib. v. Mor. cap. 8.]   (9) Mat. xi. 12.
(10) Colos. iii. 9.   (11) 3 part. Medit. xxiv.

in their bodies. All of them suffered some sort of martyrdom, either in body or in spirit, for the defence of some virtue, and dying on this cross, thus entered into glory. All of them, like " living stones," were polished with the strokes of tribulation, and so were placed in the building of heaven. All of them passed through the fire of afflictions, and issued forth tried like " gold in the furnace," for patience perfected its work in them, and made them "perfect and entire, failing in nothing,"(12) which appertains to the loyalty they owe to God.

Colloquy.—I give you thanks, O most strong and valiant soldiers, for the fidelity which you displayed in your persecutions, whilst fighting for the honour of your God. I rejoice in your invincible patience whereby you have obtained so glorious a crown. Help me, I beseech you, by your prayers, that imitating your example, I may have part in your victories. Amen.

iii. Thirdly, the saints excelled in *following Christ our Lord,* so that the life of Jesus Christ was manifested in them, for, from the foot to the head they were clothed with Jesus Christ, and for their perfect imitation of Him, each might be called another Christ, in humility, chastity, and in the other virtues, as we have mentioned.(13) This perfect imitation the saints obtained by prayer and obedience, for they were exceedingly fervent in prayer, having frequent recourse to Almighty God, in all their affairs, and placing great confidence in the divine providence; they were also most prompt and punctual in obeying the will of God, His precepts, counsels, and His divine inspirations, esteeming it a special joy to deny their own will, to do the will of Almighty God, every one excelling in some particular virtue, for which cause the Church says

(12) 1 Pet. ii. 5. Sap. iii. 6. Jac. i. 4. (13) Introd. 2. p.

of them, that of Ecclesiasticus:—"There was not found the like to him in glory, who kept the law of the most High."(14)

Colloquy.—O most high God, who showest the highness of Thy bounty in the virtues which Thou hast given to the saints, to the end that they might be conformable to the image of Thy Son; show the same also towards me, in making me like to them, that I may imitate Him whom they imitated, and that the life of Jesus may shine in my life as it shone in theirs.   Amen.

2. From these considerations I will deduce divers affections of confusion, *considering the little which I do*, and how ill I answer to my vocation, and to the benefits received from Almighty God; for our Lord says by Ezechiel, and St. Gregory declares, we ought to behold the living Temple of His saints, to confound us in our sins, and ought to "measure and meditate the marvellous building" of their lives, to blush at our own, and to reform them according to theirs, hoping in the divine bounty that He will assist us as He assisted them ;(15) and since they, frail men as they were, like myself, could do so much, relying on the power of God, that I also may do the same, because "the hand of the Lord is not shortened" in my behalf.(16)

POINT III.

The third shall be to consider how liberal our Lord has been in *honouring and rewarding His Saints many ways in this present life, and in the other.*

1. First, *before death* He rewarded many of them with rare and singular *spiritual comforts*, with the grace of contemplation, with raptures and most delightful revelations,

(14) Ecclus. xliv. 20.   (15) Ezech. xliii. 10. Moral. cap. 6.
(16) Isa. lix. 1.

with the spirit of prophecy, with the gift of miracles, and with other gifts given gratis ; in such a manner that they, with humility, flying from honour, Almighty God with His liberality honoured them, working by them most wonderful works, which caused them to be venerated by all men, and their heroic virtues excited such great admiration, that those who beheld them were moved to reverence them, our Lord fulfilling what He had said:—" Whosoever shall glorify me, him will I glorify." (17)

2. He likewise rewarded them *in their very death*, granting some *to die as martyrs* for the confession of His glorious faith, and to others, some one kind of death, some another ; which, although it were painful to the flesh, yet it was most pleasant to the spirit, He giving them to taste some part of that which shortly they hoped to receive in glory, and sending angels to assist them at their departure. Nay, the same Lord himself sometimes came to them, accomplishing what He had promised them, saying:—" I will come again, and will take you to myself, that where I am, you also may be." (18)

3. Moreover, *after their death* He honours *them in His Church militant*, causing their *sanctity to be published, and praised by all*, and many churches to be built in their honour, their images painted, feasts celebrated, and all to worship their bones, their ashes, the patched garments which they wore in their life, the chains with which they were fettered, and the very subscriptions of the letters which they wrote. He works great miracles by all these things to honour them, and chastises very severely the insults which are offered to them. So that, they who would have been wholly forgotten in the world, had they not excelled in such sanctity, as for example, the blessed St. Francis, are now in the mouths of all men, and the

(17) 1 Reg. ii. 30.   (18) Joan. xiv. 3.

princes and mighty monarchs account it an honour, and think themselves happy to have their names, and carry their relics about them for their defence, fulfilling that which Almighty God promised to His Church, when He said:—" I will make thee to be an everlasting glory, a joy unto generation and generation:" (19) that is to say, I will make thee so glorious that the greatness of the world shall esteem it an honour to prostrate itself before thy feet.

4. Fourthly, he will honour them in *the day of judgment* with a most excellent honour, *placing them upon His right hand* in great majesty, before the sight of the world, so accomplishing that which He promised, saying:— " Every one, therefore, that shall confess me before men, I will also confess him before my Father who is in heaven."(20)

5. Finally, *in heaven* He will reward and honour them with such great rewards, that only God· and themselves can declare the greatness of them. For they shall be *set near His throne, on other thrones*, exceeding bright, " clothed in white garments," of admirable virtues, with " crowns of gold" upon their heads, like kings, with " palms in their hands;" (21) and the same God, as Isaiah says, shall be their crown, their glory, and their joy, (22) employing Himself in honouring, rejoicing, and feasting His elect: all their virtues He will reward with a peculiar reward, and with a measure so full, that it shall run over with contentment. Their faith shall be rewarded with the clear vision of divinity; their hope with the perpetual possession of all the goods they ever desired; their charity with the beatifying love which unites them with Almighty God. Humility, patience, and the other

(19) Isa. lx. 15.　　(20) Mat. x. 32.　Luc. ix. 26.
(21) Apoc. iv. 4.　Apoc. vii. 9.　　(22) Isa. xxviii. 5.

virtues, with the " torrent of pleasure," (23) which inebriates them, and gives a taste of all the rewards which are promised to the eight beatitudes, as we shall see in its place. (24)

Colloquy.—O my soul, of what art thou thinking ? Why dost thou not sigh and labour to obtain that sanctity whose end is such a sovereign reward ?   If thou desire honours and excellencies, *who* are more honoured than the friends of Almighty God ?   And what principality exceeds that of His saints ?(25) And if *he* be so honoured, " whom the King" of heaven "is so desirous to honour,"(26) why dost thou not follow virtue, which is worthy of such great honour and reward ?   O infinite God, who art glorious and admirable in Thy saints, I give Thee thanks for the wonders which Thou hast wrought in them, and for the admirable rewards which Thou hast given them ;(27) and since it is for Thy greater glory that they may be many, join me to the number of them, to the end that I may serve Thee with purity and sanctity all the days of my life, and afterwards ascend to enjoy Thee in their company, world without end.   Amen.

(23) Ps. xxxv. 9.   (24) 6 part, Medit. lii.
(25) Ps. cxxxviii. 17.   (26) Esth. vi. 6.   (27) Ps. lxvii. 36.

PRINTED BY RICHARDSON AND SON, DERBY.